# AMERICAN CITIES
# IN THE GROWTH OF THE NATION

# AMERICAN CITIES

## in the growth of the nation

CONSTANCE McLAUGHLIN GREEN

Harper Colophon Books
Harper & Row, Publishers
New York

AMERICAN CITIES IN THE GROWTH OF THE NATION

First published 1957 by
University of London
The Athlone Press

Copyright in all countries signatory to the Berne Convention

This book was originally published in the United States by
John De Graff, Inc., Tuckahoe, New York, in 1957, and is here
reprinted by arrangement.

First HARPER COLOPHON edition published 1965 by
Harper & Row, Publishers, Incorporated
New York

LC 57-12021

To
LOIS ANGELL GREEN CLARK
and
ALLEN REYNOLDS CLARK
to whose insights and critical judgment
this book owes much

# Acknowledgments

MY THANKS for help in preparing this book go first to my daughter and son-in-law to whom I have dedicated the volume. Several other scholars have also contributed invaluable criticisms and suggestions: Mina K. Curtiss who, in scrutinizing the text, has pointed out lacunae; Dr Katherine Crane, formerly an editor of the *Dictionary of American Biography*; Raymond D. Jameson of the New Mexico Highlands University; and Dr Murray Lawson of the Department of State whose familiarity with the primary sources on eighteenth- and nineteenth-century American economic development has prevented my restating some widely accepted faulty conceptions. Frederick Arnold of the Library of Congress has given me endless assistance in assembling materials in this little-explored field. And, finally, I wish to thank Professor H. Hale Bellot and University College of the University of London for creating the opportunity to present this story, first in lectures for students, and then in book form for any reader interested in the problem.

CONSTANCE McL. GREEN

Alexandria, Virginia
    October 1953

# Contents

# Illustrations

# I

# Introduction

CITIES have played an important part in the development of the United States since the founding of the nation. Indeed, it was apprehensions lest trade rivalries of city merchants of the eastern seaboard destroy the new states that led to the drafting of the federal Constitution and the formation of the federal Union. As early as the seventeenth century, urban centers where men exchanged not only goods but ideas, were emerging. While the mercantilists in London were planning measures designed to keep the colonies of the North American continent as suppliers of raw materials to the mother country and as purchasers of English manufactures, cities in the New World were already growing in strength and influence. The Revolution itself and the rise of the Confederation of thirteen independent states were nurtured in the cities of America. Yet when the first Congress of the new nation ordered the taking of a first federal census, only three per cent of the people of the United States were city-dwellers, and many 'cities' of 1790 would rank today as rural towns. In 1790, a visionary might have foreseen a sparse settlement of the continent beyond the Appalachians within two centuries, but he could scarcely have imagined that within five generations the population of the United States would have grown from four to one hundred and fifty millions, with great cities rivalling those of Europe scattered across its three-thousand-mile breadth. Thomas Jefferson in 1801 could believe in his agrarian dream of 'a chosen country, with room enough for our descendants to the thousandth and thousandth generation'. Ninety years later that dream would have vanished forever.

Yet even in 1800 city-dwelling counted for much more than the number of cities or the size of their populations might suggest. 'Urban life then, perhaps more largely than today, when rural isolation has been broken down by the modern miracles of transportation and communication, formed the substance of American civilization. It was in the cities that men by mutual imitation changed toward what they considered improvement.'[1] Urban ideas, tastes, and ambitions have thus loomed large in the United States since the nation was born. City enterprise, backed by city money, looking for new products to sell and new markets to sell to, was a force as powerful in peopling the country as the restless urge that

[1] John Krout and Dixon Ryan Fox, *The Completion of Independence* (*History of American Life*, vol. v, New York, 1944), p. 10.

drove the trapper perpetually on into the wilderness and the homesteader in his wake. For hard on their heels came men intent upon exploiting the new country in other ways—by marketing furs and hides, lumber, minerals, and farm produce, by speculating in real estate, by lending money and giving credit; in short, by building up the life of older cities and by founding new. The swift rise of cities is a feature of American history no less significant and dramatic than the swift march of the frontier.

The sketches here offered seek to illustrate that theme. Originally given as lectures at University College, London, in the winter of 1951, they are necessarily limited in scope. Belief that brief analysis of the history of particular cities at particular periods would better clarify my thesis than could a series of generalizations fortified by historical data has led me to select, sometimes arbitrarily, communities that show in a certain time-sequence the westward progress of the nation. In tracing that westward progress, I have inevitably used transportation as a secondary motif: a glance at the map of the United States superimposed upon a map of Europe will reveal why transportation has been a determining factor in the development of the United States, though the map does not show the equally obvious truth that in the twentieth century mere distance is no longer important. Only in the last two cities I have chosen to discuss does geography cease to count heavily. Explanation of the narrow time-span I have allotted to particular cities lies in the schematic treatment of the whole subject. The future course of the principal Atlantic seaports had become abundantly clear by 1830, and interesting, indeed exciting, as was the later development of New York, Philadelphia, Baltimore, and Boston, and tragic though Charleston's fate was to be, each had shown early in the nineteenth century what she would contribute to American urban life. Similarly, the significance of the river cities of the interior, as cities exploiting transport by water, ceased at the time of the Civil War; thereafter, however distinguished, Cincinnati, St Louis, and New Orleans drew upon resources other than the inland waterways. Chicago, the chief railroad center of nineteenth-century America, in turn depended upon other features of her life to hold her place after 1900, as the culture and economic power of the United States progressed, while Denver, once the mining-supply city of the high plains, lost her unique position in national history about 1904 when her original function disappeared.

I should like to believe that these studies might help to explain to English readers why the American character has assumed so distinctive a form, why forces have shaped the American into a person with whom citizens of the Old World can frequently feel little kinship. Though geography determined the pattern of

American expansion across the continent and the rise of cities at strategic points, the men and women who seized the opportunities thus prodigally offered left their own indelible marks upon the country and the nation. From their boundless ambitions and their hurry to realize them, from their daring and, above all, from their creed of equality which seemingly opened all doors to all men stem their restlessness, their self-confidence, their impatience, and their belief in their own rightness.

With the maturing of the machine age in the United States late in the nineteenth century, shifting economic opportunity partly explains the impulse of Americans to be constantly 'on the move', just as the lure of free land accounted for much of it in earlier years. The result, however, is the same. Americans pushed west, south, north, and farther west, until they doubled back on their tracks, sometimes to settle places missed at first, sometimes to return to eastern cities. Even in mid-twentieth century, the number of families who move from one place to another in the course of a decade is very high. If we are not truly a nomadic people, neither are we rooted in given localities within our borders. The consequence is that few communities have much solid tradition upon which to build. Americans always look to the future; unlike Europeans, they rarely look back on their past and, accordingly, rarely learn from that past. The westward movement and its sequel, the less clearly recognized but scarcely less significant 'eastward movement', brought about a transfer of cultures from East to West and later from West to East, but so rapid and frequent has been that transplanting that deep-seated, distinctively local customs and attitudes of mind have become progressively fewer.

Reckless extravagance, moreover, has darkened the bright picture of national growth and urban development. The wreckage wrought by Americans' instinct to exploit and move on has been incalculable. They have permitted an appalling waste of human resources. 'Ghost towns' still stand in every part of the country as a reproach to the nation—even when profitably revived as tourist centers. Exhaustion of natural resources—soil, timber, and minerals—coupled with extinction of the buffalo herds and other wild life, has been ruthless. In some places it has left little for a community to live by, and every vigorous family has departed. Sometimes forces seemingly beyond human control have produced the same effect: the flourishing river port becomes a backwater when the railroad supplants the river-boat; climatic changes wither the source of prosperity of the agricultural market town. For a balanced view of this rise of a powerful nation in one hundred and fifty years, it is essential to realize that the cost has often been tragically high. In spite of Americans' self-confidence, theirs is not an unbroken suc-

3

cess story. The degree of their success, nevertheless, has bred in them an impatience at Europe's hesitancy in accepting change.

British citizens, accustomed to conscientious local administration, may well be shocked, however prepared they may be for American vagaries, at the repeated indications of indifference in the United States to corruption in city politics. The fact itself, first underscored in Europe by Lord Bryce's *American Commonwealth*, needs no elaboration. But in view of Americans' sense of mission, their belief that extension of American ways to the rest of the world would redeem mankind, their tolerance of local maladministration becomes hard to explain. Certainly the sense of impermanence, the lack of roots in any one city, has contributed to this phenomenon. Some historians would perhaps call it the fruit of 'frontier' lawlessness, the resentment of any form of control. According to the standard rationalization of the late nineteenth century, native Americans, concerned with developing the country, building railroads, and fostering industrial enterprise, let power in city government slip into the hands of irresponsible foreign-born or second-generation Americans, 'bosses' who then lined their own pockets from the city till. That glib and amoral explanation, while restating American apathy, reveals the confusions of mind among city-dwellers in the years of heavy immigration. True it is that as cities grew larger and as an extended franchise increased the difficulty of election to office without the support of an elaborate organization, men to whom other opportunities seemed more rewarding ceased to seek any part in municipal government. Taxpayers revolted only when conditions became intolerable. When roused to 'throw the rascals out', reformers tended to bend their efforts to saving the taxpayer money rather than investing in improved public service. Observation that the corrupt city political machine frequently met the needs of the rank and file of humble citizens better than did more honest administrators then encouraged the return of 'machine' rule. This situation, touched upon only lightly in the pages that follow, has long been a part of the American urban scene. Whether in mid-twentieth century it is passing forever into history is still uncertain.

These sketches of American cities will doubtless lend color to Salvador de Madariaga's characterization of America as 'vitality—vulgarity'; to which, however, Americans themselves, and perhaps many Europeans, would add the attribute 'kindliness'. The vitality of the young nation carried her across the continent. The vulgarity of much of her civilization stands out at innumerable points in her history. A recent writer on Chicago, for example, speaks of her achieving in a hundred years a growth that took Paris twenty centuries to reach. Such emphasis on size, on numbers of people and volume of wealth, is unhappily not untypical.

John Nef, distinguished American historian of sixteenth- and seventeenth-century England and France, remarks that the industrial revolution introduced into the modern world the concept that quantity possesses merit quite apart from quality. The United States, whole-hearted advocate of mass production, has been caught in the toils of that idea. Her cities have been the high temples of that creed. Nor is the doctrine today confined to America. Yet, along with this cult of material things, American cities and rural areas together have fostered a spirit of generosity. Occasionally observers on both sides of the water have averred that American openhandedness is merely a form of establishing American prestige, that Americans, unaware of the personal pleasures to be derived from wealth and leisure, give away only what they do not know how to use themselves. That judgment discounts the humanitarian elements, born less of pride than of humility, which run strong in urban communities of the United States. Helping one's neighbor, if only as a guarantee of help to oneself in time of trouble, was a distinguishing feature of both urban and frontier life in America. The strength of that feeling of obligation endures. Despite the blatant weaknesses of American civilization, evidence of its admirable qualities will, I dare hope, also emerge from these pages.

## II

## The Seaboard Cities
## at the Opening of the Nineteenth Century:
## New York; Philadelphia; Baltimore;
## Charleston; Boston

IN 1800 the United States was primarily a nation of farmers. Yet even then her few urban centers were well-springs of American civilization. The federal government listed as cities only communities with 8,000 inhabitants or more; of these cities, only five had as many as 10,000. Each was a seaport. Philadelphia, it is true, lay on the Delaware river in Pennsylvania, and Baltimore, Maryland, on an arm of Chesapeake Bay, but ocean-going vessels docked at their wharves and seaborne commerce nourished both cities. Boston on Massachusetts Bay was the principal port of all New England. Charleston, South Carolina, possessing the only safe anchorage along the four-hundred-and-fifty-mile stretch of coast between Norfolk, Virginia, and Savannah, Georgia, dominated the trade of the Southern states. New York, with the finest natural harbor in North America, outdistanced all the others both in value of imports and in population, but before 1815 her lead was not undisputed.

The United States in 1783 had won political independence; but political independence, Americans soon learned, did not automatically bring economic and cultural independence of Great Britain and of Europe. Conscious vigorous striving for the 'completion of independence' began about 1820; reliance upon European capital endured much longer. While America's troubles of the post-Revolutionary era were those any country endures after a long, bitterly fought war, the new nation nevertheless faced peculiarly difficult economic adjustments. Excluded from the privileges they had enjoyed as colonies under the British commercial system, shut off from trade with the British West Indies, and denied opportunity to sell American-built ships to British merchants, the states were forced to establish a new commercial pattern. They had to find new markets for American produce and new means of paying for imports from abroad. To the solution of these problems the seaports were the key. From the ports went the foodstuffs and materials which Americans could exchange for articles they could not produce themselves. Distribution of imports within the states depended largely

6

on coastwise and river shipping controlled by merchants at the ports of entry.

By 1800, American commerce, profiting by the protracted struggle between Britain and France, had revived. But with returning prosperity, the ancient rivalries among leading American cities, so far from diminishing, heightened or took new form. Philadelphia, Baltimore, and Boston competed with each other in striving to overtake New York, while Charleston, adding cotton to rice as a staple for export, dared believe her position forever invulnerable. All these cities aspired to being cultural centers. And, indeed, the seaports were not only vital to national economic existence; they supplied at the same time the links with the ideas and aesthetics of the Old World.

## THE LEADING SEAPORTS

Of the three largest American cities, New York, Philadelphia, and Baltimore, New York was the oldest and the least English. The Netherlanders who founded New Amsterdam in 1609 bequeathed to their successors Dutch architecture, Dutch customs, Dutch trading instincts, and a nucleus of strong Dutch families. Though most of the seventeenth-century Dutch dwellings had disappeared before 1800, some Dutch-built houses remained, with crow-stepped roofs and gable-ends on the street, and the Dutch flavor of the city lingered on even after immigrants thronging from Europe had transformed the community into one of the most polyglot in the world. Trees lined many of the broad avenues which Dutch passion for cleanliness kept immaculate. The formal New Year's call continued as a social formality long after 1800. Washington Irving speaks of the services still conducted in Dutch in the city's Dutch Reformed churches when he was a young man, and of the huge brass-bound Dutch Bibles from which the head of the family daily read family prayers in households he frequented.

Despite these reminders of her Dutch antecedents, New York then, as always, was cosmopolitan. She encompassed a diversity of interests. Old families whose wealth would send a later generation of sons on the Grand Tour of Europe still spent their money on education or pleasure at home, or on new investments. Well before 1830, the unscrupulous had begun the business of exploiting immigrants, meeting incoming ships and tempting the ignorant newcomer into houses where in short order he was stripped of his every saving or she met 'a fate worse than death'. Yet opportunity to rise in the world awaited most men. In these years, when the city covered only the southern tip of Manhattan, the northern stretches of the island were still open country, where those who had leisure could ramble, picnic, or fish. Within the city, the well-to-do entertained each other with formal dinner parties and balls, while lesser people had the gaiety of the

A VIEW OF THE FEDERAL HALL OF THE CITY OF NEW YORK,

The Federal Hall of the City of New York, 1797
Here in 1789 George Washington first took oath of office as President of the United States

taverns and hotels. Both groups could enjoy the theatre, which was already gain-ing the reputation that within a few decades would make the bright lights of Broadway the symbol for hundreds of thousands of Americans of the whole world of the stage.

Artistic and literary life in the first third of the nineteenth century, before the Hudson River school of painters emerged, revolved around the Knickerbocker group and, in the 1820's, James Fenimore Cooper's Bread and Cheese Club. The Knickerbocker leaders, Washington Irving and James Kirke Paulding, historian and satirist, both wrote with understanding of the Dutch influence about them, even while they derided its occasional pretentiousness. Around Cooper, the 'Big Loaf' of the Bread and Cheese Club, gathered men of talents as varied as those of

8

Samuel Finley Breeze Morse, painter and inventor, Joseph Rodman Drake, chemist-shop owner and author of satirical verses, William Cullen Bryant, poet and journalist, James Kent, the professor of law at Columbia University whose *Commentaries on American Law* would later earn him the title of 'the American Blackstone', and, possibly most important all for the student today, William Dunlap. For Dunlap, futile as were his efforts to win contemporary fame as a painter, a playwright, or a theatrical producer, contributed immeasurably to the growth of New York's theatre and, through his histories of the theatre and the fine arts in America, to the understanding of later generations. While doctors, teachers, and merchants, rather than professional men of letters, largely composed New York's literary circle, together the group lent the city a distinction that achievements in the business world could not alone have given.

But New York owed her main influence in the nation to her merchants and bankers. New Yorkers seemed to be endowed by nature with the capacity to amass and use capital wisely. Merchants subscribed $1,000 apiece to build the Tontine Coffee House which served also as the Merchants' Exchange. The money they poured into building warehouses and wharves paid handsome dividends in the growing volume of the city's trade. The magnificent harbor attracted enterprising merchants from all parts of the country, while liberal state auction laws, allowing foreign shippers privileges denied them elsewhere, encouraged European vessels to dock in New York. It was logical that the organizers of the first regular sailing packet line between England and the States should choose New York as its western terminus. Nothing illustrates better the imagination and vigor with which New Yorkers pushed their initial geographical advantage than their promotion of plans for a canal to connect Lake Erie with the Hudson river and thus with the Atlantic seaboard at Manhattan Island. The Erie Canal, completed in 1825 after more than seven years' work, was successful beyond the most extravagant hopes of its sponsors in making New York the major distributing point for the farm produce of western New York State and Ohio. Even before the canal was opened its full length, Manhattan's merchants, exploiting every opportunity, had made the city's commercial pre-eminence unassailable, and her bankers had assured her future as a financial center of the United States. If Wall Street with its banking houses was not yet the national symbol of money and investments, well before 1830 New York's financial power was firmly entrenched and rapidly growing.

Philadelphia, William Penn's city of brotherly love, had been the second largest metropolis in the English-speaking world at the opening of the American Revolution. Though by 1800 New York had taken the commercial lead and had 60,000 inhabitants, Philadelphia, with two-thirds that number, was in many ways still the most important city of the United States. During the decade of the 1790's when she was the seat of the national government, official society had given life here a brilliance and extravagance far removed from the Quaker simplicity of earlier years. Along her wide streets, lined with harmoniously proportioned houses and public buildings, had rolled the fine coaches of federal dignitaries and foreign ministers, and at the President's levees the brocaded coats, silk hose, and powdered wigs of the aristocrats of the new republic had astonished Europeans looking for a gathering of rustics.

With the removal of the federal government to the new capital at Washington in the summer of 1800, Philadelphia returned to many of her former sedate ways; traces of her Quaker origins had in fact remained in evidence all through her days of worldly splendor. Quaker merchants, if overshadowed for a time by the statesmen and hangers-on of the national government about Independence Hall, had continued to direct from their counting houses the commercial affairs upon which the city's wealth rested. In the early nineteenth century their enterprise still quickened Philadelphia's trade, as they drew upon Pennsylvania's rich farmlands for foodstuffs to export and imported from abroad the luxuries that were unobtainable at home. From Quaker meeting houses humanitarian ideas still flowed out and, joined with the liberal political ideas of intellectuals in the city, redeemed her from excessive materialism. Her banking experience, dating from 1781, was longer than that of any other community in the country; it encouraged her citizens to invest heavily in stock of the First and, later, the Second Bank of the United States. The parent bank of each of these semi-governmental institutions was located here and gave Philadelphia close financial connections with other cities in which branches arose. Before 1820 her banking houses ran a close second to New York's in the race to control any part of the American money market not wholly in European hands.

To keep pace with New York, Philadelphia of course needed far more than banking skill. Her prosperity was tied to Pennsylvania farms. Road-building from the city westward was already well begun when the state legislature embarked upon a vast scheme of state improvements. The plan called for a network of turnpikes and canals designed to give every village in the state ready access to market in Philadelphia. Within a decade execution of the plan was proving more costly than useful, and in the late 1820's citizens began to consider railroads. Meanwhile, skilled mechanics, English weavers, and second-generation German artisans were laying the foundations upon which in the 1830's Philadelphia's fame as a manufacturing city would rise. Her shipyards had long been noted.

INDEPENDENCE HALL.
PHILADELPHIA 1876.

The steeple is a restoration of 1828. To the left stands the 'Old City Hall', and to the right Congress Hall where the Federal Congress sat from 1790 to 1800

Germantown ironmasters had been making iron since 1717, and glass-blowing was an established art. Philadelphia carpets were in great demand. Here, after 1805, Oliver Evans, inventor and ingenious 'mechanician', built his high-pressure light-weight steam engines whose power and cheapness combined to popularize the use of steam power in America. About 1808 he put his steam-powered dredge to work along Philadelphia's waterfront. Similar ingenuity and the municipal water system—its steam pumps, reservoir, and underground pipes completed in 1801—enabled the city's fire-fighters to substitute hose and power-driven pumps for the bucket line relied upon elsewhere.

William Penn had planned his city in some detail, including a promenade to run the whole length of the river front, 'a top-common from end to end', in the manner of Rotterdam's Bomb Quai. His associates and successors carried out neither this part of his plan nor his wish to have a town of open spaces with each house set in the center of its plot; they crowded the city into a parallelogram wedged between the Delaware and Schuylkill rivers, and wharves and warehouses took the space on the river front. Terrace houses were common. In the early nineteenth-century city uniform red brick houses trimmed with green shutters and with marble steps leading up to the doors flanked many of the brick-paved streets. But the thoroughfares were wide, and public buildings stood in a large open square in the heart of the city. Independence Hall, where the signing of the Declaration of Independence took place, Carpenters' Hall adjoining, where the First Continental Congress sat, and several other beautiful buildings of some historic import gave Philadelphia an air of special dignity and endeared her to Americans as 'the cradle of liberty'.

Philadelphians found solace for losing to Washington the status of national capital and to New York the lead in commerce and finance by reminding themselves that their city was still the intellectual and cultural core of America. Here Banjamin Franklin had left the imprint of his informed and inquiring mind. The meetings of the American Philosophical Society, formed by Franklin in 1743, brought distinguished scholars and thinkers together year after year, and still do so today. His creation, the Academy for the Education of Youth, was transformed in the nineteenth century into the University of Pennsylvania. Men such as Doctor Benjamin Rush, best known for his work on the cure of mental disorders, David Rittenhouse, the astronomer, the painters Charles and Rembrandt Peale, and a host of other gifted scientists, philosophers, and artists carried on the tradition of culture. Peale's museum of natural history, the first in the United States, contained exhibits of the vegetable and mineral kingdoms and animals carefully stuffed and mounted before background paintings of their natural habitats. The museum remained for decades one of the wonders of America. The Peales, father and son, ranked among the foremost American portrait painters and played a large part in establishing the Pennsylvania Academy of Fine Arts. On the other hand, music and the theatre, significant in Philadelphia life during the 1790's, suffered an eclipse when Quaker sentiment reasserted itself after the removal of the federal government to Washington. But Mathew Carey, his son-in-law, Isaac Lea, and other publishers and magazine editors kept interest in letters alive long after New York's literary lights had dimmed the brilliance of Philadelphia's.

While Philadelphia was losing some of her metropolitan quality, she was also finding her commercial position challenged by Baltimore. The Maryland town, in 1790 less than half the size of her northern neighbor, had offered at that time no major threat to Philadelphia or to the other principal American ports. But in the decade that followed, Baltimore doubled in population and widened her sphere of influence in a fashion prophetic of the growth that would enable her in 1830 to outstrip Philadelphia to become the second largest city of the United States. By 1800, with 26,000 inhabitants, she was larger than Boston or Charleston, though those older communities had been flourishing ports for generations before Marylanders had begun the settlement on the Patapsco river in 1729. Her location on an arm near the head of Chesapeake Bay, that great indentation in the Atlantic coast, made her the natural outlet for the wheat and tobacco of central Maryland and, an advantage only partly perceived at the opening of the century, placed her a hundred miles nearer the Ohio valley than any other American seaport. Northerners, Europeans—chiefly Germans, Scots, and Irish—and ambitious young men from Maryland's back-country flocked into the young city whose geographic setting and adventurous spirit promised all comers a bright future.

Baltimore citizens quickly learned to improve upon nature. When in 1797 the town obtained from the state legislature a city charter, her merchants were already taking steps to extend the waterfront. The Wardens of the port dredged the river's mouth, filled the marshlands adjacent, and built wharves along the waterfront thus reclaimed and lengthened. Ships could now dock in numbers and pick up cargoes of Maryland flour and tobacco which would sell as well as Pennsylvania produce. Furthermore, the voyage to southern coastal ports and the West Indies was somewhat shorter than from Philadelphia or New York and was safer because vessels over the first hundred-odd miles of the run sailed the protected waters of Chesapeake Bay instead of open ocean. Baltimore merchants took charge of this carrying trade themselves. Here, as in other American ports of the period, successful merchants were at the same time shipowners and bankers, lending money and handling foreign exchange. By 1818 a seventh of the stock of the Second Bank of the United States was Baltimore-owned, an indication at once of the city's wealth and of her financial aspirations. Philadelphians held nearly a third of the shares, New Yorkers, Bostonians, and others relatively small lots. Though the pattern of Baltimore's commercial growth before 1830 was generally like that of most prospering American seaboard towns, two features of her rise to power were distinctive: the speed with which her citizens brought it about and the skill with which they shifted course as conditions altered.

To the swiftness of this achievement her shipbuilders contributed notably. In the 1790's Baltimore firms built two of the six frigates of the young United States Navy, and in the early years of the nineteenth century, as troubles with British ships on the high seas culminated finally in open war in 1812, Baltimore privateers earned a name for speed and sound construction. Baltimore clippers became famous the world over. Their rounded bottoms provided surprisingly large cargo space but, thanks to the rig and huge spread of canvas, slowed sailing times very little. The thin-keeled beauty of the later New England clippers never seduced Maryland merchants from their preference for the roomy bottoms of Baltimore design. A second factor in Baltimore's early success was her accessibility to Maryland's plantations and the farms whose produce made up the bulk of cargoes for the city's ocean-borne trade. With the settling of the Susquehanna valley in western Pennsylvania, crops shipped *via* river and Bay from that region also supplied her with exports. Tobacco, rye, and especially wheat, carried by small craft down most of the navigable streams emptying into the Bay, found their way in ever-growing mountains to Baltimore's warehouses and wharves. Ships that carried Maryland tobacco to Bremen brought back emigrants who, swelling the considerable German colony in the city, made Baltimore a brewing center. Milling the wheat and grading the flour soon became even more significant activities. Distillers turned Maryland rye into whiskey. And Baltimore rye whiskey was as profitable to sell as it was palatable to drink. Apart from a refinery for West Indian sugar, other manufacturing gained little foothold. Before 1830 Baltimore was primarily engrossed in widening her commerce.

While business affairs were conducted with an energy regarded as typically Northern, in social feeling Baltimore in slave-owning Maryland was Southern. In the eighteenth century, social barriers had set Maryland's landed gentry—principally tobacco-planters—apart from the traders of the towns, but in the early 1800's these barriers dropped to admit Baltimore merchants into the inner circle, regardless of their origins, once they had made fortunes and acquired the manner. Even Annapolis, Maryland's capital and the chief gathering place of Maryland aristocracy, ceased to look down her nose at Baltimore. Some ambitious merchants of the younger city learned to accept, if indeed they had ever questioned, the standards of planter society, the gracious hospitality made easy by the labors of household slaves, and the necessary belief in the rightness of slavery that went with it. On the other hand, other influential citizens, merchants among them, rejected slavery on principle, even while they tolerated their neighbors' contrary views. The dissidents, led by Elisha Taylor, a wealthy Quaker of the city, organized the American Colonization Society which for some years carried on its work of sending Negroes back to Liberia to build a black republic of their own. Maryland laws permitted manumission and were otherwise unusually liberal for a state south of the Mason–Dixon line, the surveyors' line that marked the Maryland–Pennsylvania boundary and thus symbolically cut off slave states from free. By

1830, nearly 15,000 of the city's 80,000 inhabitants were 'free people of color', whereas slaves numbered about 4,000. But Baltimore wanted the best of both Northern and Southern worlds, and many of her citizens persuaded themselves that blacks were better off as slaves in America than as free men in Africa or anywhere else. While differences over slavery were never wholly submerged, Baltimoreans generally shut their eyes to the problem until in mid-century it became a national issue. Meanwhile to uneducated whites, even the poorest Irish and German immigrants, the existence of Negro slavery gave a soothing sense of superiority, lightening their poverty with faith that for them there was no insurmountable obstacle to a career of rising affluence and dignity.

Unhappily a good many Baltimoreans were uneducated. Though tuition was as low as $20 a year, the well-run private schools and seminaries, the German Lutheran, Episcopal, and Roman Catholic parish schools, failed to reach hundreds of children. Despite periodic state laws prescribing free, public tax-supported schools, Baltimore's one attempt before mid-century to provide free education proved abortive, and the school of 1831 quickly turned into a 'poor school', a form of orphan institution. No organized system of public schooling appeared until the 1850's. Yet in other areas the city government was attentive to public interests. Yearly it appointed Commissions of Health, Superintendents of Streets, and 'Commissioners of the Watch and for Lighting the City'. The *City Directory* for 1810 observed with pride: 'The principal public buildings are the Court House, Union Bank, the Assembly Room, Theatre, Circus, Hospital, Penitentiary and Jail; some of the latter are in every respect handsome, as also many of the private houses.' Any person who contributed $5 annually to the Humane Society could recommend as many patients as he chose to the care of the Baltimore General Dispensary. But the city charter carefully kept the control of government in the hands of the well-to-do; no one whose property assessment was less than $1,000 could be elected to the First Branch of the City Council and no one was eligible for the Second Branch whose assessment was below $2,000. Men here might make their way up, but until they had money they could cut no swathe in Baltimore society.

That society was pleasant. Irving in his *History of New York* wrote of 'Merrylanders' as 'great horse-racers and cock-fighters, mighty wrestlers and jumpers, and enormous consumers of hoe-cake and bacon. They lay claim to be the first inventors of those recondite beverages cock-tail, stone fence and sherry cobbler, and to have discovered the gastronomical merits of terrapins, soft crabs and canvas-back ducks.'[1] Baltimore's cuisine was of Maryland's best, and the public-

[1] Quoted in Van Wyck Brooks, *The World of Washington Irving* (Philadelphia, 1944), p. 88.

Baltimore and the Patapsco river, 1831

houses in the city were famous. The city was also famous for the beauty of her women. All English visitors remarked it, and Mrs Trollope described with some surprise the elegance with which Baltimore women dressed. The leading families, furthermore, assiduously fostered the arts. They patronized the theatre with enthusiasm, and men not themselves creative literary figures took pride in the writers in their midst. Of these, the first was John Pendleton Kennedy, author of charming sketches and novels, patron of the young unknown Edgar Allan Poe and in the 1850's friend of Thackeray, to whom he supplied material for *The Virginians*. In 1814 Francis Scott Key, lying aboard a ship in Baltimore's harbor, there began the verses that became the national anthem, 'The Star-Spangled Banner', stanzas that he completed in a Baltimore tavern and, in characteristic Maryland fashion, set to the music of a popular drinking song. Other members of Baltimore's Delphian Club in the 1820's were John Neal, author of the first history of American literature, and Samuel Woodworth, today remembered for his abidingly popular song, 'The Old Oaken Bucket'. As wealthy families commissioned portrait painters to immortalize them on canvas, a group of talented artists came to live in the city. Here Rembrandt Peale, Philadelphia-born, after painting a number of Baltimoreans, deviated slightly from his father's example by opening a museum of fine arts, instead of natural history. Oddly enough, for a generation the museum was less noted for its art collection than for its gas lighting, and the success of Peale's gas works in 1816 led to organizing a company to light the city's streets.

Her growing prestige as a center of culture and the prosperity her shipping brought in the first quarter of the century did not, however, blind Baltimore merchants to new opportunities. For thirty years their first preoccupation had been to outdo Philadelphia. They had built canals inland and improved navigation on the Susquehanna river in order to snatch from their rival to the north the trade of western Pennsylvania. Now that settlement was rapidly moving still further west, they looked beyond the Susquehanna valley. They readily perceived the importance of links with the Ohio valley and saw, partially at least, the futility of relying upon either the National Road over the mountains or a new canal, a project that would require an endless number of locks to take boats over the 1,900-foot watershed. Consequently Baltimore business men listened to tales of British success with railways. In December 1826 Evan Thomas, fresh back from a visit in England, described the Stockton and Darlington railway to a group of friends. Since the Erie Canal, then in full operation, was sending to New York the riches of the new West at a rate chilling to the hearts of merchants on the Chesapeake, they listened with attention. In January, Thomas's banker brother Philip, when host at a large dinner party, repeated to his influential guests the story of what the British railway was accomplishing. The group then and there appointed a committee to study the pros and cons of attempting to build a railway over the mountains. Two weeks later the committee's report endorsing the scheme was in circulation, and on 28 February 1827 the Maryland legislature granted a charter to the Baltimore and Ohio Railroad. Every share of stock in the company was sold before the end of April, mostly to local purchasers. The City Council invested $500,000 of city money in the undertaking upon which Baltimore now believed her commercial future would depend. Within five months of hearing of the Stockton and Darlington railway, Baltimore men had explored the idea, prepared a plan, organized a company, and financed the venture. To direct part of the construction they engaged Major George Washington Whistler, father of the painter James McNeill Whistler, and a man of gifts as exceptional as those of his more famous son. In the thirties, as the iron rails crept nearer and nearer the divide, merchants of other cities reluctantly admitted that Baltimore enterprise was heightening Baltimore's power.

## CHARLESTON AND BOSTON

Although New York, Philadelphia, and Baltimore were the three leading cities of the United States before 1830, neither their greater size and commercial power nor the vigor of their intellectual life lessens the special significance of Charleston and Boston. Charleston in South Carolina and Boston on Massachusetts Bay epitomized their particular regions and represented the two extremes whose conflicting ideas and economic interests would diverge further and further until all sections of the country must take sides and plunge the nation into civil war. The social and economic conditions that by 1820 had placed the South apart from the rest of the nation found full expression in Charleston. She spoke for South Carolina, and agricultural South Carolina set the example for other Southern states. Boston was the heart of Yankeedom, destined after 1825 to sponsor the industrialization of New England and thereby widen the rift opening between North and South. Contrasts between the city home of South Carolina planters and the Boston of Yankee merchants and shipbuilders existed, to be sure, before Boston money began to build New England cotton mills. The contrasts derived in part from the differences in religion and social backgrounds of the early settlers, in part from their dissimilar geographic settings in the New World. But in 1800 these differences had not yet bred hostilities. Boston visitors in Charleston were charmed by the Southern city, and the less frequent sojourns of Charlestonians in Boston gave them, in turn, respect for the Yankee town.

'Charleston', according to traditional school geography lessons in South Carolina, 'is the place where the Ashley and Cooper rivers meet to form the Atlantic Ocean.' Built in 1683 on a mile-wide neck of land between the two rivers, Charleston from the first was virtually a city-state. After the War of Independence, the social revolution that swept all the new states brought about the removal of the South Carolina capital to Columbia in the Piedmont. For just as back-country representatives in the Pennsylvania legislature chose Harrisburg as the state capital in place of Philadelphia, and New York State farmers selected Albany rather than New York, so the up-country farmers of South Carolina sought to weaken the control of the Tidewater over the rest of the state. It was a fruitless move. Until mid-nineteenth century Charleston was South Carolina in essence. Even today state officials occasionally have difficulty in persuading elderly Charlestonians that their automobiles need South Carolina licenses as well as Charleston plates.

The first settlers, besides men from England and Virginians, included a number of planters from Barbados who came with their trained slaves and thus brought with them the makings of a West Indian plantation system. Their Negroes were preponderantly from Portuguese Africa, Angola, whence, etymologists conclude, came the name Gullah. Because of their racial fitness for the climate and for Carolina plantation life, Gullahs were always the Negroes preferred by Charleston purchasers, and the musical pidgin English dialect of the Charleston Negro is still Gullah and distinctive. The Barbadian influence made itself felt not only in the region's agrarian system but also in Charleston's architecture. Eighteenth-century buildings that survived the British bombardment during the Revolution still show traces of the West Indian admixture in the city's origins. The typical two- or three-story frame or brick 'single' house stands gable-end to the street. Along its length run 'galleries', or balconies, that serve in this subtropical climate as sheltered outdoor living-rooms. Exquisite wrought iron work on the galleries may be repeated in the gates set in garden walls flanking the street. Across the vine-clad galleries the breeze sweeps through the house built only one room wide so as to catch the air from either river or sea. The 'double' house differs only in being two rooms wide. To the rear of the main house stretched a series of outbuildings, the summer kitchen, the washhouse, and quarters for slaves.

Before the seventeenth century was out, Huguenots and French Acadians came, in the eighteenth century Scots and South Germans, and in the nineteenth North Germans and Irish, until some wit could say of the twentieth-century city that she was 'owned by the Germans, ruled by the Irish, and enjoyed by the Negroes'. But while her most influential citizens in her days of greatest power

Charleston, with St Michael's church and typical galleried houses

were of British or Huguenot extraction, all settlers then and later became passionate Charlestonians. Men excluded by their humble circumstances from sharing in the gaiety of the wealthy nevertheless felt with their social superiors that as Charleston citizens they were chosen people. The half-humorous saying 'better to be dead and buried in St Michael's graveyard than alive anywhere else on earth' expressed the common feeling. Throughout her history the number of affectionate quips about the city proclaimed men's sense of her uniqueness.

The wealth of Charleston had been founded upon indigo and rice. After the Revolution, planters abandoned indigo-growing, once supported by British bounties, but rice held first place till the end of the eighteenth century. Until very recently rice appeared three times daily on orthodox Charleston tables, where connoisseurs reputedly could distinguish by flavor the grain of one kind of seed from that of another. Rice was so much a part of their lives that old families in the tourist-ridden twentieth-century city were said to reverse the Chinese order by worshipping rice and eating their ancestors. Though rice culture made fortunes for Carolina planters, it depended, they believed, on slave labor, with the result that slavery, as an essential element of the plantation system, formed the basis of Charleston's economy. Yet few men deemed that basis immutable until the invention of the cotton gin in 1793 made the raising of short-staple cotton profitable and the extension of the plantation system inevitable. Men hastening to buy land and labor to clear and plant it created a demand for slaves that led South Carolina in 1804 to reopen her port to the African slave trade. That trade which, by the terms of the federal Constitution, Congress might close forever in 1808 was legal until then. During those intervening four years it flourished in Charleston. Later, defenders of the South's 'peculiar institution' reminded Northerners that only 62 of the 202 slave-ships entering the harbor in those years were Charleston-owned; the rest were of British or New England registry. These figures, while perhaps supporting the city's claim to humanitarian sentiments, suggest that as early as 1800 commerce was already taking a place secondary to South Carolina's agrarian interests. This final importation of Africans, many of them straight out of the jungle, fastened slavery upon South Carolina for social as well as economic reasons. Unless rigorous controls were in force, white people dared not live where blacks little removed from barbarism outnumbered the whites. In 1800, the census for Charleston listed only 8,820 free whites in a population of 18,924. Thirty years later whites numbered 12,688, slaves 15,494, and free Negroes 2,100.

Besides the slave trade, other phases of the city's commerce prospered before 1807. As war in Europe threw to the United States much of the Atlantic carrying trade, Charleston became a depot for European goods bound for the West Indies and for West Indian produce destined for Europe. Favorable prevailing winds and ocean currents enabled sailing ships out of the Carolina port to make the run to the Continent or Great Britain as quickly as ships from New York or Boston. In December 1807, however, the Embargo Act, President Jefferson's valiant attempt by economic boycott to force England and France to respect American rights on the sea, brought this trade to a halt. The later Non-Intercourse Act made matters worse. For American merchants the alternatives to ruin appeared to be defiance of the law or a switch to other interests. While the northern cities veered toward smuggling, Charleston for the most part chose the other way out. Merchants here who salvaged some capital turned to cotton-planting. Thereafter Charleston money, once invested in ships and foreign commerce, was largely tied up in cotton.

Cotton export from Charleston wharves, it is true, mounted steadily in volume after 1815, but Charleston merchants no longer controlled it. New York shippers captured the cotton-carrying trade by developing what was known as the 'cotton triangle', a system whereby New York vessels picked up the cotton from Charleston's docks, as from those of Savannah and New Orleans, carried it to Liverpool, brought European cargoes back to New York, and distributed the imports from there. Charleston had to pay New York shipping, wharfage, insurance, and commission charges on South Carolina cotton exports and similar fees for imports. New York factors or Liverpool agents resident in Charleston negotiated these deals; the houses they represented did the financing, yearly supplying credit to the planters till the season's crop was sold and then pocketing most of the cash profits. Want of ready money would later hamper Charleston's every effort to recapture commercial power, and as soon as steamships supplanted sailing vessels, lack of easy access to coal would defeat her. But long before sailing ships disappeared, the leading men of the city rarely had fluid capital. Whenever the high price of cotton cleared them of debt, they bought more slaves and more land, usually in the new country to the west, where the virgin soil of Alabama and Mississippi produced prodigious yields per acre. They ignored the fact that by constantly increasing the size of the crop, they were lessening the chance of keeping the price of cotton high and steadily reducing the value of South Carolina's older fields, which years of careless cultivation were stripping of fertility.

By 1820, moreover, Savannah, Georgia, was cutting in upon Charleston as a cotton port. Georgia cotton was competing with South Carolina's, and Georgia planters shipped from Savannah at the mouth of the Savannah river and imported their luxuries from New York and abroad by the same route. As the river forms the southern boundary of South Carolina, much of the up-state Carolina crop also went down the river to the rival port. In 1828 Charleston men had become so concerned over this growing traffic that they undertook to build a railroad to the head of navigation on the Savannah to divert up-country cotton and lumber to Charleston. They named the first locomotive of the line 'Best Friend of Charleston'. But the railroad was only briefly an asset and in the long run profited Charleston little. Unsuccessful in later attempts to bring an interstate railroad into the city to link her with the expanding West, South Carolina after 1835 would subside into an aggressive agrarianism.

Loss of commercial strength notwithstanding, before 1830 the city seldom worried for her future. Her planters who spread the gospel of cotton influenced thinking throughout the South, and even while Charleston's economic importance dwindled, the ideas she stood for gathered force to dominate the ruling

Charleston 'single' houses: in foreground the Thomas Legare house, 1760

classes of the Cotton Kingdom until the Civil War destroyed them. The uneasiness of a few farsighted citizens failed to undermine the general belief that raw cotton would keep Charleston in a position of leadership. During the troubled era of the Embargo a small cotton mill, aided by a small subsidy from the State, had operated in the city, but like most similar experiments in the North, it was short-lived. For years after it closed, David R. Williams, publisher of the Charleston *City Gazette* and a cotton-planter, stood almost alone in contending that the South must balance agriculture with manufacturing. He himself built a cotton yarn mill near his plantation in 1828. As the price of cotton began to drop at the end of the 1820's, other men gave serious thought to his arguments and a few attempted to follow his example, but the size of the investment needed, the lack of fluid capital, the difficulty of training slaves or poor whites to man machines, and the cost of engaging Northern foremen discouraged planters. Greater wisdom seemed to lie in clinging to the familiar business of growing cotton; its price, they believed, would eventually rise. Leave manufacturing to the Yankees. As long as the world wanted cotton—and that would be always—Carolina planters would command prestige. And most Charlestonians refused to worry over their dependence upon European and New York credit.

The plantation owners' way of life represented all that seemed most desirable, one that lesser citizens sought to emulate by themselves becoming landed proprietors. A plantation under a competent overseer could run itself except for the weeks of the planting season or harvest; that arrangement left the owner free to enjoy life in the city. Nearly every South Carolina planter of consequence owned a house in Charleston where he spent many months of the year. Rice-planters had set the fashion in the eighteenth century by moving their households hither during the summer months to escape the malaria of the swampy rice country. The sea breezes kept the city relatively free of malaria, and though the threat of yellow fever hung over the port, that dread disease struck with epidemic force only about one year in eight. In time, planters came to spend here much of the winter as well. At all seasons, gardens, flanking every house of any pretentions, blazed with color and made the air fragrant with scent of oleander, jasmine, and magnolia. The city was small; a half-hour's walk would take one from sea-wall to inland boundary or from the Ashley to the Cooper, and white families, before 1830 numbering only about three hundred, all knew each other. In these ways the city was scarcely a city at all.

Indeed, Charleston could be called a congeries of able families. Unconcerned about money matters, the heads of the leading families in this small community were men whose distinction in other fields would have marked them anywhere. Charles Cotesworthy Pinckney served the United States skilfully on a number of difficult diplomatic missions. His still more famous cousin, Charles Pinckney, twice Governor of the state in the 1790's, was author of one version of the federal Constitution. 'Blackguard Charlie', as he was known to his associates in Congress, was at once a swashbuckling braggart, a man of exceptional charm, and a statesman of unusual ability. Though his position and wealth might have dictated conservatism, he sponsored a bill in 1808 to extend South Carolina's suffrage to all white males over twenty-one years of age. Two years later Henry Middleton succeeded in getting the bill passed. Henry Middleton, educated in England at Cambridge, owner of the beautiful Middleton Place on the Ashley near Charleston, from 1810 to 1812 Governor of the state, was another forward-looking statesman in feudal South Carolina. Through his advocacy, a bill to establish free public schools also became law, only to fail in effect because no money was voted to support them. Staunch Unionist, he stood in vigorous opposition to proponents of South Carolina's withdrawal from the federal Union in 1832 and to the Nullification Ordinance denying validity to federal laws unacceptable in the state. At Middleton's side in the Nullification controversy stood his brother-in-law, Judge Daniel Huger, descendant of brilliant Huguenot forebears and himself a man of rare cultivation and insight. On the other side of the political fence were an equally gifted group, in Charleston led by Robert Y. Hayne, noted lawyer and orator, whose impassioned defense of 'states' rights' on the floor of the United States Senate has made his name familiar to every American schoolchild. The list of eminent Charlestonians could be lengthened by a score of others whose considerable talents were variously exhibited.

Nowhere else in America was life so truly urbane as in Charleston. Affinities were closer with Paris and London than with the rest of the country. European travellers with harsh comments on the crudities of much of the United States found the well-bred sophistication of this South Carolina community wholly engaging. It was a society rooted in a leisure unknown in Northern cities. Even in Baltimore, where slavery existed and well-trained servants cared for every menial task, the heads of well-established families still gave personal attention daily to their business affairs. Charlestonians made gracious living their first business. The concerts of Mozart and Haydn given by the St Cecilia society, the balls, the theatre, the race course, and in 1800 the only golf links in America provided endless diversion. In fine weather a promenade along the sea-wall, the 'Battery', to exchange news with neighbors and visitors was a daily routine. Here were to be seen the latest European fashions in clothes, magnificent carriages, and fine blooded horses. Religion sat lightly upon Charlestonians; without being caught up by deep devotion to the church, they attended weekly services and guided their conduct by the code of 'the gentleman'. At home, in the beautiful high-ceiled drawing-rooms, men discussed the affairs of the world over fine old Madeira, or talked of philosophy and new developments in science and the arts. Good conversation was so important that a man's social standing depended in some measure upon his 'colloquial parts'. Lawyers, doctors, ministers, and teachers, if men of learning, were welcome members of Charleston society. Though few native citizens were themselves creative thinkers, artists, or writers, they were interested in what others produced, and played host to a succession of distinguished visitors from abroad. Painters like Charles Fraser, the miniaturist, Thomas Sully, one of America's most accomplished portrait painters, and somewhat later, the versatile Samuel Finley Breeze Morse found patrons here.

Leaders of this agreeable society, moreover, accepted municipal office as a matter of course. As was still true in northern cities, men of substance and social standing controlled civic affairs, though here public office was more honor than burden. In the first quarter of the nineteenth century, the machinery of American city government was uncomplicated everywhere. Charleston's differed from that of New York, Philadelphia, or Baltimore only in details. Instead of Mayor, Charleston's chief magistrate before 1836 was called Intendant. He was chosen from their own members by the thirteen Councilmen, one Councilman elected from each ward of the city. Citizens demanded few public services. Men of property expected to provide schooling for their own children. No one asked for street paving or street lighting such as northern cities provided. Volunteers supplied the city with her only form of fire protection. A public sewerage system or municipal water supply was unthought of; cisterns on the roofs of dwellings sufficed. Public health regulation was scanty. Not until mid-century would city officials discover that Charleston lagged behind northern communities in furnishing safeguards to citizens' well-being. Yet in 1830, when the death rate in Boston was 20 per thousand, in Philadelphia 20·90, in New York 25·66, and in half-southern Baltimore 22·19, Charleston reported 25·65 for white people only. Strangely enough, the city's vital statistics showed a slightly lower mortality among the black population, figures perhaps resulting from a practice common in the South of omitting from the count slave children under three years of age, but also suggesting the slave owner's vigilance in watching over his Negroes. Although the city supported a combined 'Poor-house (and asylum for lunatic persons)' and although private philanthropy endowed other institutions for relief of the needy, the aristocratic tradition that citizens cherished encouraged belief that each family should care for its own, and the paternalistic regime bred by slave-holding placed responsibility, not with public officials, but with the head of each household. Doubtless some people suffered under this system, but men of influence were satisfied with the city as she was, and even critics of the South when visiting Charleston were moved by her charm.

Boston, on Massachusetts Bay, bred a very different kind of American. The Yankee, though Southerners during the Civil War applied the term to any Union soldier, was a product of New England's stony soil and harsh climate. His racial inheritance was English, Scottish, French, and Irish, with a dash of South European thrown in. Generally long and lanky in appearance, he usually lacked the outer graces of the Southerner. His speech was laconic, his humor salty rather than genial. With a touch of the Scot in his view of life, he considered religion a serious matter. In learning to make the most of what a niggardly nature provided, he developed a talent for improvization that sometimes wrought minor miracles. Though the soil of his home lot was infertile, the sea stretched before him. And Boston was New England's leading seaport.

Founded in 1630, Boston was more than a generation old when the first settlers landed on South Carolina's Ashley. Before 1755 she was the most prosperous town in the American colonies; her harbor and 'long wharf' saw ships and cargoes in numbers and value known to no other port on the continent. Originally the stronghold of the Puritan theocracy, Boston had come in the course of the eighteenth century to modify her uncompromising religious, political, and social views. Commercial contacts with far places of the earth had widened the horizons of the Boston merchant and given him a new tolerance. Quite as wealthy as his Charleston counterpart at the turn of the century, shrewder as a business man and much more concerned with his financial affairs, he was filled with a sense of his own dignity and rightful place of influence in American society. The comment of Oliver Wendell Holmes, Harvard professor and the great New England wit of his day, applied in 1800 as in the 1870's: 'The Bostonian considers that the frog pond on Boston Common is the hub of the universe.'

Built on a promontory jutting out into the island-studded harbor, Boston was connected with the mainland by a narrow neck of land. On the south running eastward the harbor enclosed her, on the north the Charles river with a large inner basin, the Back Bay. The geographic features of the modern city bear scant resemblance to the early nineteenth-century town, for, in time, urban growth demanded filling in the Back Bay and the southern shore line and the levelling of two of the three hills that originally gave to the locality the name Trimountaine. But before 1820 the saying held true that 'in tide-encircled Boston each street led down to the sea.' The sea opened out a career to every boy, and boys embarked on their careers at the age of fourteen or fifteen, and sometimes very much younger. In the period of adjustment after the Revolution, Boston merchants, with that genius for adaptation that had characterized them for one hundred and fifty-odd years, turned to trade with the Far East. Upon the outbreak of the Napoleonic wars in Europe they seized upon that opportunity also. When the British fleet drove French ships from the sea, Boston shipmasters, along with other American shipowners, took over the transport business of the colonies in the western world belonging to France and her Spanish and Dutch allies.

Unlike her southern rivals, the Yankee port had no agricultural staple for export. Apart from New England's forests, whence came lumber, shingles, barrel and pipe staves, pine for masts, tar and turpentine, Massachusetts' native source of wealth was fish—haddock, mackerel, and, above all, cod. Fishermen's fleets sailed every spring for the Newfoundland banks and brought back each fall the catch that, salted down, supplied Boston with that mainstay of New England diet, cod for fishballs, and, even more important, provided a commodity for export to West Indian planters to feed their slaves. When Spain opened her ports to American traders, Boston merchants found they could sell cod to Catholic Europe in exchange for the fine wines wanted at home. A carved wooden codfish still occupies a place of honor in the Massachusetts State House. Although New England's infertile soil early produced some surplus rye and barley and supported enough cattle to permit salting a little beef to supplement the trade with the West Indies, farm produce could not have formed a basis for a thriving economy. It was the fisheries, shipbuilding, and, in the early decades of the nineteenth century, an ever-expanding carrying trade on which Boston's prosperity rested. By 1805 half of the 1,000,000 tons of American shipping was New England's, and of that Boston's share was nearly a quarter. Only New Yorkers, with 217,000 tons in 1807, owned more. New England shipwrights built some of the finest, fastest ships afloat, and a Boston brig or schooner sold at a handsome profit to the builder as long as foreign governments allowed their merchants to buy American vessels. At the close of the war of 1812 European powers lifted restrictions on purchase of American-built ships, and though shipbuilding by then had declined in Boston, thereafter, as long as the sailing vessel ruled ocean commerce, Boston shipyards could sell readily anything they turned out.

Bostonians, moreover, early acquired some skill in processing West Indian and native produce. From the end of the seventeenth century onward, they had converted West Indian molasses and sugar into rum or loaf sugar. The fisheries supplied the makings of sperm oil and spermaceti candles. Rope walks and sail-cloth establishments, in spite of the crudity of the spinning equipment and looms, were local manufactures important to this seafaring community. By 1800 local enterprisers were making tallow candles, glass, paperhangings, and beer brewed from the hops New England farmers could raise. These activities were only complementary to the town's main interests, but the diversification, however slight, helped the community to survive periods of commercial depression which overwhelmed neighboring towns. Still Boston would not become an industrial city for many decades. In 1830, as in 1800, she was first and foremost a great commercial port.

Her commerce, like that of other United States seaports, faced ruin when President Jefferson imposed the Embargo in 1807. Boston's merchants, like New York's and Baltimore's, ignored it. They defied the later Non-Intercourse Act equally. Respected and self-respecting men turned to smuggling, and the Collector and Deputy Collector of the Port of Boston resigned rather than try to enforce a law they considered odious. When the United States in 1812 declared war on Great Britain, New York and Baltimore shipmasters accepted letters of marque and reprisal, but only thirty-one Boston ships became privateers. The profits of Boston's trade with Halifax, Nova Scotia, which the British encouraged, was one good reason for this, and the money to be made in privateering was not sufficient bait to win New Englanders to support of the war. In fact, Boston's indignant protests over the federal government's interference with her commerce resulted in 1814 in Massachusetts' sending delegates to a convention in Hartford, Connecticut, to plan a withdrawal from the misguided Union. The war's end cancelled the agitation. Yet Boston benefited more than she suffered from the turbulent years between 1808 and 1815. By leaning upon her small manufactures and by judiciously timed smuggling, she weathered the storm that reduced rival New England ports to insignificance. She emerged the undisputed mistress of the whole region. In the year 1830 more than a thousand foreign ships discharged cargoes at Boston wharves, and Boston ships numbered in the hundreds.

Her citizens repeatedly demonstrated their shrewdness in finding new money-making ventures. At the end of the eighteenth century, Boston merchantmen were carrying gewgaws, rough clothing, and hardware to the Indians of the Pacific Northwest where captains and supercargoes bartered these inexpensive articles for sea otter pelts to sell in China in exchange for tea and silks; when the sea otter was killed off, they substituted trade with the Sandwich Islanders whose sandalwood commanded high prices in China. Less well-known but equally ingenious was the business developed by a Bostonian of shipping ice to the planters of the West Indies, ice cut at slight expense in winter on New England ponds and needing only a coating of sawdust to prepare it for transport. Men could make fortunes—and did—in two or three bold voyages.

Nor were snowballing profits poured only into commercial enterprise. Bostonians increasingly put money into banking and insurance. Marine insurance naturally appeared early and was well established in the 1780's. In 1798 the Massachusetts Mutual Insurance Company was organized to offer protection against losses from fire and some years later added life insurance. By 1807 seven private insurance offices were doing a large business. Banking was slightly older in Philadelphia, but in 1784 the Bank of Massachusetts opened in Boston, and by 1811 the town had four banks—including a branch of the Bank of the United States—and by 1824 had nineteen. The Provident Institution for Savings founded in 1816 was the first savings bank in the United States. Boston, with half the banking capital of New England, had made herself one of the financial centers of the

American continent as early as 1820, and that position she has held to this very day. The merchant might have his capital tied up for a year or two while his ships carried valuable cargo to distant ports and landed the return cargo safely in Boston harbor, but his financial commitments were of far shorter duration than the Carolina planter's with his capital vested in land and slaves. The Bostonian never lost sight of the importance of cash as well as credit and kept some capital available for investment in whatever might turn up. Daring and imagination characterized his financial dealings throughout the nineteenth century, whether he was shipping prefabricated frame houses around the Horn to San Francisco during the gold rush, developing the copper mines in the wilderness of Michigan's upper peninsula, or building railroads in the Colorado mountains.

Samuel Adams, the Revolutionary leader of Massachusetts, had dubbed Boston the Christian Sparta. Certainly she prided herself on the simplicity of her ways. High thinking and plain living, however, were only relative. Compared to the gaiety and lavish display to be seen in southern cities, Boston was sedate. She had no concerts, and yet her theatre in the early decades of the century ranked among the best in the United States. She lacked the cosmopolitan air of New York and the varied experience of Philadelphia, but her great merchants lived in far more than mere comfort. Their roomy houses were furnished with the work of renowned English cabinet makers or talented American imitators, carpeted with French or oriental rugs, equipped with fine silver and exquisite porcelain. Their portraits painted by Gilbert Stuart or John Copley show strong ruddy faces, tinted perhaps by years of drinking port, Madeira, or rum, and lacking any hint of the ascetic in cast of features or expression. Except in midsummer they rarely used their country houses; life in town was satisfying. If their hospitality usually reached only to well-to-do Boston families, their formal dinners and balls nevertheless were of the utmost elegance. In this era, high society still opened its doors to professional men and wealthy shopkeepers, provided their fortunes were a generation old. Before mid-century those doors would close, and thereafter only birth would give entrée. Even early in the century, marriage outside the fold of this close-knit society was taboo; only black sheep would stray. The lesser people of the town—the small tradesmen, the vendors of local farm produce, the cobblers and tailors, the carters and draymen, and the host of clerks who kept the books of Boston's commercial houses—accepted their place as ordained. On a modest scale they too lived well. Their houses contained sturdy American pine and maple furniture, pewter and earthern tableware; they had decent homespun clothing, ample, if simple, food, wood for their fireplaces, and stoves to fend off the bitter cold of New England winters. The crowded tenements and the filthy slums of a later day had not spread far in 1830, and though waterfront grog shops and sailors' rooming-houses were undoubtedly both unsightly and insanitary, the town and city of the 1820's was still orderly-looking and substantial.

While Spartan attributes were largely imaginary, the Christian epithet was justified. The Congregational church was state-supported until 1833, though the Episcopal church had some adherents in Boston, and Roman Catholicism was gaining a foothold as Irish immigrants poured in to build the canals, factories, and railroads for New England. Religious orthodoxy had ceased to dominate the Massachusetts community a hundred years before, but the proper Bostonian still expected what he termed Christian behavior of himself and his fellows. The tinge of sombreness in his character usually prevented his turning his wit upon anything so important as his faith, but in one sentence it flashed forth: 'The Bostonian believes in the Fatherhood of God, the Brotherhood of Man, and the Neighborhood of Boston.'

In opposition to the Deistic rationalism of Boston intellectuals who were mainly Unitarian Congregationalists, the trinitarian wing of the established church was beginning to stress an emotional humanitarianism. It was, in the phrase of Lyman Beecher, pastor of Boston's Hanover Street Church, 'clinical theology', healing to the souls of sinful men. Emphasis upon kindly behavior rather than dogma was giving new meaning to the word *Christian*. In Boston it meant churchgoing, respect for the minister and contributions to his salary, but also consideration for others, a heeding of civic conscience. In contrast to the earlier Puritan view that poverty was an act of God calling for no human intervention, *Christianity* now embraced the Good Samaritan creed. What Boston provided in her almshouse was unquestionably far from munificent, but the town and townspeople individually accepted the obligation to care for the helpless. The Overseers of the Poor were town officials. In 1812 public-spirited citizens formed the Washington Benevolent Society and a dozen years later a charitable eye and ear clinic partly supported by state funds. At the turn of the century, when slaves were to be found in every other seaport of the United States, all Negroes in Boston were free. The growing sense of the community's responsibility for community ills distinguished Boston from cities to the south. Quaker benevolence did much for Philadelphia, generosity of individuals in New York and Baltimore often rescued others from want, and Charleston families took care of their own dependents, but nowhere else in early nineteenth-century America did men so generally acknowledge public duty and so promptly act as in Boston.

Equally significant was Boston's attitude toward schooling. Massachusetts had

Boston, 1828
The domed building is the State House on Beacon Hill

always contended that a Christian society could not endure unless people could read the Scriptures and that schools were therefore essential. This doctrine was, of course, neither new nor peculiar to Massachusetts. Its distinctive feature lay in its application. Boston accepted the concept that taxpayers' money must support public schools open to poor and rich alike. In 1818 when the School Committee reported that 526 children between the ages of four and fourteen were receiving no schooling, townspeople voted money to establish another school. As yet no law required attendance, and in the 1840's Theodore Parker would plead passionately for public attention to the vagrant children in the city: truant officers would not appear until the 1860's. Nevertheless, social custom made school attendance for Yankee children virtually obligatory, because illiteracy was the mark of the immigrant and the social upstart. Though the quality of the schools left much to be desired, the ideal remained. Schools of sorts existed, open to any child whose parents wanted him or her to attend. Whatever its shortcomings, this scheme of public education was well in advance of those in other American cities and was in sharpest contrast to the casual private-schooling of Charleston. New York made her first move to establish free public schools after 1805, and until 1828 a private society, not public taxation, supported them; Philadelphia had none before 1818; Baltimore waited still longer. As a result both of her schools and of her uncomplicated religious views, Boston society before 1830 had a unity greater than anything to be found in England and only rarely to be matched elsewhere in America. Everyone knew what made a good life and everyone— merchant, clerk, or tradesman—behaved accordingly.

Allied to awareness of citizens' material and spiritual needs was Boston's interest in municipal improvement. Early in the eighteenth century, private enterprise had installed underground sewers drawing out through wooden conduits. Street lamps lighted the streets until ten o'clock unless the moon was shining. Tar-coated pebbles paved the main thoroughfares before the opening of the nineteenth century. In the 1820's a gas company began laying gas mains. Up to 1822 town constables, instead of a police force, patrolled the streets. For before 1822 Bostonians refused to abandon the town form of government. The first settlers of Massachusetts Bay had introduced the town system already in effect in Plymouth Plantation. At the annual town meeting all freemen—that is, all men accepted by their fellows as full-fledged, responsible members of the community —met to discuss town affairs. After electing a moderator to preside, the freemen chose three Selectmen and officials, such as a surveyor of weights and measures, the Constable, and the members of the School Committee, to manage town business during the year ahead. The town paid them according to the number of days they spent on public matters. If an emergency arose, the Selectmen would call a special town meeting. In a small community this system could be the essence of democracy, though established leaders, notably the clergy, at times rode rough-shod over lesser men. But for a town of 25,000 inhabitants, like Boston in 1800, the system was cumbersome, and in 1820, when she had over 41,000, men found it unworkable. Reluctantly in 1822 townspeople voted to seek a city charter. It pro-vided for a Mayor, a Board of Aldermen, and a Common Council, to be elected yearly. In 1823 Josiah Quincy, later President of Harvard College and author of a history of Boston, became Mayor and was re-elected four times; under his re-gime, town turned into city easily. Friction would come in the 1840's and 1850's with the enfranchisement of newcomers and the rise of the Irish to political power. Before 1830 men of substance and, by New World standards, of ancient family continued to run the city.

While Boston called herself the Christian Sparta, she was convinced that she was also the Christian Athens. In Cambridge, across the Charles River and some four miles west of Boston, stood Harvard College where young men had been trained for the ministry since 1636. Ties between the Harvard Yard and Boston counting houses on India Street and Battery March grew up in the course of the eighteenth century so that Boston boys who did not ship to sea were likely to en-roll at Harvard. Though the College struck a low point in the first decades of the nineteenth century, and for a generation ceased to be a center of scholarship, its graduates acquired a social stature quite unrelated to any intellectual achievement. The connections between the one-time seat of learning and the commercial sea-port endured, and in the 1840's and 1850's when intellectual vigor revived in the College, Harvard's influence upon Boston would be pronounced. In the preced-ing generation a more solid basis for claiming intellectual distinction lay in the collections of books and the existence of learned societies. The American Aca-demy of Arts and Sciences founded in 1780 and the Massachusetts Historical Society created in 1791 were the first. Perhaps still more notable was the opening of the Athenaeum in 1807. The rare books and pamphlets available to members and guests of the society—the very name Athenaeum proclaiming its classical association—made its rooms a rendezvous for scholars and literati. It includes most of George Washington's books and ranks today among the finest libraries in America. Furthermore, every well-to-do household contained books. Before the transcendentalists of the Concord group had formed a creative literary com-munity in that part of New England, the Bostonian regarded books, their con-tents as well as their bindings, as part of the equipment of every citizen whose opinion could carry weight. As in Charleston, few native citizens earned a place in literature equal to that attained by New Yorkers and Baltimoreans, but in 1815 a group of Harvard classmates, staunch Unitarians all, gave birth in Boston to one of the first great periodicals of the United States, the *North American Review*. No later American publication has surpassed the quality of this American counterpart of the *Edinburgh Review*.

Boston's architecture also was distinguished. The layout of the original town with its home lots and Common had not allowed for growth. Because narrow streets twisting away from the Common literally followed the cowpaths made by the cattle pastured on the Common in early years, broad vistas, like those in Philadelphia, were rare. Nevertheless, the town had an outer mien of dignity and affluence scarcely less noteworthy than Philadelphia's or Charleston's. Wealthy merchants at the turn of the century were building harmoniously proportioned houses in a style of architecture which is known in the United States as Federal, and closely resembles English Regency. Bostonians, realizing that Federal preceded Regency in time, compared London to Boston, not Boston to the older city. In 1795 Charles Bulfinch, recently returned from wanderings in Europe, was engaged to build an imposing new State House on Beacon Hill. In the years that followed he displayed his taste to even better advantage in the private residences he designed. Perhaps imitating John Wood of Bath, he built a crescent of brick houses which reputedly was the most beautiful row of houses in America. Unhappily, a later generation destroyed the famous crescent to make way for 'modern improvements'. Yet today a section on Beacon Hill and Louisburg Square, with its private garden fenced by iron grilles, still stands as a testimonial to Bulfinch's art.

One aspect of Boston's life, rarely mentioned but still of significance, was the fate of her women. Boston men were always sailing off on long voyages, often lasting two or three years; hence there were always too many lone women about. Sweethearts and wives left at home had to make out as best they could. The yearly crop of sailors' widows was big. After 1800, moreover, a growing number of spinsters weighted Boston society. From the ranks of the well-born spinsters whose schooling had been quite as thorough as their brothers' came a group of literary females, some of them early engrossed in good works and espousing causes, others subsiding into gentle obscurity at home, but always well-read and possessed of opinions. Among the poorer classes, single women turned to running shops and taverns, thus taking a place in the daily business world of the seaport long before the business woman was accepted elsewhere. Before 1830 Boston was still a masculine city dominated by men and men's interests; but the influence of women was gradually permeating her life, and forty years later women would not only set the tone of social intercourse but also control many of Boston's large fortunes.

The 1820's saw marked changes in nearly every American community. The generation familiar with British colonial administrators and schooled to observe the niceties of Europe's social forms was gone. Men trained only in the rough and ready ways of the frontier were pushing into national politics, and in the cities men neither rich nor well-born were clamoring for a share in municipal affairs. As British liberals moved slowly toward the reforms that would become law in 1832, state legislatures in the United States, one after the other, extended the franchise. If 'the rise of the common man' took place between 1830 and 1850, the forces that brought it about were nevertheless at work before 1820 and were clearly visible by 1828 when General Andrew Jackson of trans-Appalachian Tennessee was elected to the Presidency. Jackson, largely self-educated, Indian fighter, idol of frontiersmen, and 'the hero of New Orleans' in saving the city from British capture in 1814, represented to his countrymen a new America. The election made unmistakable the fact that the old order was passing, giving way to one where European manners no longer counted as an asset and the western trade vied with the European in the calculations of merchants.

As urban life fostered the exchange of ideas, the new concept of the United States as a nation spread rapidly through the cities. Despite the interest of the Atlantic seaports in maintaining their commerce with Europe, they were swept into the movement directed toward a fuller national economic and cultural independence. Charleston, wedded to Europe and European cotton markets, was less affected than most seaboard cities, though, while successfully fending off social change, she too strove to establish ties with the West. The other Atlantic port cities were feeling the new social pressures and were increasingly aware that whoever captured the bulk of the Ohio valley trade would prosper at the expense of all other competitors. New York relied upon the Erie Canal; Philadelphia and Baltimore sought their own waterways to the West until the Marylanders ventured upon building their railroad, and Philadelphia, with skilled workmen in her midst, northern Pennsylvania's anthracite coal fields at her door and iron deposits nearby, turned to manufacturing machinery and iron wares, and, as a prop to her commerce, to shipping coal. Boston, a hundred and fifty miles east of the Hudson and over two hundred and fifty miles farther than Baltimore from the Ohio country, could not compete for the western trade on terms of equality. She must wipe out that inequality or find some new source of strength, if she were to maintain her place among the great cities of the East. Local agricultural products could no longer bolster her commerce; New England farming, never much above the subsistence level, was now producing little more than enough to feed New England's growing population. The answer to Boston's quandary lay in developing manufactures and building railroads. Her small home industries had helped tide her over crises before; New England factories turning out goods in quantity would do even better. A railroad to the West would distribute the manufactures inland and create trade with the interior.

Before the mid-1820's most Bostonians saw neither the problem nor its solution with clarity. Yet the process had already begun of turning New England's water-power to account by using it to drive factory wheels. From the early seventeenth century onward, Yankee farmers had put it to some use; undershot water wheels installed on swift-flowing brooks had supplied power for grist and saw-mills in every New England village. But these were not factories equipped with expensive machinery. The industrial revolution in England had of course spurred American ambitions. In 1790 Samuel Slater, emigrating to the United States, had brought in his head the essential features of Arkwright's spinning frames. Financed by two Rhode Island merchants, he had then built and successfully run a cotton-spinning mill near Providence. In Massachusetts, too, small spinning mills had started up and failed, only to be succeeded by others when embargo and war afforded artificial protection. During that brief interval, Baltimore men also had tried cotton manufacture, but they, like the owners of ill-equipped Massachusetts mills, abandoned it as soon as English goods returned to the American market after the war.

Boston capitalists up to that time had taken no interest in manufacturing enterprise. It was Francis Cabot Lowell who, after a trip to England, made the first converts when in 1814 he induced his brother-in-law and a few other friends to join with him in forming the Waltham Company. With the help of a gifted mechanic, Lowell designed and built for his factory both spinning machines and, still more important, a power loom. The loom enabled the company to weave rough cotton cloth cheaply enough to compete in price with English goods. The success of the Waltham Company made its mark; in the course of the next decade Boston capital founded several other textile companies in nearby towns. Mounting profits, a powerful argument for further investment, persuaded more and more merchants that in New England mills, as much as in New England ships, lay New England's future. For Boston the turning point came in 1826 when the city opened Faneuil Hall—the market hall given to the town in 1742 by Peter Faneuil, a local merchant of Huguenot descent—to a fair, spring and fall, for display of New England manufactures. Opposition of influential importers put an end to these fairs in 1832, but by then Boston men had made too much money in industrial ventures to be deterred. As Massachusetts railroads in the 1830's and 1840's pushed steadily westward, new factories appearing along their routes would tie transport and manufacturing into one complex of Boston interests.

The cities of the Atlantic seaboard which controlled the commercial life of the United States in 1800 were still important economic and cultural factors in 1830. Here were to be found the money and credit to finance new ventures, here the intellectual stimulus and opportunity for artistic expression. All of them, indeed, except Charleston, would continue till the end of the century and after to exercise a powerful influence upon the growth of the nation. By 1830 American ideas had changed about what its future should be. Jefferson's prayer for a nation of husbandmen was being rejected by an ever larger number of men who saw in commerce and the country's incipient industrialism a promise of wealth and power which agrarians could not command. Confidence in American expansion had not yet found voice in the slogan of the 1840's, 'Manifest Destiny', but men no longer felt bound to Europe, though they would still seek foreign capital to develop the resources of the continent. In the cities, where a man's native wits made him his place, aristocracy of birth now weighed no more than individual achievement. The flood of European immigrants which later would inundate the eastern cities was just beginning to gather force, but the mixture of peoples that made up America had already produced a new amalgam. No city in America but had a somewhat heterogeneous population. In the cities, as in the villages and on the farms, poverty existed, stark want virtually never. Ambition and the opportunities of a vast unsettled hinterland gave Americans faith that they were the way and the light.

# III

# The River Cities:
# Cincinnati; St Louis; New Orleans

THE Atlantic seaports governed American economic life at the opening of the nineteenth century, but within two decades new rivals beyond the Appalachian mountains were challenging that domination. Before the back-country of the original thirteen states was more than thinly settled, the push into the virgin lands to the west was under way. The woodsmen of 'the dark and bloody ground' of Kentucky had peopled the region south of the Ohio river sufficiently to bring Kentucky into the Union as a state in 1792 and Tennessee in 1796. The great forested stretches north of the Ohio had been organized as the Northwest Territory in 1785 and when defeat of the Indians and a treaty with the tribes of the Ohio country in 1795 removed the fear of the tomahawk, the stream of wagons and river-boats carrying families to the new territory grew with every year. The region between the mountains and the Mississippi river would by 1830 contain a fourth of the population of the whole United States. By the autumn of 1802 the easternmost unit of the Northwest Territory could claim enough inhabitants to seek and gain admission to the Union as the state of Ohio.

In the years immediately following the Revolution, the new nation, hard pressed to pay its debts, had chosen to sell land in the territory acquired from Great Britain, instead of adhering to the usual colonial system of practically giving land to pioneer farmers as reward for their venture. Surveyors appointed by Congress had set off in 1785 to mark out the northeasternmost area, surveying it into townships six miles square, each divided into thirty-six rectangular sections, of which, in keeping with New England precedent, section sixteen was to be reserved as public property for school support. Congress had hoped to sell at a minimum price of a dollar an acre, and the Northwest Ordinance had stipulated that purchasers must buy an entire section of 640 acres in order to prevent the United States' having left on its hands odd pieces of undesirable and unsaleable land. Few could buy at that price. But when the surveyors returned, their accounts of the fertility of the Ohio country so fired imaginations in the East that in 1786 and 1788 two groups organized to negotiate for purchase of large tracts. They persuaded Congress to accept from men who had fought in the Revolutionary war the 'certificates of indebtedness' they had received as mustering-out pay,

'The Jolly Flat Boat Men'

and by that arrangement the companies were able to get men to participate who could not otherwise have afforded the venture. The first company, the Ohio Associates, formed in Boston, settled in 1788 on the upper Ohio river at a spot the founders named Marietta. John Cleves Symmes of New Jersey sponsored the second enterprise; he undertook to buy land and find settlers for a million acres between the Great and Little Miami rivers, some two hundred miles farther down the Ohio. By advertising, Symmes induced several other men to join with him, and although in the end the purchase shrank to a third of his original proposal, on this tract arose the settlement that became the city of Cincinnati.

The river formed the natural highway to this fertile region. Once householders had carted their belongings over the mountains to the headwaters of the settlement of Pittsburgh they could load their possessions on to rafts and flatboats and float themselves downstream to their selected site. The voyage was dangerous. Before 1795 the Ohio country was still an Indian hunting ground, and the river itself was perilous to navigate. It is a mighty river. From 'the forks' where the Monongahela and Allegheny rivers join in western Pennsylvania to make the Ohio, it flows southwestward 980 miles to empty into the Mississippi about a hundred miles below the confluence of the Missouri with the Indians' 'Father of Waters'. Longer than any river in western Europe except the Danube, the Ohio drains an area over five times as large as the United Kingdom. Along its upper reaches 'La Belle Rivière', about a quarter-mile wide, cuts through high hills that come steeply down to its edge. In spring its banks are pink with Judas trees in bloom and starred with dogwood. Islands dot its course. In its lower stretches the river widens to nearly a mile and flows through gently rolling green hills. For much of the year the current is swift and during the spring torrential floods occur, uprooting trees and undercutting the banks at one place to build them up at another, or carrying earth downstream to form treacherous new shallows and sandbars. The shallow draft of the flatboats that carried the first settlers down the river frequently saved them from wreck, but submerged logs could rip into the clumsy, hard-steering rafts so that passengers were dumped into the chilly water and precious supplies were lost. Only the rich promise of the new country could have persuaded men to risk the journey for themselves and their families.

## CINCINNATI

The first twenty settlers of the Symmes tract arrived in late December 1788 after a voyage made particularly difficult by floating ice. Symmes, writing the following May, announced: 'They landed safe on a most delightful high bank of the Ohio, where they founded the town of Losantiville, which populates considerably.' By the end of January 1789 log cabins had been built to accommodate eleven families and twelve bachelors, and some months later the federal government erected a fort. When the Governor of the Northwest Territory arrived to look over the new settlement and the fort, he objected to the name Losantiville, chosen in a display of knowledge of Latin to indicate the village opposite, *anti*, the mouth, *os*, of the *L*, or Licking river in Kentucky. General Arthur St Clair was a member of the Society of the Cincinnati, an association of officers who had served in the Revolution, and he decreed that the place should be named Cincinnata. Cincinnati it became. The location of the settlement was not only delightful, it was peculiarly well suited to river trade. At this point, some 450 miles downstream from Pittsburgh, a semi-circle of protecting hills, giving way toward the south to lower hills, enfolds a basin bordered by the river. Between two and three square miles of the basin is flat land lying just above normal high water level. River boats could tie up here easily.

In 1789 oak and beech trees, sugar maples, hickories, and sycamores covered most of the region. Since the forests abounded in deer, bear, squirrel, turkey, partridge, and quail, and in autumn flights of duck, geese, and pigeon darkened the skies, the settlers lived on game until they had cleared their fields and harvested their first crops. They sold any surplus to the garrison of the fort. Indeed, trade with the soldiers stationed here was the mainstay of the little community during its earliest years. Until a defeat in 1795 forced the Indians to withdraw to the northwest, Cincinnati grew slowly. Then new settlers began to pour into the area round about, and in 1803, when the federal government withdrew the garrison, Cincinnati, incorporated as a town the year before, numbered nearly eight hundred inhabitants.

The form of town government was prescribed by the charter granted by the territorial legislature ten months before Ohio was admitted to the Union. Administration of public affairs was vested in a Select Council—consisting of a President, seven Trustees, and a Recorder—an Assessor, a Collector of Taxes, and a town Marshal, all elected yearly in town meeting. Any freeholder and any householder who paid the considerable sum of $36 annual rent could vote. After 1815 suffrage was restricted to white men with the necessary property qualifications. Voters decided what services the town should perform, and the Assessor then distributed the charges. The charter forbade levy of a poll tax. The Marshal, the local agent for law enforcement, was empowered to use the county jail to imprison men for non-payment of taxes, to impose fines for refusal to accept public office, and to expel undesirables from the town, usually women of doubtful morals. This simple, direct scheme of self-rule, put into effect by leaders in the community, kept order.

During these early years Cincinnati served as the supplier of household wares to new homesteaders and as the market for the crops of established farms in the neighborhood. A few miles to the west of the town the Great Miami river, flowing into the Ohio, watered a valley so fertile that the fields, once cleared of trees, grew hay and grain high enough, one traveller reported, 'to cover a man on horseback'. Cincinnati dealers sold this produce to newcomers in the vicinity, to immigrants stopping briefly before moving on, and to merchants in New Orleans, fifteen hundred miles south near the mouth of the Mississippi. How productive the Miami valley had become may be surmised from the creation in 1803 of the Miami Export Company, a community project of farmers and Cincinnati merchants who organized for collective buying and selling and thus incidentally provided a much-needed system of credit. The formation of the company points to Cincinnatians' awareness of the importance of maintaining good relations between town and country. This local merchants never forgot.

By 1810 the agricultural prosperity of the surrounding farmlands and the shrewd marketing of the traders at the river port were telling. The population of 1803 had tripled. Eight brickyards, several tanneries, and a number of slaughter-houses for the swine driven in from the oak and beech forests where they fattened themselves, indicate some of the main occupations. Carpenters, mechanics, merchants, teachers, Presbyterian and Methodist preachers, and lawyers, always to be found in a growing town in America, were making their way. In 1817, in recognition of Cincinnati's leadership in the western country, the Second Bank of the United States established a branch here; thereafter financial connections with the money centers of the East aided Cincinnatians seeking to expand their business ventures. A constant flow of strangers into the town, and often out again, prevented any stagnation of ideas and schemes even during the brief periods of hard times: The river brought to Cincinnati's wharves an infinitely various assort-ment of men, women, and children—families of peasants from the Old World, young men from eastern cities, ready to take a turn at anything; skilled Penn-sylvania and New Jersey artisans, traders, farmers, and always the river boatmen. For Cincinnati's well-being was tied to her shipping interests. Inland though she lay, four hundred miles as the crow flies from the Atlantic seaboard and further still from the Gulf, her export trade *via* the rivers and New Orleans during half a century was her very life.

One young physician had perceived clearly the diversity of opportunity con-tained in the town. Daniel Drake had arrived in 1800 as a boy of fifteen. Appren-ticed to the only doctor for miles about, Drake, by study, by observation, and eventually by some schooling in Philadelphia, made himself into a full-fledged doctor. His intense interest in teaching medicine and surgery and in building up a great medical school in Cincinnati was equalled only by his passionate wish to see the town and city become the business and cultural metropolis of the West. Over a period of years he assembled data on the Miami country and in 1815 published a book, *Picture of Cincinnati*, which sold widely both in the United States and Eu-rope and brought thousands of people to Cincinnati. To the day of his death in 1852 Dr Drake spoke of Ohio as the promised land and, with the flamboyant elo-quence characteristic of men who had shared in turning wilderness into a city, he voiced his faith and pride in Cincinnati. He was an early vigorous advocate of railroads for the river city. Determined to give the community stature as an in-tellectual center, he organized a debating society and, with the help of others, opened a library and a museum where he put in charge a little known young naturalist, John James Audubon, in later life to be famous the world over for his paintings of birds and other wild life. For many years Drake and his wife held informal soirées to which the most distinguished visitors to the city came. He founded Cincinnati's Medical College and taught there off and on for thirty-five years, withdrawing periodically when quarrels with his associates led to forced resignations. His greatest service reached far beyond the immediate locality. He edited for a time and wrote most of the articles for *The Western Journal of Medical and Physical Sciences*, of which Drake's biographer writes:

> Travelling in the packs of the pony express, carried on snow shoes to the far north, *The Western Journal* was read in log cabins while wolves and coyotes howled outside. . . . And moccasined doctors who had never seen a medical school or read a text not fifty years behind the times, stared at Drake's journal with amazement that so much was known of which they had never dreamed. Backwoodsmen whose arrow wounds had festered or who were stricken with mysterious fevers, pioneer women writhing in abnormal pregnancy, all these had cause to bless Daniel Drake that their physicians could consult the dog-eared pages of *The Western Journal* and apply the new scientific technique there in the shadow of the pre-Adamite forest.[1]

Dr Drake's reputation elicited a letter from an obscure Illinois lawyer named Abraham Lincoln who sought advice on how to treat his attacks of melancholia. The last ten years of his life Drake dedicated to writing *A Treatise on Principal Diseases of the Interior Valley of America*, volumes based upon exhaustive first-hand observation and a work that served as a text for two generations of American doctors after him. A controversial figure in Cincinnati during his lifetime and a man of limited means, he was nevertheless always recognized here as a force. He was Cincinnati's first booster.

If no other one citizen made such significant contributions to the community, most men who arrived early in the century made money, some of them a great deal of it. As the town grew, fortunes were made astonishingly quickly. In 1806, before the boom was well begun, one enthusiast reported, 'Merchants here allow themselves 50 to 100 per cent on all their goods.' Thirty years later a German resident wrote that 500 per cent profit was 'regular'. On the other hand, before 1820 commercial risks were great. Though one shipper who sent logwood to New Orleans cleared $4,000 in one eight-month trip in 1813, that was an extraordinary feat. If the river froze, as occasionally happened, traffic ceased, produce piled up in warehouses, and carrying costs became ruinous. In spring and fall mud might make farmers' trips into town all but impossible, thus cutting off from the town's merchants both export supplies and profitable sales to the farmers' households. Once a cargo was loaded on a river-boat for New Orleans, a thousand misfortunes could overtake it. A snag could rip the barge apart and a season's or even a

[1] James T. Flexner, *Doctors on Horseback* (New York, 1939), pp. 214–15.

life-time's profits could go to the bottom. If a boat grounded on a sandbar, so much time and labor might be spent in getting free that the cost of the voyage would equal the price to be got for the goods in New Orleans. Always there was the chance that a shipment would arrive when the market was glutted and prices low. The very length of time of a round trip added a certain hazard. A record set by a barge in 1811 for the fifteen-hundred-mile return voyage from New Orleans was seventy-eight days. As long as boats had to be poled and dragged by ropes upstream at the rate of ten to twelve miles a day, imports from New Orleans were few and expensive. Eastern manufactures carried over the mountains and shipped down the Ohio by keelboat were even costlier because the difficulty of getting produce upstream to Pittsburgh and thence to eastern cities tended to preclude barter, and hard money was scarce in the West. River commerce before 1820 was neither safe nor sure as a means of making money. But it had an abiding appeal for Cincinnati.

Before the introduction of steamboats to the western waters, the volume of Cincinnati's trade was thus necessarily small. It was the steamboat that made the city great and won her the right to call herself the 'Queen City of the West'. Just as Boston enshrined the codfish, Cincinnati might well have erected a monument to the river steamboat. Perhaps a dozen steamboats had appeared on the Ohio before 1817, clumsy affairs that skeptics declared would never survive a trip over the shoals or through the rapids. Survive they did. Cincinnati built her first steamer in 1817 for a New Orleans firm and in 1818 a 176-ton vessel for a Cincinnati owner. That was the beginning of a vital industry. The boats were of ocean-going size. To the merchant the steamboat spelt some reduction in time and, at a later date, a lower cost, in shipping his goods downstream, but on the return trip from New Orleans the saving was tremendous. The record of 1811 looked insignificant when in 1817 the *Washington* made the voyage from New Orleans to Louisville, Kentucky, ninety miles below Cincinnati, in twenty-five days. Though such a run was unusually fast, on ordinary voyages steamboats in the next decade cut trip times in half. Firewood piled at some twenty-five-mile intervals along the river banks made refuelling easy. When Henry Shreve put to work 'Uncle Sam's toothpullers', the nickname of specially built boats that removed the dangerous snags from the river beds, voyages to and from New Orleans became still faster and risks diminished. Merchants could now market imports brought *via* New Orleans at prices within the reach of all but the very poorest householder in Cincinnati. The eastern seaboard cities were as disturbed at this threat to their commercial supremacy as the towns and cities of the West were rejoiced.

Public Landing, Cincinnati, 1855

Quite as important for Cincinnati as the immediate commercial effects of steamboats were the new occupations that steamboats created. Early in the century the town had contained a large number of 'mechanics'—blacksmiths, carpenters, wheelwrights, and skilful jacks of all trades who repaired and mended everything from wagons to household looms. The coming of the steamboat to the western rivers opened to these men a host of opportunities. To some it offered careers as captains and pilots; to others new challenging jobs on land. Before 1820 Cincinnati had built twelve of the seventy-one steamboats constructed in the West; in the next ten years she outstripped every competing city. Nor were the boats and the shipyards alone important. Steamboats meant steam engines; steam engines meant foundries, forges, machine shops, and, in time, machine-tool shops. Coal and iron lay within reach; here were workmen as skilled as could be found anywhere in America; the prospects of fat profits produced capital—and initially no vast sum was needed; enthusiasm was boundless. The result was inevitable: Cincinnati became a machinery-manufacturing center. Shops that could build steam engines could build other machinery. In the mid-twenties one local mechanic built five sugar mills for some New Orleans sugar-planters by copying the drawings of a Scottish mill which they supplied. The Cincinnati engine and mills cost the planters a fraction of what they had paid for the imported product. Thenceforward Louisiana sugar-planters purchased processing machinery in Cincinnati.

The social effects of these new specialized occupations were tremendous. Unlike New England's multiplying textile mills which required dozens of spinners and weavers, the early machine shops and foundries were sparsely manned. No workman here was anonymous. With luck, a skilful man after a period of working as a hired help could branch out for himself. Mrs Trollope, author of *Domestic Manners of the Americans*, that sharp commentary on the United States, and on Cincinnati in particular, spoke of the behavior of the Cincinnati mechanic with some asperity. The aggressiveness to which she objected sprang from something more basic than native American bad manners. It derived in large measure from the self-confidence of the foundryman and engine-builder who knew he was a valuable citizen, might one day be wealthy, and, in any event, felt himself his own master. He was sometimes mistaken, but his behavior remained unaltered.

Since steam engines could turn factory wheels as well as drive paddles on riverboats, other manufacturing enterprises also developed. A little flour-milling, some woodworking, a great deal of whiskey-distilling, and even more slaughtering, meat-packing, and tanning had gone on for some years, but about 1830 all these took on new importance. By 1838 the business in packing pork, lard, and

House of Nicholas Longworth, Cincinnati

hams amounted to some $3,000,000; Cincinnati hams, shipped east by river and canal, were an advertised delicacy in New York hotels. Butchering offered chances to many men to climb in the world. Harriet Martineau was astonished to learn that her host at some lavish party had been a household servant ten years before. So many pork kings arose in the Queen City that in the 1840's she was dubbed Porkopolis.

Transport of this growing array of products in the 1830's included more routes than the Ohio river. The Erie Canal connecting the lower Great Lakes with the Hudson river and New York City had inspired Ohioans to construct a chain of canals from the Miami river to Lake Erie, which, when completed in 1832, made shipping by the northern route easy and inexpensive. Eastern money began to pour into Cincinnati, whose products were coming to be known on the seaboard and whose future looked bright enough to warrant investment. In the mid-forties, Cincinnati, with some financial support from the East, began to build rail-roads out from the city. By 1855 she had rail connections with the growing city of St Louis on the Mississippi and by 1857, *via* the Baltimore and Ohio, with the principal Atlantic ports. But railroads were still only supplements to the long-established routes. Cincinnati, the hills at her back, faced south toward plantations whose owners bought foodstuffs in order to keep their land in cotton or sugar. The city's commercial ties with the Southern states were too old and strong to be broken by anything less than civil war. Her steamboats, and down into the fifties flatboats too, gave her cheaper shipping than could canals or the rail-roads of the day. Up to 1861 she remained a river city, her expanding industry strengthening and enlarging her commercial domain.

While most Cincinnatians thus looked to the river, others eyed the town itself. Cincinnati illustrates as well as any city in America how men could make fortunes not by enterprise, ingenuity, and hard work, the vaunted pioneer virtues, but by buying land and sitting tight. Speculation in real estate made millionaires again and again. It often unmade them too, for sooner or later panics and depressions succeeded booms. In 1819 the town, with 9,000 inhabitants, became an incorporated city. That year came a country-wide depression, the result of delayed adjustments to the peace following the war of 1812. Another panic struck in 1837 as a consequence of excessive land speculation, and still another in 1857, that time because of a decade of industrial and commercial expansion at a pace too rapid for the growth of population and wealth of the United States to support. But always the city recovered and then real estate speculation was resumed. Two years after the panic of 1837, lots that had sold in 1789 for 83½ cents an acre were priced at $382 a square foot. The buyer who had been able to hold on was made. The best single example of the successful land speculator is Nicholas Longworth who came to Cincinnati in 1810, 'hung out his shingle' as a lawyer and, having saved his first client from the gallows for horse-stealing, accepted as fee a copper still. He promptly traded the still for thirty-three acres of land on the town's outskirts. Twenty-odd years later those acres lay in the heart of Cincinnati's business district, and Longworth still owned them. Similar purchases left him at his death one of the richest men in the United States. A grandson married Alice Roosevelt, daughter of President Theodore Roosevelt, and a grand-daughter became the Marquise de Chambrun, an authority on Shakespeare and an historian of her native Cincinnati.

The amassing of fortunes, whether by gambling in land, by building and operating steamboats, or by packing pork, produced early in the city's life pronounced economic discrepancies. Before the pattern of the city's life was firmly set, a kind of equalitarianism had prevailed, but after 1830 that gradually disappeared. With a few notable exceptions, men won prestige by having money. How they acquired the money mattered little. The butcher turned large-scale pork-packer took equal place with the banker, the leading lawyer, or the merchant-steamboat owner. Wealth became the measure of a man's importance and social standing, and for most of his fellow citizens the gauge of his wealth was his manner of living. Where Charleston, Philadelphia, and Boston deferred to men related by birth or marriage to old, established families, in this new western city pride of ancestry could play little part. Although, it is true, the scion of the honored family of Boston or Philadelphia or Baltimore had an entrée upon coming to Cincinnati, unless he soon showed he could make money, his social position dwindled. Mrs Trollope owed the coolness of her reception as much to her poverty as to her caustic tongue. Men not yet rich were impelled to ape as nearly as they could the elaborations of house and furnishings, of horses and carriages and clothes, which marked the unmistakably rich.

Thus after the passing of the pioneer era in the 1820's, pretentiousness was everywhere in evidence. Cincinnati was intent on proving to Boston and New York and Charleston that she was just as sophisticated as they. Because patronage of the arts would create an aura of culture, well-to-do men now commissioned portraits and bought landscapes, until the compiler of the city *Directory*, doubtless seeing the advantages of double advertising, listed local painters not only by name and address but by their works and their patrons as well. Big houses set in wide lawns on the hills at the edge of the city also proclaimed Cincinnatians' new awareness of art. Architects trained in the East and skilled local builders erected a number of handsome houses, some of them exceptionally fine examples of Greek Revival. Not all of these were built to show off their owners' wealth, but all of them bore witness to it. In furnishing these mansions—so contemporary writings describe them—socially ambitious householders poured out money for rugs, Empire furniture, paintings, and statuary, some good, much ugly, but all expensive.

Yet along with this ostentation went an increasingly genuine search for what were termed 'the better things of life'. Though the informed and literary conversation that nourished Charleston and Boston society was transmuted here into talk of business affairs and city or national politics, citizens were reaching out for an understanding of the intellectual and artistic. A city library, a literary society, and, somewhat later, picture galleries attest to mounting interest. When Nicholas Longworth perceived talent in Hiram Powers, the sculptor who had made the wax figures for Mrs Trollope's 'Infernal Regions', Longworth sent him to study in Florence. While Powers, though exposed to the society of the Brownings and other cultivated Europeans, failed to hasten the 'American Renaissance', his marble, 'The Greek Slave', made a great stir in the late forties, not, to be sure, because of its beauty, but because of its daring: it was nude and female! Exhibited at the Crystal Palace in 1851, it was draped when Queen Victoria paid her visit. Charles Cist, the city's biographer in 1841, made a point of the opportunity for local artists. In language that seemed to contemporary Cincinnatians wholly appropriate, he wrote:

> The field of art in Cincinnati is perfectly unbounded, both for the arts of design and expression. It is only necessary to think of the freedom of man, the marked individuality resulting therefrom, the multifarious nations and characters here congregated, the endless variety of occupations here carried on, the romantic history of the aborigines and the pioneers, the grand and beautiful features of western scenery, the unconscious and almost wild spontaneity with which the infant world of the great valley has been and is now in all things developing itself, and the deep moral and physical interest of the great social movements of the times—it is only necessary to reflect upon these things to be struck with the extent and richness of the practical field of art upon which the true artist of the west may enter.[1]

But it was music, not painting, that caught Cincinnati's imagination. In the 1850's German singing societies made concerts popular, and in 1859 a wealthy brewer, moved by hearing Jenny Lind, the 'Swedish Nightingale', built Pike's Opera House. Within a generation Cincinnati would be one of the musical centers of America. The theatre was widely patronized, though American stock companies staging current melodrama drew as large audiences as barnstorming troupes of

[1] Charles Cist, *Cincinnati in 1841* (Cincinnati, 1841), p. 138.

English actors playing Shakespeare. Had Mrs Trollope, who thought the society of Cincinnati's élite dull, frequented the taverns and saloons along the river front she might have seen real gaiety and native artistry in the carnivals held regularly for the boatmen waiting for cargoes to be loaded.

In spite of some snobbery, class distinctions were neither sharp nor fixed. Men in all walks of life were likely to rub shoulders in the course of the week's work or play. The election polls, by the terms of a new city charter of 1827 now open to all citizens with or without property provided they were neither felons, females, minors, or Negroes, gave undeniable power to the common man. Realization of that fact stirred uneasiness in the minds of the group that would have liked to call itself the ruling class. The election of President Jackson in 1828 and the rise of the Democratic Party dashed all hopes of halting 'mobocracy'. In 1831 that penetrating observer de Tocqueville asked a leading Cincinnati lawyer if he were not disturbed at 'this excessive development of the democratic principle'. Lawyer Walker replied: 'I wouldn't say so in public, but between ourselves I admit it. I am frightened by the current that is carrying us on. The United States, it seems to me, are in a crisis; we are at this moment trying out a democracy without limits; everything is going that way. But shall we be able to endure it? As yet no one can say positively.'[1]

All things considered, Cincinnati's government was then, and up to the Civil War continued to be, neither much better nor much worse than during its first thirty years. The community's rapid growth, rather than the change from town to city rule or to the widened suffrage of 1827, accounted for most difficulties. The 9,600 inhabitants of 1820 had become nearly 25,000 by 1830. In the next ten years population increased to 46,000, and by 1850 to 115,000. Mayor and Councilmen still represented the interests of the well-to-do, but night watchmen on the police force, street paving, city-owned water-works, and, in the 1850's, a system of drainage became imperative. Rivalries between the volunteer fire companies turned into open conflict, resolved only in 1853 by the establishment of a paid fire department. A still more bitter feud developed between the Marshal and the Chief of Police when a state law widened the authority of the city's police; but that struggle grew out of the Marshal's determination to lose none of his fat fees and ended with the abolishing of his office. After the Civil War the city would fall prey to a peculiarly vicious boss-rule sustained by openly purchased votes and secure in power until rebelling citizens organized a vigorous campaign of reform in 1916 and in 1924 introduced a successful City Manager system. Be-

---

[1] Quoted in George W. Pierson, *Tocqueville and Beaumont in America* (New York, 1937), p. 561. Quoted by permission of the Oxford University Press.

fore 1860 certainly it was not 'democracy without limits' that created problems of city administration.

Nevertheless, to safeguard against possible evil consequences of the 'excessive development of the democratic principle', Ohio took steps in 1830 to force communities to establish public tax-supported schools. Cincinnati was reluctant. Private schools had existed here since the early years of the century; a public school system seemed to some men to be the equivalent of substituting charity for individual obligation. But, following the imposition of a state tax for school support, Cincinnati opened her first public schools in 1830–1. While many parents continued to send their children to private academies or parochial schools, people came to take pride in the quality of the city's public schools, which, Cincinnatians announced, attracted settlers from St Louis and New Orleans. William McGuffey's *Readers*, first published in Cincinnati in 1836, set the standard. Indeed, generations of school children in every hamlet in America received most of their basic education from the McGuffey *Readers*. Although immigration after 1820 brought to Cincinnati non-English-speaking Germans and illiterate Irish, and though the city excluded Negroes from the public schools, people here, by and large, could read and write. Cincinnati's colleges and seminaries founded before mid-century point to the stress laid upon higher education.

Upon this confident prosperous community in the 1830's the problem of the Negro and Abolitionism thrust itself in peculiarly distressing form. All Negroes in Ohio were free. The Ordinance of 1787 had forbidden slavery in the Northwest Territory and all the states to be carved out of it, but that had not prevented Ohio from enacting a Black Code designed to keep Negroes from moving into the state. The Code required a $1,500 bond for good behavior from every Negro, refused his children admittance to the public schools, and denied him right to testify in court against a white man. These laws had been unenforced in Cincinnati before 1829. In that year the city, discovering that she had an uncomfortably large colored population, suddenly invoked the Code. Negroes now found themselves stripped of all protection against white knavery and violence. They emigrated from the city as quickly as they could. Twelve hundred found haven in Canada, some in a town appropriately named Wilberforce. By 1834 fewer than eight hundred remained in Cincinnati, and against these the Marshal made no further attempt to enforce the Black Code rigorously. But their position, already difficult, was soon made worse by the rise of vociferous anti-slavery groups in the city. The first Cincinnati converts to the American Anti-Slavery Society, founded in Philadelphia in 1833, were at the Lane Theological Seminary, where men trained for the Presbyterian ministry. In 1834 the Seminary became the scene of a bitter controversy when a group of students, led by a member of the faculty, insisted on mingling with Cincinnati Negroes as equals. Local businessmen were outraged. Much of the city was Southern in temper. A quarter-mile away across the Ohio river lay Kentucky, where slavery was legal and where well-to-do families owned slaves as a matter of course. Cincinnati's principal market was New Orleans in slave-owning Louisiana. Cincinnati merchants had no quarrel with the 'peculiar institution' of their Southern neighbors. The radicals at the Theological Seminary, rebuked by the conservative Board of Trustees, moved out *en masse* to Oberlin College in northern Ohio.

This was only a beginning. Two years later an Abolitionist newspaper began publication in the city. After one preliminary demonstration, an angry mob broke into the shop, threatened the printer and publisher, and dumped the press into the river. The city Marshal then chose to restore peace by ordering the editor to cease publication. That order injected the issue of freedom of the press. The editor left the city, and his successor modified the tone of the paper, but the passions aroused did not entirely die down. Negroes were subjected to some persecution, and more than one sober citizen witnessing the violence done them felt compelled to accept the doctrine of legal equality between the races. Harriet Beecher Stowe's years in Cincinnati gave her the ideas that made *Uncle Tom's Cabin* a best-seller after 1852 and the most effective single piece of anti-slavery propaganda in the United States. In an appeal to Lord Denman to enlist further British support for this crusade, Mrs Stowe explained: 'I wrote what I did because as a woman, as a mother, I was oppressed and heartbroken with the sorrows and injustice I saw—because as a Christian, I felt the dishonor to Christianity—because as a lover of my country I trembled at the coming day of wrath.' In the forties and fifties Cincinnati became a station on the Underground Railway, that chain of householders who smuggled escaped slaves across the border into Canada. Still, many people disapproved of that defiance of the law, and most men were torn between their business interests and their humanitarian feelings. The rift was not to be mended until the Civil War forced a choice.

Meanwhile a lesser and shorter-lived conflict arose over the treatment of the foreign-born. Numbers of Germans and some Irish had come in the early years, but about 1835 the small stream swelled to a flood. In 1840 a third of the population was German-born, and by 1850 there were thirty thousand Germans, nearly fourteen thousand Irish, and enough people of other nationalities to reduce native Americans to a minority. At this army of newcomers native workmen looked at first with misgiving and then with resentment. Here were competitors for jobs. The owners of this land of the free were going to be pushed out by foreign riffraff, and Roman Catholics among them at that! Anti-foreign sentiment and an organized anti-foreign movement were country-wide, culminating in a national political party called the Know Nothings, who nominated a candidate for the Presidency in 1856. In Cincinnati feeling ran strongest against the Germans because they were the most numerous as well as the most industrious and most skilled. Native Americans fought one or two pitched battles with the German colony living in a sector called 'Over the Rhine', until the attackers were roundly defeated. Then almost as quickly as it had flared up, the feud subsided. Well-to-do citizens had consistently deplored it, and working men concluded that the newcomers after all had solid virtues. In fact, Cincinnati now began to preen herself on being cosmopolitan.

In spite of the earlier antagonism to the Germans, German customs quickly spread throughout the city. The beer gardens of Over the Rhine became popular resorts. German dishes appeared on nearly every table, and every housewife treasured a good recipe for Wienerschnitzel, Sauerbraten, or Apfelstrudel. *Turnen* became a vogue, and American-born gymnasts were soon competing with German-born. German music was sung and played everywhere. In late December candle-lit Christmas trees decorated the houses of native Americans and German-born alike. Most extraordinary of all, the public schools offered courses in German. By 1860 the German flavor was so unmistakable that Americans elsewhere considered Cincinnati a German community.

The commercially powerful city of mid-century, though proud of her past, was at once ambitious and faintly apprehensive of her future. City promoters in the 1850's were arguing that domestic trade was of far greater value to the nation than foreign and that the commercial leader of the interior must be proportionately more significant than the Eastern seaports. Charles Cist announced in 1851:

> Cincinnati is the grand centre of the United States, not geographically perhaps, but the centre of the forces and influences which, when readjusted after the introduction of the great disturbing cause, the railroad, must settle and determine the destiny and relative position of the various cities or centres which are now struggling for supreme ascendancy on this continent.[1]

Such statements were tinged with anxiety. Before 1860 dawned, the upstart city of Chicago, strengthened by her network of railroads, was threatening Cincinnati's control of the country's pork packing industry, and St Louis, of whom Cincinnati had spoken condescendingly in 1840 as 'the busy, go-ahead little city of St Louis', had overtaken the Ohio city in the river trade. Cincinnati would suffer

[1] Charles Cist, *Cincinnati in 1851* (Cincinnati, 1851), p. 370.

as much as Chicago and St Louis would benefit from the Civil War, and in the 1870's 'the great disturbing cause, the railroad' would enable St Louis to outstrip forever the 'Queen City of the West'.

## St Louis

St Louis, founded in 1764 by a company of French traders from New Orleans, had first come under American jurisdiction when President Jefferson purchased the Louisiana Territory from Napoleon in 1803. Located on the west bank of the Mississippi river ten miles below the point where the turbulent Missouri joins it, the little settlement for a generation had been a center of the French civilization of that inland empire lost to France in 1763. When the Treaty of Paris gave Great Britain the domain east of the Mississippi, a number of traders and peasants, preferring Spanish to British rule, had crossed the river into Louisiana, where Spanish overlordship did not diminish French influence. Long before the Territory fell to the United States, the fur trade had enriched St Louis; trappers and Indian traders, using the village as the point of departure for the wilderness beyond, brought back yearly otter, beaver, fox, and buffalo skins which commanded high prices in New Orleans. In the early years of the nineteenth century the value of these pelts averaged annually over $203,000, a huge sum for that era. The St Louis merchants who shipped the furs down the river spent their profits with discerning taste on spacious houses, French furnishings, paintings, and the works of Voltaire, Rousseau, Diderot, and other authors of the Enlightenment, occasionally including the writings of Jefferson and Thomas Paine. In the library of Auguste Chouteau, at the age of thirteen a founder of St Louis and a highly respected citizen throughout his long life, a fourth of the books were listed in the *Index Expurgatorius*. St Louis was, in short, a stronghold of freethinkers who, while nominally Catholics, paid scant attention to the priests sent to redeem their souls. Their intellectual kinship with educated American 'Jacobins' doubtless eased the transfer of the Territory to the United States.

On 9 May 1804, when the American flag was raised over the village, the men of the Lewis and Clark Expedition, standing there at attention, foreshadowed the future role of St Louis. Here was the starting point of that famous expedition commissioned by President Jefferson to explore the Northwest, and it was to St Louis that seventeen months later the party returned from its four-thousand-mile journey up the Missouri river valley and across the continental divide to the headwaters of the westward-flowing rivers and on to the Pacific. While men the country over marvelled at this bold, fruitful venture, St Louis profited directly, for she became the 'Gateway to the West'. In 1804, only two of the resident families had been American, but American 'scouts' and traders now moved in upon the village; exploring and trading parties fitted out here before setting forth upon the dangerous trails into Spanish Mexico or deep into the Indian country of the upper Missouri. Usually, like Lewis and Clark, they returned to the town on the Mississippi with their furs, their Mexican silver, and their tales of adventure and hardship. Fur, not money, was the medium of exchange until American and Spanish coins began to supplement barter on the frontier, and the fur trade remained a significant feature of St Louis' life down into the forties. Yet, despite this activity, since many of the traders were transients, the town grew slowly. In 1817 she had few more permanent residents than the 1,400 of 1808, though, after the creation of the Territory of Missouri in 1812, the territorial legislature met here.

Amid the comings and goings of American traders and politicians, St Louis gradually lost her French atmosphere. To this change, the opening of an English school in 1808 doubtless contributed. Even though children of well-to-do French families were educated, as formerly, in Europe or by private tutors at home, French nevertheless quickly disappeared as the language of the streets; most business was conducted in English. The *Missouri Gazette*, the first newspaper published west of the Mississippi, carried, to be sure, some columns in French but still helped to break the barriers between old residents and new. The houses built by prospering Americans followed the general architectural style of the French, but the newcomers lacked the means and usually the taste to equip their households with equal elegance. Before the arrival of Protestant 'missionaries' in 1817 and Bishop DuBourg with Jesuit priests in 1818, the town was little touched by religion and the early boast that 'God would not cross the Mississippi' approached truth. Local priests found it hard enough to keep a parish going at all, and were perforce indulgent. Cock-fighting and card-playing carried over as pastimes from earlier days, while frequent street brawls added a new kind of excitement. Duels fought on Bloody Island in the river were so commonplace that when in 1817 the future senator from Missouri, Thomas H. Benton, killed his opponent on the 'field of honor', the incident cast no shadow on Benton's political career.

With the coming of steamboats to the western rivers, St Louis began to grow more rapidly. The *Zebulon M. Pike* took six weeks in 1817 to make the trip from Louisville on the Ohio, but in 1819 the *Harriet* steamed up the Mississippi from New Orleans to St Louis in twenty-seven days. This voyage marked the revolution in St Louis' life that the *Washington* had brought to Cincinnati's. As the crude transports, made by laying planks across two pirogues, gave way to steam-powered ferries, commercial ties with the settlements of southern Illinois east of the river strengthened, and, far more important, trade with New Orleans doubled. Down into the forties, economic development largely repeated the Cincinnati pattern, though lagging by nearly twenty years; in 1830 she had scarcely 6,000 inhabitants, and in 1840, when Cincinnati claimed 46,000, St Louis had little more than a third that number. Here, as on the Ohio, river shipping with its concomitant, supplying necessities to westward-bound settlers, was the town's first interest, second came fur-processing, some flour-milling, and, in time, a little manufacturing of iron wares made from Missouri ores. Speculation in real estate went hand in hand with all business.

In 1822, two years after Missouri was admitted to the Union, the state legislature had incorporated 'The Mayor, Aldermen, and Citizens of the City of St Louis', vesting in the new corporation the usual municipal powers. But the city's political influence was now confined within her own limits. For, unlike Cincinnati's merchants, the merchants of St Louis had failed to develop cordial relations with the settlers of the hinterland, and rural representatives in the legislature stoutly refused to make the river city the state capital. Meanwhile, the work of the Jesuit fathers had taken effect in St Louis, and the Baptist and itinerant Methodist preachers, at first fiercely opposed by all Catholics and largely ignored by everyone else, had made headway. An Episcopal church was built in 1819, and by the mid-twenties St Louis was ready for the honor that befell her. Denied the status of political capital, she became the formal Catholic capital of Missouri, when, upon creation of a new Roman Catholic diocese in 1826, she was selected as the cathedral city. Catholic sisters opened a hospital two years later, and as parochial schools began to appear, the erstwhile godlessness of the town vanished. Freethinking lingered in some quarters, fortified in the early thirties by the arrival of German liberals, scholars, and professional men who, like their French predecessors, had no patience with 'priestcraft'. But the city as a whole settled down into orthodoxy, if not into religious devoutness.

The thirties were a period of preparation for the burgeoning growth of the decades ahead. European immigrants—English and Scottish tradesmen, Irish day laborers, German furriers and other skilled artisans—found their way to the city on the frontier's edge, while the restlessness foreign travellers observed as a national trait was driving other Americans, also, westward. From the Southern states, especially Kentucky and Virginia, householders came to the young western city where slavery was legal. In the city *Directory* of 1838 the newly organized St Louis Insurance Company advertised: 'They will also insure the *Lives of Slaves*, whether working on land or on boats navigating the rivers.' In the face of the invasion of newcomers, while Catholic French influence widened, the remnants of the earlier French civilization disappeared. Well-to-do French families inter-married with well-bred Southerners and remained among St Louis leaders, but now marked more by French names and manners than by French customs. By 1839 scarcely a house was standing that had graced the village of 1803. New buildings arose, the cathedral of St Louis with its impressive Greek columns of tawny Missouri limestone, seven other churches, and two markets. Work was beginning on an imposing, domed Renaissance Court House. The Planters' Hotel, newest of nine, was already famous when Charles Dickens, in 1842 critical of most things American, admitted to admiration for the Planter House service. The city built water works, laid out new streets, and bragged of her waterfront, one hundred and fifty feet wide, most of its length graded and paved. The Bank of Missouri opened its doors. Besides several parochial primary schools, 'an Academy for the education of females and a University, conducted by the Order of the Jesuits', a St Louisan wrote in 1838 of 'two Public Schools in this city with male and female departments'. By present-day American definition, these, though non-sectarian, were not public schools, because they were neither supported by public money nor directed by state or city officials. But St Louis, city of a slave state where sympathies and customs in these years were more Southern than Yankee, accepted the view that education was a private or Church responsibility. Four newspapers were publishing daily editions, and the *Anzeiger des Westen* was appearing weekly. Prophetic perhaps of her later literary interests, the city at the end of the thirties had seven printing offices. St Louis' challenge to Cincinnati waited only for the full tide of western settlement to reach the Mississippi and beyond.

The decade also brought St Louis troubles. A severe epidemic of cholera in 1832 led the city to establish a Board of Health with a physician in charge, though its efforts were less effectual in restoring public health than was St Louis' advertised natural 'salubrity'. Plans laid in 1836 at a convention held here to charter, not one, but eighteen railroad companies in Missouri died in the panic of 1837. Most alarming of all for the river city was the threat from the river itself. Shifting currents were swinging the Mississippi's course eastward and building sandbars above St Louis' waterfront which, were the process not halted, would leave her wharves high and dry. The United States government saved that situation. Just as Lieutenant Jefferson Davis in 1833 had safeguarded a Lake Michigan harbor for a small town named Chicago, so Lieutenant Robert E. Lee rescued St Louis. Lee, in 1837 stationed at Jefferson Barracks, the army's western headquarters, built jetties and revetments along Bloody Island near the Illinois shore and thus turned the river back into its old channel. Twenty-four years later General Lee would

St Louis, 1846–7

command the Confederate army, serving under Jefferson Davis, President of the Confederate States of America.

Activity on the river front of the forties heightened yearly. Westward expansion into the lands beyond the Mississippi was gaining momentum, and St Louis was at the crossroads. The Oregon country, which Lewis's and Clark's men had looked on with wonder, was beckoning to missionaries and intrepid farmers, and the new Republic of Texas, its independence of Mexico declared in 1836, was welcoming Americans who would help stave off interference from Europe. The Mississippi river-boats weekly landed in St Louis dozens of families bound for these new regions and some who, seeing a sure livelihood in the growing city, went no farther. Here householders heading for Oregon embarked upon the Missouri river-boats that would carry them northwestward as far as navigation permitted, while St Louis merchants equipped parties setting forth by wagon trains for the lands of the 'Lone Star Republic'. When President Polk announced the annexation of Texas in 1845, Missourians, St Louisans among them, took credit for acquiring that new state for the Union. As farms inland began to raise surpluses to sell, the wharves at St Louis, in the local phrase 'the chief emporium' of the central Mississippi valley, were piled higher and higher with produce to ship down river to New Orleans and thence to eastern cities and to Europe. Joining the chorus of Westerners contending that the value of internal trade outweighed foreign nine times over, St Louis boasted, and truthfully, that five thousand miles of navigable rivers fed her commerce. The river-boats also brought curious travellers who, like Dickens, would write of the vulgarities of this new world but at the same time betray envy of its vitality. Alexander Mackay, the London journalist whose sympathetic volume *The Western World* brought balm to Americans, described the river city in 1847 thus:

> St Louis is a most striking town as seen from the river. The ground on which it is built slopes gently up from the water, its flatter portion being occupied by the business part of the town which adjoins the quays. For some distance the river is lined with piles of lofty and massive warehouses, indicating the existence of an extensive 'heavy business.' The wharves are thronged with craft of different kinds, but from the inland position of the town, the steamers greatly predominate. The city is handsomely built, chiefly of brick. . . . The principal streets run parallel with the river. . . . The country behind it is rich and picturesque, whilst its river prospect is imposing both for the character of the foreground, and the bold sweeping lines of the Illinois bank opposite. Within its precincts, particularly about the quays, and in Front and First streets, it presents a picture of bustle, enterprise and activity.[5]

[5] Alexander Mackay, *The Western World; or Travels in the United States in 1846–47* (London, 1849), iii, 52.

The 'Forty-niners' increased that 'bustle'. How word of the gold found on Sutter's creek in California travelled east so fast is one of the mysteries of American history inexplicable by any factual chronicle. Within two months the news was common knowledge in eastern cities three thousand miles away and through all the farm-lands of the Mississippi valley. Men dropped everything to join in the rush for the gold fields. Prospectors setting out by the overland route congregated in St Louis. Her merchants knew from long experience what supplies men would need to sur-vive the two-thousand-mile journey across the continent. Steamboats filled with men and equipment lined up in the river so many deep that freight had to be rolled over the decks of twenty vessels to get it ashore. St Louis thus occupied in the California gold rush much the role that fifty years later Seattle would assume in the stampede to Alaska. By 1850 the Mississippi river port had nearly 77,000 residents, an increase of 60,000 in ten years.

The next decade repeated the material successes of the forties. River traffic mounted steadily in value and put the city as a center of the river trade ahead of Cincinnati before 1854. While Senator Thomas H. Benton addressed Congress with arguments for federal support of a transcontinental railway, St Louis began construction of a railroad westward through Missouri, and almost simultaneously one eastward to link her by rail to her competitor on the Ohio. The panic of 1857 interrupted work on the Missouri-Pacific, but citizens clung to the vision of St Louis as the great railroad city of the Middle West. Despite the setback caused by the panic, population by 1860 reached 160,000. Only the rise of Chicago, in the fifties still a far smaller city than the mighty river ports, could imperil St Louis' commercial leadership in the new West. Manufacturing, moreover, was gaining —iron plow shares to turn the tough sod of the prairies, other farm tools, en-gines, ornamental iron work, clothing, and shoes. Though fur-processing shrank in volume as westward settlement reduced the supply of skins, the city remained— and still is—the fur center of the United States. Even some manufacture of chew-ing tobacco went on, for, in the days before cigarettes, Americans found chewing tobacco relaxing; 'spittoons' were standard equipment in all public buildings. German-born citizens began brewing the beer that at the end of the century, when baseball had become the national game, would inspire the saying: 'St Louis, first in shoes, first in booze, and last in the American League'.

The phenomenal growth in population created housing shortages and necessi-tated new municipal services. A second epidemic of cholera awakened citizens to the need of a sewerage system and wider powers for the Board of Health. A destructive fire on the waterfront brought about building ordinances restricting construction to brick and stone in the heart of the city. Since parochial and private non-sectarian schools no longer sufficed, in 1853 the city opened public tax-supported schools, with primary and grammar grades and high school all under the direction of a city superintendent. A police force, instituted in 1840, was enlarged, the waterworks were extended, gas street lights were introduced, and, in 1859, horse-drawn trams.

Though the city's population in mid-century included people from nearly every state in the Union and from most of northern Europe as well, Negroes in St Louis were surprisingly few. Even more surprising, a third of the 4,000 Negroes in 1850 were free, and in 1860 the 1,800 free blacks outnumbered slaves. The explanation is twofold. Slaves brought high prices farther south; in the city they could be used chiefly as household servants, although occasionally a master, like Dred Scott's owner, would rent out the services of his Negroes. Inasmuch as German and Irish immigrants could be hired for a pittance, economy apparently dictated the selling of some slaves. In St Louis, moreover, Northerners now predominated, and public opinion, strengthened by the arrival of German liberals following the revolution of 1848, was largely opposed to slavery. Certainly manumission was a common practice here in the fifties. Yet the Negro and slavery in these years was a problem constantly in the minds of St Louisans. In the still unfinished domed Court House in 1847 lawyers opened the argument on perhaps the most important legal case in antebellum America, *Scott, a Man of Color* vs. *Emerson*, later, in the federal courts, *Dred Scott* vs. *Sandford*. Appeals in 1850 and 1852 were also heard in St Louis. Here the ignorant Negro, Dred Scott, became the symbol of the struggle between the advocates of the extension of slavery and their opponents not only in Missouri but the country over. Represented by skilful lawyers eager to establish a principle, Dred Scott pleaded that earlier residence with his master in a free territory of the United States made him a free man. Finally settled in 1857 by a seven to two decision of the United States Supreme Court, the suit ended with the pronouncement that Dred Scott, because 'a Negro of African descent', was not a citizen of Missouri and therefore could not sue. The decision, denying as it did the authority of Congress to prohibit slavery in the territories, contributed directly to the outbreak of the Civil War four years later. Within St Louis, Negroes, now refused citizenship, fared no worse than before. Today a plaque commemorating Dred Scott stands in the Court House grounds.

In spite of the deepening shadows cast by the slavery conflict, St Louis in mid-century was at once stimulating and gay. Money-making and developing new country were exciting occupations, and, apart from the Negroes, everyone dared believe in the fortune the future would bring him. Further removed from the eastern seaboard than Cincinnati and influenced by early ties with Louisiana,

St Louis Court House, 1854

The Court House was the scene of the hearings in the Dred Scott case

the city enjoyed a social life patterned as much on New Orleans as on New York and Philadelphia. Trips down the Mississippi on the luxurious river-boats of the fifties combined business with pleasure and permitted St Louis' well-to-do to buy Paris clothes in New Orleans. Wealth and taste in some families, inherited possibly from French forebears, gave this western city a culture unexpectedly varied and original. Some of its characteristics were common to most of urban America of the period—the enthusiasm for the theatre, the patronage of portrait painters, and participation in the singing of the choral societies here fostered by the Church and trained by the professor of music at the Jesuit St Louis University —but some aspects of this culture were distinctively western or peculiar to St Louis.

The 'show boats' were a Mississippi river institution, though they also steamed up the Ohio. When the steam calliope announced the arrival of a show boat at the wharves, eager St Louisans hurried to find a place in its saloon. In 1852 when 2,500 people crowded aboard the new *Floating Palace*, some of them were obliged to stand on deck and peer through the windows to see the performance. As late as 1925 river show boats were still docking at St Louis. Panoramists contributed a second form of art long little known in the East. Painters, fascinated by the great sweep of the river, the stretches of open prairie, and the Indians of the Missouri river valley, undertook to transfer to long rolls of canvas a continuous picture of this strange western world. In 1839 five St Louis painters shared in making a panorama which, unrolled before an audience in Boston, constituted the first American 'movie'. The best-known works were first those of John Rowson Smith, in 1832 a scene painter in a St Louis theatre, whose 'four miles' of canvas depicting the West was exhibited in 1844 in eastern cities and in Europe. Second were the scenes of the upper Mississippi painted by English-born Henry Lewis in 1848. Before the Civil War, St Louis was also beginning to evolve a special architectural style. Private houses and public buildings, it is true, followed the fashions current in the East, Greek Revival, then pseudo-Renaissance, and, in the Central High School completed in 1856, a narrow-windowed, high-shouldered form of Gothic. Warehouses, offices, and commercial buildings near the waterfront, on the other hand, were arising, built with iron columns and wide windows which anticipated some of the architectural innovations of Chicago in the eighties. Begun here by using the prefabricated iron store fronts shipped west by that curious genius, James Bogardus, watchmaker and iron founder of New York, this type of construction was taken up by St Louis iron-makers and builders. Using iron joists instead of wood and designing on simple lines throughout, these men were creating a nearly fire-proof and distinctly utilitarian business section such as few older American cities could equal.

St Louis' newspapers encouraged writers who, realizing that the frontier with its color and adventure was yearly receding, used local themes. 'Tall tales' of the West appeared frequently in the *Weekly Reveille*, and a predecessor of Mark Twain, Joseph M. Field, published in its pages the classic *Death of Mike Fink*, a story of a fabulous river keelboatman. The *Western Journal* published also more serious works, the *Life and Times of George Rogers Clark*, a history of the Revolutionary War hero who captured the British outposts of the Northwest Territory, and *The North American Indians*, one of the first American anthropological studies.

Most remarkable of all, here at the end of the fifties a school of Hegelian philosophers was emerging whose intellectual vigor would furnish the spark to younger men in all parts of the country. Led by William T. Harris, in 1857 an Easterner teaching in St Louis' public schools, and the learned Henry C. Brokmeyer, emigrated from Germany in 1858, the group took shape following the appearance of Brokmeyer's translation of the works of Hegel. Some of the group were New Englanders like Harris, some, like Brokmeyer, were German-born intellectuals, and some were native St Louisans who seem to have carried over from earlier days the freethinker's spirit of inquiry. They remained relatively obscure until after the Civil War, but then they launched *The Journal of Speculative Philosophy*, the most significant publication of its kind in America, the pages of which would carry the articles of unknown young men, such as William James, Josiah Royce, and John Dewey, who could obtain a ready hearing nowhere else.

The Civil War interrupted not only creative movements like that of the Hegelians but, for a time, all business as well. Sympathies in Missouri were divided between North and South, and though Union supporters soon won the upper hand in St Louis, the river port suffered until she made the adjustment to serving as a supply depot for the army of the West. Vulgarians and unscrupulous contractors who profited from the war would give a new cast to the city in the post-war era, but that change itself would yield to others, as railroad building turned men's attention from the river toward the unsettled western lands.

## NEW ORLEANS

Thirteen hundred miles downstream from St Louis and fifteen hundred miles from Cincinnati lies New Orleans. New Orleans was founded by the French in 1718, became Spanish territory in 1763, was reacquired for France by Napoleon in 1800 and sold along with all the Louisiana Territory to the United States in 1803. For nearly eighty years New Orleans had been the capital of the Louisiana Territory, and as such, even when little more than a village, ranked as a city, a city

66

set in a watery waste of swamp and bayous, the brackish inlets of river and sea, a hundred miles and more from the open Gulf but with the Mississippi river making her the gateway to a vast inland empire. Resident French and Spanish colonial officials and governors had maintained some semblance of pomp and circumstance and had kept New Orleans aware of her connections with Europe. An archiepiscopal palace, parish church and cathedral, Ursuline convent and hospital reminded men that, though they lived on the edge of the wilderness, Mother Church had them under her care. At the same time a river city and a seaport, New Orleans had probably more of the flotsam and jetsam of two continents than any other city in North America—rascals and thieves, refugees from justice, pimps and pirates, down-and-outers. Thus even in 1800 she was the Marseilles of the New World.

Though Spanish occupation was briefer than French, the Spaniards left their impress upon New Orleans architecture. 'Stuccoed wall and iron lattice, huge locks and hinges, arches and gratings, balconies, jalousies, inner courts with parterres, urns and basins with fountains, and statues half-hidden in roses and vines' gave an appearance more Spanish than French. But the inner spirit of the place was French. Need to protect this outpost of empire, coupled with French gregariousness, had led French governors to build the city into a compact unity about the Place d'Armes, the parade ground facing the river. Two miles inland stretched Lake Pontchartrain guarding the settlement's rear. After the United States took over, an American quarter arose along the river bank north of the Vieux Carré. Both quarters of the city rested on swampy land subject to periodic overflow from the river, in spite of the earthen dikes, the levees, early built along the river bank. At most seasons mud was so deep that citizens, believing that paving blocks would fast sink out of sight, for years made no attempt to pave the streets. Some buildings stood on pillars to keep them above mud and flood. The city lies on the outer arc of a great bend in the Mississippi where river currents ran too strong to build wharves out into the stream. Planking laid over the levee served for wharfage along the crescent river front. Ships appeared to dock almost in the city streets. Masts towered above the tallest buildings, and from ship decks sailors could look down into the city itself. It had an alluring, foreign air.

The Creoles of New Orleans, the French and French colonials of the eighteenth century, were a mixed lot—Breton and Norman, French Canadian, colonists from the French and Spanish West Indies, Canary Islanders, refugees from Acadia in 1755, and San Domingans at the end of the century. Rather Gallic in type, they were a fine-looking people, intelligent yet ridden by conventions and taboos, proud almost to arrogance, yet easy-going and intolerant of any rigorous restraint save what their own customs decreed. Their attitude toward the Negro was unique in America, for while slavery was widespread, 'free people of color', mulattoes, quadroons, and octoroons, had a recognized and honorable place well above the lowest ranks of New Orleans society. In the city's theatres seats reserved for Negroes could not be occupied by whites, and *vice versa*, but blacks and whites attended the same performance. The Creoles' continental Sunday, their opera, and, after its introduction by students returned from Paris in 1827, the Mardi Gras carnival, their distinctive cuisine, and their conservative dress marked their civilization as apart from that of the rest of the United States.

They despised *les Américains*, the backwoodsmen bringing their boatloads of lumber and produce down from up-river, the Yankee traders and farm boys agog at the sights of the busy port and out to taste for a few days all its pleasures. As long as the city was ruled by Spanish or French, soldiers and gendarmes could keep these rough up-country bumpkins in check, but when New Orleans became United States territory, Americans roared in and out, an uncouth horde bringing welcome business but threatening to upset the accepted tenor of Creole life. The Creoles, bewildered at first by their new status as Americans and for a time believing it only temporary, were at pains to avoid social contacts with the brash *Américain*. They maintained that aloofness for some years. Intermarriages for a generation would be rare, and not frequent for two generations more. But business—that was different! The flatboats and keelboats landed their cargoes, and, purchases made for the return trip, the boatmen were then 'loose on the town'. Brothels and grog shops in the new American faubourg profited and, as much of the land was owned by Creole citizens of the French quarter, ground rents poured money into Creole pockets. *Les Américains* in their place were all very well, but it took close to two decades of business association to make even gentle Kentucky-bred residents socially acceptable to the Creole.

The United States had completed the Louisiana Purchase at the cost of $15,000,000, some twinges of President Jefferson's conscience, and a promise to admit Louisiana to the Union on an equal basis with the other states. Louisiana posed a new problem. In addition to the great territory to the north and west, encompassing no one then knew exactly what, Louisiana was seaboard territory. How could country about a port like New Orleans become a state until the federal government could build and man custom houses, make provision for ordering international commerce, and put a legal system into force? Louisiana laws were a tangle of Spanish and French codes and customs; to superimpose the common law and English legal procedures upon such a welter would make chaos out of confusion. Most of the inhabitants spoke French or perhaps a little Spanish, but not English. Consequently Congress temporarily organized the area about New Orleans as Orleans Territory with a territorial government like that of Mississippi just east of the river. The law evolved gradually, in considerable measure through the work of Edward Livingston, member of a distinguished New York family and in 1801 Mayor of New York City, who won for himself further fame and fortune by acting as the lawyer for the pirate brothers Laffite. The common law has never run in Louisiana. Instead, a system based largely on the Code Napoléon took form, a system more important today than a hundred years ago, if only because the federal government cannot levy inheritance taxes on widow or widower. With courts established, custom house officials installed, and more than 60,000 free inhabitants counted in the territory, in 1812 Louisiana was admitted as a slave state. That some Louisianans were known to be rogues and scalawags could not stay her admission.

The terms of the Purchase Treaty had included another stipulation, inserted because Napoleon had expected to reclaim Louisiana: French and Spanish ships docking at New Orleans were to pay tonnage fees greatly below those exacted in eastern American ports. Accordingly the New Orleans rate had been set at six cents a ton for French, Spanish, and American vessels alike, whereas in the Atlantic ports the charge was a dollar and a half a ton for foreign ships. Eastern cities screamed 'Discrimination!' but Congress asserted that, as Louisiana was not yet a state, the internal commercial discrimination forbidden to states under the Constitution was not involved. The consequences were an increase in the volume of New Orleans' foreign trade that soon doubled and tripled the $5,000,000 of 1803. Ocean-going vessels could dock at the Quai at the foot of the Old City; river boats were kept to the upstream wharves of the American quarter. In comparison with the Atlantic seaports, she suffered little from the restrictions that preceded and accompanied the war of 1812. While her strategic location at the portal to the interior of the whole continent made her an obvious British target during the war, the siege of New Orleans, postponed till December 1814, and the American victory had only one effect upon the city. For the country as a whole it had long-term significance: it made General Andrew Jackson, the Hero of New Orleans, a national figure and seated him in the White House fourteen years later. For New Orleans the battle and its aftermath spelt the end of the large-scale business in slave-smuggling which had flourished since 1808.

Before 1808, while importation of slaves was still legal, the slave trade into New Orleans had been active, and long after that West Indian planters, thronging in to settle in Louisiana, brought slaves with them. United States agents were too few to prevent their entry, and it was difficult to distinguish between slave and free

View of New Orleans, 1803

The eagle and banner symbolized for Americans the satisfaction of New Orleans residents at coming under the protection of the United States

black immigrant. Sizeable though this illicit importation may have been, it was a small matter compared to the business run by the organized slave-smugglers. And here enter the brothers Laffite, Frenchmen who migrated to the New World in 1809. The maze of streams and bayous of the delta country between New Orleans and the Gulf was ideally suited to small craft carrying black contraband or other valuable merchandise. The handful of federal customs officials and few revenue cutters could not cope with such topography. In fashion foreshadowing the methods of the bootleggers of the 1920's, the Laffites 'muscled in' upon the small fry of the trade and before 1810 had an elaborate organization with headquarters on two islands off the coast. One brother presided over the establishment on Grand Isle. Pirates, posing as legitimate Cartagenian privateers against Spain, brought in shiploads of Negro slaves and other readily saleable cargoes. They were sold in New Orleans by the other brother. The Laffites guaranteed delivery. Their profits can be estimated: sometimes with a good haul three or four hundred Negroes could be sold in one day; and prime field hands brought from $800 to $1,000 apiece. Public opinion in New Orleans regarded the situation with a tolerant eye. After all, sugar-planters wanted the slaves, and the Laffites were colorful characters. During the war of 1812 they co-operated with the American army and navy to dispose of the British, with the result that the pirates were officially pardoned for the sins of their past. When they attempted to resume operations after the war, they found that New Orleans' easy acceptance of them had vanished. Some of the gang were eventually hanged as pirates, and the brothers transferred themselves outside the jurisdiction of the United States. Slave-smuggling continued for the next forty years but never again attained the proportions of the Laffite enterprise.

Planters considered that slaves were as essential to sugar cultivation as to cotton- or rice-growing. Sugar-raising had turned into a profitable business in Louisiana practically in a single season. Jesuit fathers in mid-eighteenth century had tried growing cane, and a Frenchman named Debrueil had granulated sugar, but the short growing season put the region at such a severe disadvantage in competition with the West Indies that Louisiana planters, after repeated profitless experiments, let sugar cultivation languish. World events of the 1790's reversed this order. In 1791 the slave insurrection in Haiti which drove white men from the island halted sugar-growing there, and in 1792 the outbreak of war between Great Britain and the French Republic disrupted trade with their West Indian colonies. Hence, when in 1794 Étienne de Boré, a Frenchman who had come to manage his wife's plantation near New Orleans, decided to try sugar, the time was propitious. De Boré bought cane stalks from two Spaniards in the neighborhood, planted, harvested, and, by devising an improved method of granulation, cleared $12,000. That was encouragement to others. The Negro uprising of 1796 in San Domingo brought about the emigration of experienced San Domingan planters to Louisiana, and the Napoleonic wars in Europe gave American growers some twenty years of artificial protection. After 1815, as competition heightened, the infant sugar industry of Louisiana was saved by three developments, first, the substitution of steam for animal power to drive the sugar mills, second, protective tariffs passed by Congress in 1824 and 1828, and, third, the introduction from Java of a better variety of cane which could withstand cold. In the 1820's sugar took over in Louisiana much as had cotton in South Carolina and Georgia twenty-five years before. While Louisiana planters did not follow the South Carolina–Charleston custom of living for months of the year in the city, their standards and mode of life affected New Orleans in subtle ways, and some of their wealth, represented by the hogsheads of sugar and molasses rolling on to New Orleans wharves and off again into the holds of ships, enriched the city's merchants.

In the 1820's and 1830's, as planters from the Carolinas and Georgia, where the soil was wearing thin, began to buy and bring under cultivation land in Mississippi, western Tennessee, and the Arkansas Territory, New Orleans had cotton and some tobacco to ship. Though Louisiana at first grew little cotton, by 1835 two steam presses in the city were baling half a million bales a year. Only less commercially important than the slave crops were the mountains of foodstuffs, whiskey, furs, lumber, and hides yearly brought down the river from the Ohio, the upper Mississippi, and the Missouri valleys. Flatboats, cheap to build even if slow-going, continued in use into mid-century, for thus any farmer, or two or three together, could ship in his own boat direct to market, there knock the boat apart, and sell the lumber along with his cargo. Yet as early as 1825 the river steamboat was cutting in upon the flatboat, and passenger travel was almost wholly by steamboat. Five hundred and two steamboats docked at New Orleans in 1825, five times that number—and bigger boats at that—twenty years later, and 3,566 in 1860.

Lloyd's of London is said to have prophesied in 1821 that New Orleans would become the greatest port in the world. That year her exports were valued at $16,000,000. Her imports included sugar from the West Indies, to eke out the Louisiana supply, coffee, tropical fruit, mahogany and rosewood from Central or South America, British cutlery, tools, china, and cotton goods, French wines, brandy, silk, broadcloth, and linen, Mexican silver, cochineal, and pimento. Certainly the makings of the world's busiest port were there. Even the ocean-going vessels of today can unload from their holds right into the warehouses on the levees, with no cartage at all. But in 1821 and for several years after, New Orleans had no warehouses on the levees and few anywhere in the city. She had not troubled to build so much as a roof over her wharves. Cargoes stood out on the levees in all sorts of weather. The losses of perishables were on a scale a Boston merchant would have called criminal—$100,000 in tobacco in one season. Flour and pork went mouldy; hides dried out. The Orleanians shrugged, laughed, said easily that if insurance did not cover the loss, another shipment and another deal would. Until 1833, the city had no central market, no public warehouses, no auction rooms, no exchange. A captain landing an unconsigned shipment had himself to scurry around to find a buyer. Men conducted their business on a personal basis, frequently in one of the wine shops or restaurants. There was neither business organization nor wish for it. Life was gay, easy, leisurely. Citizens let themselves believe that the city's position made her forever immune to attack from competitors.

The first shock to New Orleans complacency came before the 1820's were done. In the autumn of 1825 the first boats had gone through the Erie Canal from Buffalo on Lake Erie to Troy on the Hudson and thence to New York City. Freight costs from Buffalo to New York dropped from $100 to $10 a ton. Now farmers of the northern Ohio country and beyond turned attention to getting their produce to Lake Erie to ship east to New York, instead of sending it by the Ohio and Mississippi to New Orleans. The opening of the Pennsylvania Canal and, after 1832, the waterways from Cincinnati to Lake Erie made further inroads on New Orleans-bound traffic. Farmers and merchants, tired of having their goods spoil on New Orleans wharves, shipped east when they could. New Orleans as yet lost little of the Ohio trade, but the volume increased less rapidly than that siphoned off by the canals. Even carefree Louisianians were jolted.

Meanwhile New York firms had been organizing their affairs to take over the cotton-carrying trade out of New Orleans as they had the trade out of Charleston. Here was a tougher nut to crack than Charleston: New Orleans had the whole Mississippi valley at her back. In 1835 her commerce was valued at nearly $54,000,000, and her exports exceeded New York's. New York's banking and factoring system, however, was gaining, and by 1850, when cotton composed 60 per cent of all United States exports, New York City had taken the lead from New Orleans, and taken it forever. New York credit was financing western as well as Carolina planters. New York ships were carrying much of the crop to Liverpool and Le Havre, and New York merchants and bankers were pocketing forty cents on every dollar of cotton raised. New Orleans, like Charleston, remained unconcerned until it was too late.

The Creoles were more prone than American residents to let matters take their course. Creoles viewed as extravagant folly the laying of cobble stones in 1817 along Gravier Street in the American quarter, until the practicality of that experiment persuaded the French-born Mayor to pave two thoroughfares in the Vieux Carré. Yet in 1835 only two streets were paved full length. The easy-going attitude of the Creole irritated new citizens as much as their readiness to change the established order annoyed descendants of the French. Mutual exasperation reached such a pitch in 1836 that the state legislature was induced to grant a new city charter creating three separate municipalities tenuously bound together by a nearly powerless Mayor and advisory Council. During the next sixteen years the First Municipality, the Old Square, was free to ignore the Second Municipality, the American quarter, and the Third Municipality on New Orleans' outskirts; and the newer sections, in turn, were free of the Creole. Each municipality had its independent fiscal system and, strangest of all, its own municipal currency, popularly labelled 'shin plasters', with which to pay its employees and settle its debts. Endless confusion and added friction naturally developed within the city. Alexander Mackay, commenting in 1847 on the contrasts between the Creole and the American municipalities remarked: 'You not only, in crossing Canal Street, seem to bound from one century into another, but you might also fancy that you had crossed the boundary line between two coterminous nations.'

Faulty administration or insufficient taxation to meet demands for new municipal services had by 1848 brought all three corporations close to bankruptcy. The First Municipality found particular difficulty in carrying out state instructions of 1841 directing cities to open public schools; in the Vieux Carré classes had to be taught in both French and English, thus requiring two staffs of teachers and two sets of textbooks. In the American quarter, the municipality assigned its harbor fees to school support but had to impose a special tax as well. Throughout New Orleans, as in Cincinnati a decade earlier, citizens objected to tax-supported schools, and public school attendance was small. By 1850 the three corporations were ready to reunite, but the state insisted that before it could abrogate the charter of 1836, New Orleans must conduct a referendum on the question. Unhappily the new 'consolidated charter' of 1852, though ending much of the internal political turmoil, could neither change the natural climate nor solve the city's health problems.

At this point let us talk about the weather, for, as the noted historian, Ulrich Phillips, says in opening his *Life and Labor in The Old South*, the weather 'has been the chief agency in making the South distinctive'. Before the science of epidemiology was born, before the sources of malaria and yellow fever were so much as guessed at, before fine-meshed window screens were known, New Orleans was at the mercy of her weather and her environment of swamps. Her climate is debilitating, muggy, warm or hot for about eight months of the year, damp, raw, and chilly for the rest. Temperatures rarely rise above 95° or drop below 40°, but the humidity, averaging 70 per cent, is oppressively high. The swamps and bayous bred malaria- and yellow-fever-bearing mosquitoes, the more deadly because unrecognized as carriers. Cholera broke out yearly. New Orleans' death rate, always much higher than that of equally large northern cities, in periods of epidemics was appalling. In the great yellow-fever years of 1853-4 and 1855 there were more than 25,000 deaths in a city that in 1850 numbered 116,000 inhabitants. The Medico-Chirurgical Society that before 1855 did duty as the Board of Health was helpless. Quarantines could not be enforced. Sanitary engineering was nowhere far advanced. A sewerage system seemed impossible because much of the city lay below the level of the Gulf. The distaste of citizens for anything demanding vigorous effort was the outcome in no small part of New Orleans climate and topography. The rapidity with which Northerners on becoming residents accepted the New Orleans tempo shows that it did not stem from innate sloth. The energy and business acumen displayed by New Yorkers in preempting New Orleans' cotton trade might soon have wilted in the southern port.

Yet to picture all New Orleans as lacking in enterprise and vision would be as false as to paint her social life as one long round of dissipation, frivolity, and duelling. Climate notwithstanding, James Robb in the thirties embarked upon an energetic career that proved highly constructive for New Orleans. Beginning by buying and exchanging 'uncurrent' money, that is, speculating in coin and paper that was not legal tender, then by purchasing at a bargain price the New Orleans Gas Light and Banking Company when it was hard hit by the panic of 1837, and then by using the huge profits from that transaction to open the 'Bank of James Robb', he built up the most powerful banking house in the Southwest. He early sensed the importance of rail connections for the river cities and vigorously promoted the New Orleans, Jackson, and Great Northern Railroad, until the panic of 1857 enmeshed him. That panic, particularly acute in the financial centers of the East, convinced New Orleans of the folly of relying on northern banks, and in the two years preceding the Civil War southern banking made notable progress.

Nor were Robb and his associates alone in seeing the wisdom of making New Orleans independent of northern capital. In 1847 J. W. B. De Bow, a Charlestonian come to New Orleans, began publishing *De Bow's Commercial Review*,

'New Orleans, La. and Vicinity', 1863

which almost overnight became the most widely read and frequently quoted periodical in the South. His motto was 'Commerce is King,' and, harping constantly on that theme, he published a series of articles year after year exhorting Southern merchants to bestir themselves to prevent Northerners' making further inroads upon Southern prosperity. His flowery style had mighty appeal for his Southern contemporaries who ranked bombastic oratory as a great art. New Orleans read what he wrote, pondered his proposals, but delayed acting on them. His plea for direct trade with Europe was based on clear perception of the plight of the South. In 1858 he summed up his views in an unusually tersely worded article entitled 'Who Profits by our Commerce?'

> The doctrine that Cotton is King [he wrote] is taught to the South; it is a fallacy . . . That cotton might be King may be true, if Commerce could be made Queen. As matters stand, they form different dynasties. . . . The total exports of the country in 1857 were $340,000,000, of which the South supplied one half. . . . But the ships of the North convey our products to the North, and, with the European ships, thence to Europe. . . . New York City has become the great medium for the exchange of the country.

Yet how by that date could New Orleans hope to overthrow New York's financial overlordship? New Orleans was making headway when the Civil War broke out, but she was forty years too late in organizing a business empire to compete on even terms.

In the antebellum era, whatever the businesss ups and downs, whatever the Creole-American bickerings, and however enervating the weather, New Orleans maintained a kind of spontaneous gaiety peculiarly her own. Wealth and the leisure created by slave labor gave birth to a society where manners were important, but warm and friendly manners. By 1850 too many 'nouveaux', so-called, had permeated New Orleans to make family background count heavily, though having Creole ancestry was always an asset. The city was at once cosmopolitan and provincial. When the 'nouveau', whether European, Yankee, or Southerner, acquired the manner and conformed to the Louisiana pattern of behavior, New Orleans accepted him. While slave-owning was general among the well-to-do, it was not a matter of prestige as in Charleston; in New Orleans wealthy merchants, shippers, and bankers held equal place with the sugar-growers of the neighboring plantations. The small householders minus slaves and the transients in and out of the city could enjoy most of the city's diversions along with the rich. The restaurants served the best food in North America; Thackeray considered New Orleans' bouillabaisse superior to that of Marseilles. French, English, and German theatres, a French opera company, and in mid-century a local orchestra offered good entertainment the year round, and the carnivals provided very special festivity in the pre-Lenten season. Among the literate the atmosphere of the abidingly French city nourished a taste for romantic literature—Scott's novels, Lamartine's and Schiller's poetry, Carlyle's essays. Everyone felt the mellowness of the city's life; even the slaves seemed to share the feeling. Nowhere in the United States was life more agreeable, nowhere less American in quality. Never a typical boom town even in her days of greatest commercial activity, New Orleans kept her distinctive charm when war and political reconstruction wiped out her prosperity.

The peak of river trade was reached in the 1850's. Some freight still goes by river-boat, but the extension of railroads through the country's interior doomed cities that relied primarily upon river traffic to a steadily shrinking significance. In the era of railroad expansion after the Civil War, St Louis, capitalizing upon her location in the heart of the central valley of the continent, enlarged her power by making herself a railroad center of some importance. Cincinnati's well-being, in turn, as the century wore on, came to depend more upon railheads than riverboats. New Orleans, still a port for ocean-going commerce but too far south to share in the profits of the first transcontinental lines, had to wait till Northern capitalists saw the advantage of a southern railroad route across the United States.

Each of the river cities had drawn upon the older seaboard cities. River traders long depended on eastern credit, and the Atlantic ports in the days of water transport were the chief markets and distributing points of western produce. Eastern cities also fed people to the new settlements on the Ohio and Mississippi, tradesmen and artisans who saw no attraction in farming but who were eager to profit by the opportunities opening up as western villages grew into towns and towns into cities. Teachers, ministers, and newspapermen bred in Boston, New York, Philadelphia, or Baltimore carried their ideas to the young cities of the new West, while Charleston men gravitated toward New Orleans, metropolis of the Southwest. In time, the transfer of culture, in its broadest sense, would work also from West to East. Before the Civil War that reverse current was still relatively slight, though a gifted few—people like Dr Drake with his contributions to medical knowledge, Harriet Beecher Stowe, and William McGuffey—influenced life in eastern cities as in the Middle West. From the river cities, in turn, men would move on to share in building new cities in the country beyond.

# IV

# New England Manufacturing Cities: Holyoke and Naugatuck

WHILE South Carolina planters were dedicating Charleston to King Cotton and while the river cities of the West were widening their spheres of commercial influence in the country's interior, New England began shaping a new economic pattern for herself. The upper Mississippi valley and the shores of Lake Michigan were still Indian country when New Englanders, led by Boston capitalists, first turned from the sea to look inland. Their gaze for a generation after 1830 would be divided between the sea and the back-country; but they saw that New England's ocean-going commerce would profit as much from native exports as from a carrying trade dependent on the whims of foreign governments or of rival states in the Union. Merchants with contacts in distant ports, and shipbuilders too, saw the wisdom of developing a hinterland on which to draw. To draw from a remote back-country meant developing transport facilities, canals, roads hard enough to be passable at every season and wagon trains to traverse them, or, best of all, railroads and steam-powered cars. Eventually New England railroads could reach out into the rich farmlands of western New York and beyond, but until then something more than New England forests and the meagre surpluses of New England farms would be needed to feed the steam roads with freight. Manufactured goods would supply exports, and the feasibility of cotton manufacture using New England streams to provide water power to run machinery had been proved well before 1820. New England's first mills had been located near the seaboard. To supply freight for roads running into Boston from the west would necessitate building factories inland. Thus it came about that the spread of manufacturing through all the interior of New England and the development of New England railroads were inextricably intertwined.

Manifestly conversion to an industrial economy could be neither immediate nor universal. The canny Boston merchant who observed the success of Francis Lowell's Waltham Company could plan to invest money in imitative ventures, on the principle that diversification was a hedge against losses in trading voyages. Building a factory, however, constructing machinery, and recruiting hands to run it might still look risky, even after the tariff of 1828 gave substantial protection to infant industry. That mercantile capital nevertheless flowed in to multiply cotton mills in New England bears testimony to the adventurousness and self-confidence of the New England merchant. Other goods besides cottons were needed by the expanding young nation, but in the 1830's and 1840's textile manufacture was the one essential industry in which mechanization had gone far and hence in which large-scale production was possible. Though makers of firearms and clocks were already using a few machine tools which enabled them to produce interchangeable parts, neither muskets nor time-pieces could command the wide market waiting for sturdy cotton cloth. Plantations owners needed it in quantity for field hands, and every housewife in America welcomed a chance to buy cheap fabrics instead of having to spin and weave at home. Boston capitalists, once won over to industrial investment, therefore concentrated their resources upon cotton mills and the machine shops to equip them.

## HOLYOKE

In 1833 Boston enterprisers, anticipating the day when railroads from the city would reach across Massachusetts, built a dam and cotton mills at the falls of the Chicopee river tributary to the Connecticut. Chicopee prospered so remarkably that her promoters began looking for other mill sites in western Massachusetts. New England's mightiest potential waterpower lay mid-way between Springfield, just below Chicopee, and Northampton, eighteen miles north, where the Connecticut river dropped sixty feet over rapids and falls within the space of a mile. Easy access to the locality was provided by the Western Railroad, which by 1845 stretched from Boston a hundred miles to Springfield and on to the New York State border. But tracks from New York City also ran into Springfield, meeting there with a line from Northampton. Consequently, New Englanders reasoned, if Boston, not New York, was to control the Connecticut valley, Boston money must develop the region. If Boston capitalists could acquire the site at the Great Falls of the Connecticut and harness its power, they could build and direct the fortunes of the greatest cotton-manufacturing city in the world. That was their hope.

In the summer of 1847 the scheme began to materialize when landowners on the right bank sold their farms to a newly incorporated company, the Hadley Falls Company. The power rights were assumed to be appurtenant to the land. As nearly every important man or business firm in Boston bought shares in the venture, the list of stockholders read like a Boston *Social Register*, the local equivalent of Debrett. Directors immediately engaged an experienced engineer to plan the layout of the company town and direct the building of a dam and canal system.

Two and a half years later their 'New City' came into being, with a score of mill sites available for sale. Eventually, the directors believed, there would be space and power for forty-eight huge factories; England's Manchester would take second place to this manufacturing mammoth. Directors named the place Holyoke, in honor of a seventeenth-century Puritan pioneer of the Connecticut valley. Everything necessary for a booming mill town seemed to be in readiness—rail connections, vast power, the financial backing of successful Bostonians. Possibly even the charm of the natural setting would prove an asset.

Above the dam and the great bend of the river, wooded hillsides came down to the railroad along the river's edge, while, on the other shore, farm and pasture lands rolled off to the east. A few miles north rose the wooded shoulders of Mt Tom and the pine-clad sweep of the Mt Holyoke range, between which the river cut. In the nearby towns of Amherst and South Hadley Center stood two institutions of learning, already famous, Amherst College founded in 1821 by Congregationalists opposed to Unitarian rationalism, and Mt Holyoke Seminary where young women trained as missionaries and from which, a generation later, would come some of the foremost women scholars of America. Dignified Springfield and Northampton, with two centuries of New England town life behind them, were Holyoke's downstream and upstream neighbors. New England tradition pervaded the countryside. The mills built up in Chicopee, to be sure, were foreshadowing a little of what sudden industrial development might bring. Stockholders of the Hadley Falls Company, however, saw no reason to doubt that they were about to reap fat dividends and simultaneously to shed prosperity and other urban benefits upon the Connecticut valley.

But something went wrong. Not only were Holyoke's founders doomed to disappointment; succeeding generations of ambitious men also failed to infuse into the community the civic consciousness and unity that characterize a vigorous city. Holyoke is not decayed; on the contrary, she may in time find her way out of her confusions to take a distinguished place among the smaller cities of the United States where life is the richer for being simpler than it can be in a great metropolis. But Holyoke, now over a century old, has never flowered. For a brief period, perhaps from about 1878 to 1893, she gave signs of sturdy growth. Then a slow paralysis set in, and the promise was not fulfilled. Today she has far more to recommend her than a dozen other New England manufacturing cities— Manchester, New Hampshire, where abandonment of half the cotton mills has crippled the community; Fall River, Massachusetts, where one-time busy textile mills today house a series of virtual sweatshops; or Gardner, where furniture manufacture, once flourishing, has petered out with the exhaustion of New

England's lumber supply. Nevertheless, if Holyoke is not one of New England's dreary mill towns, she is still far from realizing the hopes her founders and later comers alike had for her.

The first troubles of Holyoke grew out of the Boston stockholders' basic concept: from this community they planned to derive profit—profit from cotton manufacture, from sale of power and real estate, and from freight fed to their railroads; but they planned to make the profits as absentee owners. Since flimsy structures would be a poor investment, company directors were determined to have nothing shoddy in the 'New City'. The company tenements were models for their day. The harmonious proportions of the brick rows and the pine panelling in the foremen's houses were unusually fine. Mills built for sale or company use were solid in construction. But no stockholder had the remotest intention of personally concerning himself with life in the town. Build well, sell property at good prices, and hire agents to live on the spot to watch over the investment and manage the cotton mills. Boston investors would live in Boston and occasionally, from handsome offices in Milk Street, issue orders that might leave mill hands in Holyoke jobless and hungry or bring hordes of new workers to crowd into the tenements. Company policy was to discourage small enterprise. By holding its property for high prices, the company hampered the growth of a solid middle class. Because in 1847 the locality had been farmland, there were no roots for a community other than what the company planted; and the planting was shallow. The absentee owners intended to control Holyoke's economic life, but wanted no responsibility for her social or spiritual well-being. Men who in Boston still shared in civic affairs were unwilling to extend their civic obligations to their own distant creation.

The second difficulty was closely related to the first. Into the New City, with its lack of indigenous social patterns, the Hadley Falls Company poured immigrants fresh from Europe to serve as mill hands and unskilled labor. Before native Americans who arrived on the scene could lay the foundations of a New England community, they were inundated by a flood of Irish, mostly County Cork and County Kerry men, hardworking, but completely alien. The system that Lowell had inaugurated and other Boston millowners had followed was to employ in their factories farmers' daughters from the neighborhood. By housing them under careful chaperonage in company boarding houses, companies had stilled parental objections. Until about 1850 this plan had worked well. Harriet Martineau had described with admiration the arrangements provided in Lowell where young women of education served as mill operatives and spent their leisure in high-minded discussion and in publishing their own magazine, the

*Lowell Offering.* As the 1850's wore on, this system ceased to function, partly because farm girls were no longer tempted by the long hours and low pay, and partly because uneducated immigrants seeping in as fellow employees stripped factory work of its one-time dignity. In Holyoke native mill hands were nearly unobtainable almost as soon as the factories opened. The incoming Irish families were ignorant of American ways, were largely illiterate, spoke a brogue often so broad as to be scarcely understandable, were usually penniless, and, worst of all in the Protestant Yankee view, were staunchly Roman Catholic. Before the 1850's were out, a number of French Canadians came from Quebec Province to add another foreign element and another brand of Catholicism. By 1860 most New England mill towns had a sizeable admixture of foreign-born in their population, but none was so lacking as Holyoke in an established social order on which to build.

That adjustments between native Americans and foreign-born were not made readily and permanently can probably be attributed to the economic ills that beset the village in its early years. Some of those misfortunes can again be laid at the door of the Hadley Falls Company. Miscalculation of the demand for manufacturing property in the United States of the 1850's left the company in straitened circumstances, its capital tied up in power rights and real estate which did not sell. Furthermore, though directors were obliged in 1854 to deviate from their policy of holding mill sites for cotton manufacture and sold two sites for paper mills, they clung to their original scheme long after events showed it unsound. For a decade the town scarcely grew at all. Depression in the cotton industry caused occasional layoffs of the work force in the two cotton mills that had been built, and general doubts about the future of the community prevailed well before the panic of 1857 struck the country. The panic was not the fault of the Hadley Falls Company, but the effects upon both company and town were disastrous. The company was eventually forced to sell out at auction at a small fraction of its original investment, and meanwhile Holyoke all but fell apart. Although the paper mills and a small wire factory started in 1857 managed to operate, unemployment spread. Householders with means to take themselves elsewhere moved away, leaving behind only the poverty-stricken and those who could not quickly get rid of their commitments. Gloom, anger, and hunger stalked the streets. It was not an atmosphere in which to build cordial community feeling.

Thus when a group of Hartford, Connecticut, men bought the Hadley Falls property in 1859, the new Holyoke Water Power Company acquired overlordship of a discouraged town along with possession of valuable industrial potentials. The canals were skilfully laid out and well built, mill sites were ready for factories,

**Time Table of the Holyoke Mills,**

To take effect on and after Jan. 3d, 1853.

The standard being that of the Western Rail Road, which is the Meridian time at Cambridge.

**MORNING BELLS.**

First Bell ring at 4.40, A. M.    Second Bell ring in at 5, A. M.

**YARD GATES**

Will be opened at ringing of Morning Bells, of Meal Bells, and of Evening Bells, and kept open ten minutes.

**WORK COMMENCES**

At ten minutes after last Morning Bell, and ten minutes after Bell which "rings in" from Meals.

**BREAKFAST BELLS.**

October 1st, to March 31st, inclusive, ring out at 7, A. M. ; ring in at 7.30, A. M.
April 1st, to Sept. 30th, inclusive, ring out at 6.30, A. M. ; ring in at 7, A. M.

**DINNER BELLS.**

Ring out at 12.30, P. M. ; ring in at 1, P. M.

**EVENING BELLS.**

Ring out at 6.30,* P. M.
* Excepting on Saturdays when the Sun sets previous to 6.30.    At such times, ring out at Sunset

In all cases, the *first* stroke of the Bell is considered as marking the time.

and a machine shop existed equipped to make the water wheels and machinery for any new enterprise. Dirt roads as well as the railroad connected Holyoke with Springfield and Northampton, while a swing ferry served for crossing the river below the great dam to the South Hadley shore. Beyond the shanties of the Irish immigrants on the outskirts of the town stretched the fields and hills of the enchanting New England countryside. Along the alternately muddy and dusty streets within the village stood several rows of mill tenements, frame boarding houses, scattered private dwellings, a few stores, and a bank. Three Protestant churches had built places of worship in the course of the ten years since the town had been organized, and Roman Catholics, urged on by a resident priest, had somehow found money to build St Jerome's church. A district schoolhouse not far from the dam and several schools in the outlying areas of the township supplied the legal minimum of education for future citizens of the Commonwealth. But uncertainty about what lay ahead long cast shadows over the village.

The Holyoke Water Power Company made perfectly clear its intention of letting the town run its own civic affairs. As for industrial promotion, the new resident agent decided to make haste slowly. The new company could afford to wait, for it had purchased what had cost the Hadley Falls Company over $2,000,000 for only $350,000. On the other hand, the locality with its abundant cheap power was unusually well situated to manufacturing enterprise, and in the months before the outbreak of the Civil War hope for the future stirred. The cotton mills were running full time, machine-shop orders increased, and the two paper companies, once despised by Hadley Falls directors as too insignificant to bother about, were making money. Unemployment disappeared, and a few newcomers moved into the town. Still, troubles were not yet over. The Civil War cut off the supply of southern cotton and in the summer of 1862 shut down the chief cotton mill in Holyoke altogether. The Union army took off the younger men, and prices of necessities shot up.

The turning point came in 1863. Demand for clothing for the Union armies, together with passage of a high war tariff, gave new incentives, and the agent of the Holyoke Water Power Company, seizing the opportunity to attract new enterprise to Holyoke, persuaded company directors to build a mill for lease and to adopt a policy of lending money to men to launch new ventures. In this way a machine shop and two woolen mills were started. At the end of the war suddenly the town began to grow.

Most Massachusetts manufacturing towns concentrated upon a particular type of article—to begin with, cotton, woolen goods next, and then, in one town or another, boots and shoes, tools, furniture, or small wooden wares; before the end of the nineteenth century few communities developed diversified manufacturing. Contrary to the expectations of her founders, Holyoke became, not a cotton, but a paper city. For paper-making she had the all-important advantages of abundant cheap power and chemically pure, soft water. Ample power was essential because paper machines, once started, had to be kept running until the batch of halfstuff was run through; interrupting the run meant costly breaks in the paper. Operating the heavy machines required great, as well as steady, power. Furthermore, washing the rags for the preliminary processes needed not only gallons and gallons of water but water of special chemical properties. These the Connecticut river had. In spite of the earlier troubles of the town, the paper mills established in the 1850's had flourished, and men who had been clerks and salesmen in these concerns now saw the chance to use their experience for themselves. The Holyoke Water Power Company's new policy of advancing credit enabled men to organize paper companies with very little initial capital, to pay off indebtedness from profits, and then to expand. Between 1865 and September 1873, eleven paper mills began operation in Holyoke. And these were largely locally owned and locally managed. Absenteeism all but disappeared.

Nothing succeeds like success. Though paper-making was Holyoke's speciality, as the town began to boom, new textile mills and new machine shops also appeared—a thread mill, factories for manufacturing heavy overcoatings and

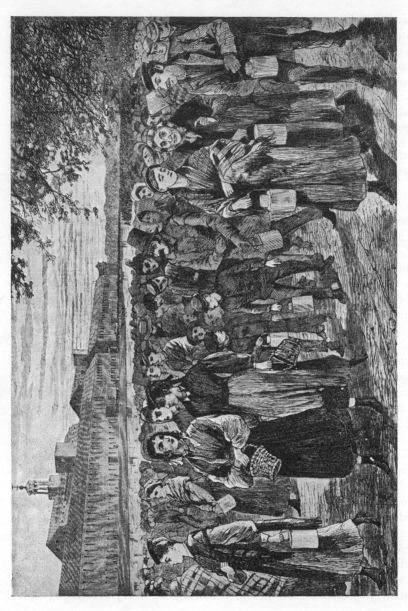

'New England Factory Life—"Bell Time"', 1868
The scene depicted is Lawrence, Massachusetts, but is typical of Holyoke at the same period

dress goods, shops for making machinery and water wheels, and job shops for repair and maintenance work. As new mills required more mill hands and more housing, brick kilns and lumber yards sprang up to supply building contractors. One cheerful promoter described the scene in the summer of 1873 in typical American style: 'The spirit of hustle and bustle pervaded the busy town.'

The rapid growth brought its penalties. Tenements had to be located near the mills because workpeople had only shanks's mares for transportation. Mill whistles sounded at six in the morning and at six at night, and walking through heavy snow in winter or mud in spring meant that people must live within a mile or two of their work. People crowded into tenements, sometimes ten to twelve families in a house built for two or three. The charming spot just above the dam with a beautiful view of the river and hills became a slum. The newcomers were usually ignorant of the most elementary rules of health and sanitation, and, had they been educated, poverty and lack of facilities would still have made their quarters uncomfortable at best, foul at worst. By the mid-seventies Holyoke's death rate was higher than that of any town or city in Massachusetts, save Fall River, and as late as 1890, when doctors and householders knew more of preventive measures than in the 1870's, Holyoke's infant mortality was 312 per thousand of the population under one year of age. In 1873 the town was prospering, confident, expanding; it was also filled with poverty, disease, and human wretchedness. Contrasts were sharpened, where they were not actually created, by the swiftness with which a rural countryside had been turned into a mill city.

One may at moments be tempted to curse the Boston capitalists whose greed, or ambitions, or notions of material progress converted lovely country into industrial hideousness. On the other hand, having created the havoc, many of these same Bostonians joined with men of conscience in other parts of the Commonwealth to force enactment of state laws creating a Bureau of Labor Statistics to investigate conditions in Massachusetts mill towns. The first annual reports of the Massachusetts Bureau of Labor Statistics, published yearly after 1870, were based upon facts collected by state inspectors who saw with their own eyes. In the section on Holyoke the report of 1875 gave details too precise to be challenged:

> Holyoke has more and worse large tenement houses than any manufacturing town of textile fabrics in the state. . . . The sanitary arrangements are very imperfect, and in many cases, there is no provision for carrying the slops from the sinks, but they are allowed to run wherever they can make their way. Portions of yards are covered with filth and green slime, and within twenty feet, people are living in basements three feet below the level of the yard.

With specific details such as these in print, Massachusetts citizens of the 1870's

and 1880's could know what industrialism was imposing upon the Commonwealth and could struggle to mitigate its ills. The resulting social legislation made
the Massachusetts Labor Code a model for other enlightened states.

In 1873 Holyoke became an incorporated city. Selectmen paid by the day for
occasional services could not cope, men believed, with civic problems as well as
could Mayor, Aldermen, Boards of Public Works and Health, and all the formal
officialdom of a city government. Unfortunately, new machinery of government did not remake the community, and during the 1870's citizens chose city
officials from the Yankee Protestant group who had dominated the town during
the years when Holyoke's immigrants were too new to know their way about
amid the mazes of American municipal politics. Then, because the Irish learned
quickly and were eager for office, after 1880 naturalized Irish officials invaded the
betowered granite City Hall in full force. Native Americans were not only in an
overwhelmed minority, but the difficulty of making Holyoke a decent place to
live in made holding public office a thankless task. Competent Yankees, grown
reluctant to run for office or to campaign vigorously for election, were, by im-
plication, now ready to let the foreign-born take a try. Problems remained. Probably the Irish politicians did very little worse than native-born could have done,
though the Irish saloon keeper and the liquor interests in general had undue power
in the city administration.

The inroads on local politics, made with steadily mounting vigor by the erst-
while immigrants, intensified Yankee hostility to the foreign-born. Resentments
focused on the Irish because they were the most numerous and the most aggressive. They seemed to New Englanders to be a different breed of human, super-
stitious at times, always emotional, lacking in discipline, not perhaps of spirit but
of behavior, disconcertingly prone to assert themselves to be as good as the next
fellow. Brawny, generally good-humored, occasionally stirred to violent anger,
they were a force to reckon with. Their growing numbers stirred nameless
apprehensions in Protestant native Americans. In proportion as the Irish rose in
the economic scale and outgrew any one of their original colonies, the 'Patch'
or the 'Flats' or 'Tigertown', native Americans disliked them the more. As
the power of the Roman Catholic church grew in the community with the increase of Catholic immigrants, Protestant apprehensions mounted still higher.
French-Canadian and German Catholics came to be regarded by the more rigid
native New Englanders as lesser and almost innocuous evils. In fact, native Americans nourished faint and vain hopes that differences between the French-speaking
Catholics and the English-speaking Irish would cancel out each other's influence.

The prolonged perpetuation of this feud stemmed partly from Yankee guilt.

The ignorance and poverty of the immigrants put upon property-holders—and they were predominantly Protestants—a heavy burden of taxation to provide schools. The alternative of acquiescing in Catholic parochial schools hurt New Englanders' conscience, for it meant abandoning the New England ideal of free, public, non-sectarian schools where all received the same education. The emotional conflict set up by this choice was real, even if unacknowledged. Yet the increasing number of Holyoke children who attended parochial schools as time went on heightened the sense of difference between Protestant and Catholic. Furthermore, the determination of both Protestant leaders and Catholic priests to prevent intermarriages between young people of the two faiths entailed the restriction of social contacts. Yankees, seeking to protect themselves from the discomforts of rubbing elbows with people bred in a different world, educated in different schools, and steeped in a religion that was anathema to the Puritan, took refuge in an air of superiority that incensed the people they excluded. Irish and, to a lesser extent, French-Canadians retaliated by sneering at the 'uppity Yankee'. The insecurity of each group contributed to the widening and deepening rather than the gradual disappearance of the cleft.

The panic of 1873 and the five-year business depression that followed curtailed Holyoke's prosperity until at the end of the seventies the city was rescued by another boom. A silk manufacturer and an alpaca company built mills, prospered, and became employers of large numbers of operators. Paper-making resumed at a quickened pace. New companies emerged, some coming from outside, more of them offshoots of existing local enterprises. Like the earlier paper companies, the new were owned and run by men who made their homes in the city. By 1890 about 80 per cent of the country's fine writing and bond paper was made here. The fifteen years preceding the panic of 1893 marked Holyoke's hey-day. The Paper City's business activities expanded, employment and population mounted steadily, and, in spite of social cleavages and political wrangling, the community began to see herself as overshadowing in wealth and importance her older neighbor, Springfield. A successful paper manufacturer built an Opera House in Holyoke which far surpassed anything rival cities in the valley could boast. Fine carriages drawn by thorough-breds raced along the city streets, and elegant clothes and European tours came to be part of the scheme of things for the prospering mill owners.

But Holyoke's distinction was tied to paper-making, and by the mid-nineties her career as a paper city was doomed by the increasing use of wood pulp. Since 1880 sulphite papers had been encroaching upon rag, and by 1900 for most purposes sulphite had wholly supplanted rag papers. Despite rail connections with

Quebec Province and Maine, Holyoke was now too far from the pulp-wood supply to compete easily. Where spruce chips were available, there pulp mills went up; paper mills followed. Most of New England's spruce forests were gone. Maine and Canada supplied the East, Wisconsin and the Pacific Northwest the rest of the country. With her natural advantages for paper-making thus lost, Holyoke ceased to be America's leading paper city. Well before men comprehended the full force of this technological change, the panic of the 1890's began to take heavy toll. And then at the end of the depression a group of New York stock manipulators hit upon the plan of consolidating Holyoke's paper companies together with a few located elsewhere. The promoters argued that economies in purchasing materials and in marketing the product, plus elimination of competition between separate companies, would make more money for all. They slid over the obvious fact that their plan spelled monopoly if it worked. All but three of the local paper manufacturers were seduced, and what was to have been the great writing-paper trust was formed. The attempt at monopoly failed, and the 'combine' was soon operating at such a loss that it was forced to close several of its mills in order to avoid bankruptcy. Today, as for fifty years past, Holyoke's most successful paper companies are those that refused to sell out to the combine and maintained their independence.

The community never entirely recovered. The local textile companies for a time fared better, and down through World War I men dared hope that the setback in the local paper industry need not blight the city's growth. Then textiles also suffered reverses. The zest and confidence that gave Holyoke promise in the era when she ruled the paper world were gone. The South, having found in the 1920's that her cheap labor offered an industrial advantage and that cotton manufacture need no longer be a New England preserve, captured the coarse cotton trade entirely, made inroads upon the fine cotton market and, with the introduction of synthetic fibres, was able to compete with northern mills on an equal footing. Changes in fashion and the increasing use of heated automobiles wiped out the market for Holyoke's woolens and worsteds; by 1950 only one woolen mill remained. Meanwhile, the introduction of automatic looms reduced employment at the silk mills. The machinery and machine-tool plants, universally sensitive to industrial fluctuations, here suspended operations during most of the thirties until the war clouds in Europe in 1939 rained sudden new business upon American firms. After the war, demand again dropped. Fortunately, toward the end of the decade several enterprises new to the city appeared. Establishing themselves in buildings left empty after the demise of local companies, these concerns, though none of them large, between them dispelled fears of widespread unemployment or a general exodus of workmen. Yet citizens today, in so far as they remember the grave economic and social problems of Holyoke's recent past, dare not believe in an untroubled future.

## NAUGATUCK

Naugatuck, named for an Indian tribe of the region, is a very much simpler community to understand. One of several score small Connecticut manufacturing towns and cities, Naugatuck today is distinguished for the uninterrupted success of her most important industries and, perhaps a corollary, the relatively peaceful course of community development. Unlike most Massachusetts mill towns, she has had some diversification of manufacture from the early nineteenth century onward. Located in western Connecticut some twenty miles north of Long Island Sound, she never fell within Boston's orbit but was linked by river and Sound, and later by rail, to New York City. Naugatuck's history is one of gradual evolution from a one-hundred-and-fifty-year old agrarianism through intermediate steps of small-scale manufacturing to full industrialism in the twentieth century. Where Holyoke was created by a sudden artificial imposition upon a nearly empty countryside, Naugatuck grew slowly through each stage, feeling her way as she went. In 1950 Naugatuck's population was 18,000; Holyoke's was 55,000. In the smaller place adjustments to an industrial society came little by little, whereas the Bostonians' New City had to struggle with a revolutionizing new order at once. It should therefore not be surprising to find the lesser place the less troubled and possessed of the more immediately promising future.

Naugatuck was an offshoot of the very much older, wealthier town and city of Waterbury, Connecticut. Waterbury had been settled in the 1680's, at about the same time as Charleston, South Carolina. Toward the end of the eighteenth century the settlers of the southernmost stretch of Waterbury had requested and were granted the privilege of setting up a 'winter parish', in order to be relieved of the necessity of weekly attendance at meeting in the town center. For Waterbury, like other eighteenth-century Connecticut towns, was an orthodox Congregational community in which churchgoing was obligatory. The winter privilege, so-called, eventually became a year-round privilege, dependent on settlers' supporting their own separate ministry and their own place of worship. Fifty years later, in 1844, Salem parish of Waterbury was separated from the mother town to become the independent town of Naugatuck.

The Naugatuck valley is a slit in the high hills of western Connecticut. Five miles from Long Island Sound the Naugatuck river flows into the Housatonic, the chief river between the mighty Connecticut and the Hudson. At Naugatuck's site the valley widens slightly, leaving between the steep hills to the east and the west enough level land to attract eighteenth-century farmers. And the eighteenth-century village, six miles downstream from the Waterbury town center, had been primarily a farming community. But save at the 'intervales', formed by the river where slowing of the current permitted alluvial deposits to collect, the soil was thin and far less suited to agriculture than the fertile country beyond the mountains in New York State and the Ohio valley. Hence early in the nineteenth century, as news of the rich lands to be bought in the West spread through the Naugatuck valley, dozens of farmers sold their holdings and trekked westward, leaving behind them the men whose interests lay less in tillage than in using other resources of the region. The main resource was the water power of the mountain brooks tumbling down the wooded hillsides into the Naugatuck river. Men had set up water wheels along these streams early in the eighteenth century to saw wood or grind meal or full cloth, and in time they discovered that they could turn out various farm and household wares to sell to their neighbors. The upshot was a kind of natural selection: farmers moved west, the tinkerers remained.

The objects men could make profitably in this hillbound locality were few. Because of the lack or roughness of roads in the early nineteenth century, saleable goods had to be small wares that pedlars could pack on their backs—'Yankee notions'—pins, needles, wooden bowls, mousetraps, buttons, clocks, knives, Britannia-ware forks and spoons. The pedlar of Yankee notions was preeminently a Connecticut product. He was accused by people of other states of peddling wooden nutmegs, so that Connecticut is often called derisively the 'Nutmeg State'. Naugatuck, decades before the town was separated from Waterbury, was producing her full share of Yankee notions. As turnpikes and railroads began to thread through Connecticut and peddling as a method of marketing vanished, reason would suggest that the village producing these wares on so small a scale would shrivel away for want of links with the world outside the narrow valley. That this did not happen was due to luck and perspicacity combined.

In 1843 chance in the person of Charles Goodyear brought unique opportunity to Naugatuck. Though Goodyear had discovered in 1839 how to harden rubber by vulcanizing, he had failed to find anyone to put faith in his invention until he returned to Naugatuck, his boyhood home, to demonstrate the process to his two brothers-in-law. Both were shrewd business men, William DeForest, owner and manager of a small woolen mill, Milo Lewis of a cotton-warp mill. Goodyear brought with him several strips of raw rubber, two shoe lasts, and his oldest daughter. In the tiny office of DeForest's mill, the seventeen-year-old Eleanor showed her uncles how to shape the soft rubber over the forms. Her father then vulcanized the rubber still on the lasts. When DeForest and Lewis saw the result, a pair of durable rubber overshoes, both men were sufficiently impressed to put up money to organize the Goodyear's Metallic Rubber Shoe Company. Thus the enterprise began that first made Naugatuck famous. The adage that the world beats a path to the door of the man who makes a better mousetrap held true for the village. Even before a railroad, built up the valley in 1849, solved the transportation problem, the home of the product unobtainable elsewhere was becoming a manufacturing center of some importance.

Just as new paper companies sprang up in Holyoke once paper-making was well launched there, so, following in the wake of the shoe company, other rubber companies appeared in Naugatuck. Here was a new industry and only here were people to be found with any experience in making rubber goods. A rubber glove factory, opened in 1847, was soon producing surgeons' gloves, ponchos for the army, and other rubber wearing apparel. Later companies made rubber balls and tennis shoes. But always most important of all were rubber 'arctics' or galoshes. Indeed so successful were the Goodyear plants that both the original investors, DeForest and Lewis, eventually abandoned woolen and cotton manufacture to concentrate upon rubber. The DeForest woolen mill continued under new ownership, but when in 1869 the cotton-warp mill burned, Lewis did not bother to rebuild it.

For a generation after 1844 the new rubber factories, the small textile mills, and the old Yankee notions shops alike used the water of the river or its tributary brooks for power. But, as the village turned into a factory town and new workers' families arrived, need of housing led builders to strip the hillsides barer and barer of trees, until the brooks dried to mere trickles and the 'raging Naugatuck' to a shallow stream. Then only the shops that converted to steam power could survive. For the individual owner of a shop 'up the brook' the cost of carting coal up the hillsides or of moving to a site along the river was usually ruinous. Still the safety-pin maker and several cutlery firms carried on to the end of the century, and the woolen mill ran, though at a steadily slackening rate, till after the first World War.

The survival of these small enterprises could not alone have saved Naugatuck from becoming, like most Massachusetts mill towns, dependent upon a single industry. It was the malleable iron foundry established by Bronson Tuttle in 1858 that provided the redeeming balance. Tuttle, starting at the age of twenty-two with his father's blessing and some of the profits of his father's hoe shop, formed a

Naugatuck from the east, 1865

The straight road cutting from right to left flanked the river. The tall spire is that of the Congregational church. The chimneys belonged to the Goodyear's Metallic Rubber Shoe Company

partnership with John Whittemore, the penniless twenty-year-old son of a Congregational minister in a neighboring town. The partners made an ideal team. Whittemore early displayed a genius for finance, and Tuttle, despite his inexperience, showed unusual abilities as a 'production man'. Malleable iron castings in the days before Americans had learned to make steel were in great demand for a variety of purposes. Malleable iron was cheaper than imported steel and far stronger and more easily worked than ordinary iron. The foundry's first big order, placed in the early months of the Civil War, was for wagon hub-caps for the Union army. When domestic steel manufacture began to relegate wrought and cast iron wares to the background, Tuttle and Whittemore skilfully shifted their production to new articles for which steel was unsuited. The 'fish plates' that tie together the rails on a railroad, brackets to hold the insulators to telegraph poles, and a host of other items individually small and inexpensive but, ordered in quantity, highly profitable to make, kept the foundry busy and brought a fortune to its owners.

Operatives to man the rubber shops and the malleable iron foundry soon had to be recruited from outside the town limits. As elsewhere in New England, the immigrants at first came largely from Ireland. Some Scottish families followed and, slightly later, Germans and a few Swedes. By the end of the 1880's the town was distinctly polyglot. Towards the end of the century Poles and other Slavs came in some numbers. Crowding and unwholesome living quarters appeared in Naugatuck, as in all industrializing American communities, but since her growth was never rapid, social adjustments were relatively easy. Naugatuck took fifty years from the beginning of her career as a factory town in 1844 to reach a population of 9,000, and fifty years more did not double that number. Townspeople made the religious adjustment well, partly because the influx of aliens was gradual and partly because the men guiding the town's religious life were exceptionally wise. Under the aegis of intelligent and humane Congregational and Episcopal pastors and Catholic priests, Protestants and Catholics arrived almost at once at a *modus vivendi* as wholesome as it was rare. A larger mutual tolerance of different faiths still obtains in Naugatuck than is usually to be found in New England cities where the proportion of Catholics to Protestants is high. In fact, though most people in Naugatuck attend church every week, religion is not a divisive element in the city's social structure.

Other adjustments were less successful. Connecticut leaders of the nineteenth century blandly assumed that their first men of industry could do no wrong. There were none of the careful factory inspections that Massachusetts insisted on, no Connecticut laws limiting hours or stipulating safety devices. In the absence of state or local records, the historian must guess at conditions in Naugatuck's mills. The golden picture old residents like to paint of mill-owners and mill hands as all one happy family looks suspect. Hours were long and, thanks to the seasonal character of work in the rubber shoe shops, annual earnings for employees of the town's chief enterprise were low. During shutdowns wage-earners eked out a livelihood by farm work in the neighborhood or by domestic labor. At the foundry a contracting system, common in many metal-working shops in nine-teenth-century New England, put workmen at the mercy of the foremen who, having entered into contract with the company-owners to perform certain jobs for a flat yearly sum, hired their own help at the lowest wages men would accept. Choices of occupation for semi-skilled workmen were too few to encourage protest. Before the first World War no unions emerged, save a few feeble organizations among carpenters and bricklayers. Indeed, Naugatuck industrial-ists prided themselves on having no unionization—proof, they contended, that everybody was supremely satisfied with things as they were. Employers clung to this view in the face of a ten-week strike in the rubber shops in 1919. Yet in the mid-1930's when the Congress of Industrial Organization began its campaign for members, even in this paradise agitation for unionization appeared. Upon the passage of the National Labor Relations Act, Naugatuck's rubber workers organized and, forcing union recognition, won a satisfactory contract. Thus it was twenty years after collective bargaining had been accepted in most of New England before Naugatuck employers succumbed.

Town government, meanwhile, had given way to borough government. The reasons that impelled townspeople in 1892 to petition the Connecticut legislature for a borough charter, if nowhere officially recorded, are nevertheless easy to surmise. Were Naugatuck, under the influence of rapidly expanding industry, suddenly to grow greatly, the system of administering town affairs through selectmen who gave to their public duties only a few days a year would no longer suffice. Local newspapers, moreover, obliquely hinted at gross mismanagement of town business in the years immediately preceding when petty political bosses appeared to be running the selectmen. The town needed a new broom; a borough charter might supply it. A chartered borough, in the United States a form of muni-cipality peculiar to Connecticut, has an elected Warden and advisory Board of Burgesses who have more responsibility and authority than town selectmen but less power than a city mayor and councilmen. As under the town system, citizens in town meeting yearly approve a detailed budget of proposed public expendi-tures, and money voted for one purpose cannot be spent for another. Hence, although the Warden is empowered to disburse funds, control of the purse strings remains with the citizens themselves. In Naugatuck the chief advantage of borough government derived from the concentration of authority in the hands of a single official. This arrangement, in contrast to the diffusion of responsibility among three Selectmen, a Superintendent of Roads, a Fence Viewer, a Hay-Warden, and a dozen other town officials, enabled the Warden to direct municipal planning effectively.

Shortly before the inauguration of borough government, a change occurred that ultimately was to have more far-reaching consequences for the community than new political forms. In 1892 the rubber companies of Naugatuck and several elsewhere combined to form the United States Rubber Company. The consolidation came as no surprise, for as early as 1853 rubber manufacturers had toyed with the idea. The new company had no immediate effect upon Naugatuck. Indeed for the next thirty years each local superintendent ran his own shop as if it were an independent mill. Then, as technology called for specially educated chemists and engineers to revolutionize methods of production, significant changes began: the autonomy of the local superintendent vanished, automatic machinery wiped out the distinction between the skilled craftsmen and the semi-skilled, and the special consideration formerly accorded to old employees disappeared. The depression at the end of the 1920's, requiring of manufacturers greater efficiency and more careful financial management in order to compete and survive, emphasized these changes. The culmination of this local revolution was reached about 1930 when the United States Rubber Company embarked upon a regime of switching its key men from one plant to another, a practice now standard in many big American corporations with branches in a dozen cities. After 1930 few important executives in Naugatuck's rubber plants remained there more than four years. In nineteenth-century Naugatuck such shifting about as occurred was among the wage-earners, who moved on if jobs looked better elsewhere; the white-collar and employer group stayed put. In mid-twentieth century it is the top level that most frequently moves and the working people who are rooted. Thus the men who a generation ago would have been community leaders, the men of most education, experience, and vision, now have no sense of being part of the community and take little responsibility for it. Naugatuck is just one way-station on the course of their industrial and business careers.

The policy of deliberate detachment from local affairs which the United States Rubber Company developed and maintained after the late twenties may have been partly the result of determination to escape the charge of making the borough a company town, where company patronage controlled major decisions and company interests received first attention, but where, when anything went wrong, blame fell upon the corporation. Naugatuck was small enough and sufficiently dependent upon the rubber shops to have given such accusations plausibility. The official explanation was even simpler. In the 1920's, as the company opened new plants in a number of cities, directors reportedly decreed that all must be treated alike. The easiest way to act upon that resolution was to remain rigidly aloof from every community. Certainly during the depression responsibility for any town or city was a heavy burden to bear. Yet a company decision saved Naugatuck in the thirties from the unemployment and suffering that most of New England, and indeed most of the country, faced. Company directors chose to keep Naugatuck's mills running and to concentrate here work formerly done elsewhere. Thus the borough's chief industry, so far from curtailing operations, brought in new people, thereby giving merchants new customers and causing a small building boom. Old residents who growl at the Rubber Company's impersonal behavior concede that its action, though taken without special thought for the borough, benefited the community as nothing else then could.

While United States Rubber Company officials rank themselves as temporary residents and accordingly tend to be indifferent to community concerns, among other citizens local pride runs high. Artificial social barriers and unwarranted discriminations are rare, and this virtue redeems any lingering complacency. Furthermore, the constant coming and going of industrial executives has combined with the family automobile and the steady rise in the general level of prosperity to dispel Naugatuck's provincialism. Physically the borough is unlikely to grow very much more; the hills and surrounding townships hem her in geographically, and nothing points to any large increase in population within these boundaries. Scant space remains for new industrial plants and increasing mechanization in existing factories makes creation of more jobs improbable. But as rising pay scales promise people already employed in Naugatuck a steadily improving material standard of living, bigness ceases to be a borough goal.

Holyoke, deliberately conceived and unloved offspring of Boston, and Naugatuck, spontaneous product of the Connecticut hills, represent two facets of New England's industrial growth. The story of other cities would reveal still other forces at work—New Bedford, for example, whaling port converted to cotton manufacture; Meriden, rural village become a silversmithing center; or Bridgeport, grown powerful through the transformation of tiny shops into mighty machine-tool and machinery plants. Yet these and other New England mill towns, turned into cities, were ancillary rather than essential to the sweep of urbanization across the continent. The course of events in the rest of the country would have been no different had any particular New England manufacturing city never arisen. Nevertheless, the cumulative effect of the rise of this congeries of industrial cities was considerable. While capital for new settlement rarely stemmed direct from these sources, and while the westward movement drew its strength less from mill hands than from other elements of the population of the East, the growth of these small industrial centers enlarged the markets in the West and, in turn, created new stores of manufactured goods to supply western towns. Furthermore, by feeding the railroads of New England and the New York area, individually unimportant cities of New England tightened the unity of the country and contributed to the shift from an agrarian to an industrial economy.

# V

# Chicago, the Railroad Center

NO city in the world has a more extraordinary tale to tell than Chicago
in the nineteenth century. In the hundred years 1830 to 1930 she grew
from a settlement of fifty people to a city of three and a third million. In
the half-century between 1840 and 1890 the rapidity of her development outstripped that of every other city on earth. By 1920 only London, New York,
and Berlin exceeded her in size and commercial importance. Today, in spite of
having shed her one-time flamboyance, she is still very much herself and un-
abashedly provincial. 'In Chicago,' a shrewd observer wrote in 1950, 'anybody
who is anybody knows everybody who is anybody... New York, San Francisco,
New Orleans, Miami aren't America; Chicago is.' From her earliest years she
stirred in men a passionate loyalty and faith in her destiny that gave her a compelling vitality. If to visitors of recent years she seems to have subsided into an
ugly commonplace where semi-sophistication has replaced the engaging brashness
of earlier days and where now neither wickedness or righteousness has any color,
to Chicagoans she remains the most interesting and challenging city in the world.

While human beings supplied the enthusiasm to boost village, town, and city,
geography furnished the basis for their success. In 1803 when the federal government established Fort Dearborn in the marshy wilderness at the mouth of the
Chicago river, the site was chosen for sound reasons. The Indian name Checagou
is believed to mean onion or garlic; wild garlic covered the banks of the stream.
The sluggish little river, formed by the confluence of two branches a mile west of
its Lake Michigan outlet, provided a waterway with only a half-mile portage to
the Des Plaines river, some ten miles southwest, and thence to the Illinois and
Mississippi. Indians had used the Chicago portage for centuries, and French missionaries and explorers traversed it from 1673 on. The fifteen-foot elevation between the Chicago and the Des Plaines rivers formed the watershed between the
Great Lakes–St Lawrence valley and the Mississippi. Thus for all its 'desolation
of dullness', as Margaret Fuller of Boston later described Chicago's setting, the
location was strategic both for frontier defense and for trade. Captain John
Whistler, father of the Major Whistler who planned much of the Baltimore and
Ohio Railroad and grandfather of James McNeill Whistler, built the first Fort
Dearborn. Destruction of the first fort early in the war of 1812 was followed by

the building of a second in 1816. For the next seventeen years, trade with the Indians sustained the settlement until, after an Indian uprising in 1832, the Black Hawk War, the tribes of the region west of Lake Michigan agreed to move themselves beyond the Mississippi.

It is important to observe that the territory about the Great Lakes was scarcely settled at all for more than two decades after white men had occupied lands adjacent to the Ohio river. As the Ohio was the main highway down which homesteaders moved, southern Illinois along the Ohio and its tributary streams, and later along the Mississippi, was peopled long before northern Illinois was touched. Farmers of southern Illinois made up the population that entitled Illinois to statehood in 1818. It was the Black Hawk War that called attention to the northern stretches of the state. The year 1833 marks Chicago's true beginning. During the Black Hawk War, militia and regulars pursuing the Indian had seen the fertility of the prairie land of northwestern Illinois. Their reports on the richness of the region brought hundreds of settlers in the next years. At the same time, the importance of the Chicago river to the development of this new country so impressed a young army engineer, Jefferson Davis, that he persuaded Congress to vote $24,000 to dredge the river and make a safe anchorage for lake shipping. In 1833 the Illinois legislature incorporated Chicago as a town.

Back of Illinois' campaigning for federal assistance was a plan that had been under discussion since 1815. It was to cut through the Chicago portage so as to open a canal linking Lake Michigan with the Mississippi and the Gulf of Mexico. The state had sponsored surveys in the 1820's, appointed a succession of canal commissions, and chartered a private company to build the canal, only to find eastern capitalists unwilling to put money into it. Finally in 1827 Illinois obtained a federal land grant to get the job started. Some of the lots of the government grant lay along the river within Chicago's limits; the rest bordered the proposed canal route in alternating sections on right side and left. Once immigration into northern Illinois was well started, new settlers, many of whom came to the region because of the canal in prospect, now brought every pressure to bear to have construction begun. The Illinois legislature accordingly authorized a loan to be floated in the East to provide immediate funds, and in the summer of 1835 the federal Land Office in Chicago began sale by auction of the government lots along the line of the canal. Within two weeks over $350,000 was in hand, and early the following year, upon passage of the State Canal Bill pledging the state's credit to meet interest payments on canal bonds, money enough was available to let contracts for the work. Digging began that summer.

The land boom in Chicago from 1833 to the summer of 1837 was more irrational than in a gold rush town, for Chicago had nothing in her sand and clay soil but the hopes men planted there. By the fall of 1833 the village, 'a chaos of mud, rubbish and confusion', as an English visitor described it, was thronged with feverish speculators. Some 350 inhabitants grew to 1,800 in a year's time. The soberest citizens were caught by the mania, and by 1836 a local newspaper boasted of property that had 'risen in value at the rate of *one hundred per cent per DAY*'. The second public auction of canal lands that summer brought in $1,041,344 from the sale of 186 lots in Chicago alone. Not only people on the scene, but men in towns and cities all over the country employed agents to buy for them. Cincinnatians added Chicago real estate to their portfolios. It is not surprising that the 1837 census listed seventeen lawyers' offices in a community of 4,170 people. Real estate changed hands at ever-rising prices but rarely with more than a quarter of the price paid outright. Easy credit increased the speculation. Rising land values raised rentals. Insufficient housing for the inpouring crowd pushed them higher. Food was expensive because much of it had to be carted from Wabash valley farms nearly two hundred miles away until lands nearer Chicago could be settled and made productive. The town naturally attracted gamblers of every stripe. Yet not all of the new arrivals came as speculators. Artisans and merchants came to earn a living, perhaps later a fortune, by supplying the needs of the families moving to the prairie lands to the west.

People arrived in any kind of conveyance they could find or afford. Single men came on horseback; some came afoot. An American Dick Whittington, 'Long' John Wentworth, carrying his shoes, walked barefoot into the town where twenty-five years later he would preside as Mayor and where he would own more real estate than any other one citizen. Most families in the 1830's came by wagon over roads deep in sand, mud, or snow. The well-to-do sometimes chose to travel by Erie Canal boat and lake steamer from Buffalo, though steamboats, stopping daily to load wood to keep the fire boxes filled, took nearly two weeks for the 1,100-mile trip and in stormy weather might take a month. Not until coal-burning steamboats appeared in the 1840's would the duration of the voyage shrink. People who dreaded the long voyage through Lake Huron, the Straits of Mackinac, and down Lake Michigan might disembark in Detroit and take wagon across southern Michigan and around the end of the lake. Before a pier was built in 1835, steamboat passengers landed in Chicago by lighter. Eastern wares were nearly always shipped by water to what was the only improved harbor at the southern end of Lake Michigan. Before 1840, Chicago had little to ship east in return but the deeds to local real estate, an occasional barrel of salt pork, or beef, and a yearly dwindling supply of furs.

When in the summer of 1836 President Jackson, in an attempt to halt the un-wholesome speculation in western lands, issued the famous Specie Circular, requiring government Land Offices to accept only gold or silver in payments on government land purchases, one might have expected Chicago's pyramid of paper prosperity to tumble at once. Actually it was another ten months before panic swept the country, and by then the canal was under way. The contractors succeeded for a time in keeping some semblance of livelihood available for the swarms of ditch-diggers and draymen, but as state banks closed and credit evaporated, prices fell, merchants went bankrupt, and gradually work on the canal petered out. Chicago refused to accept defeat. The town had obtained a city charter early in 1837, and leading citizens now exhibited the courage and determination that, more than Lake Michigan and the ill-smelling Chicago river, were to make the city great. Two local insurance companies issued certificates of deposit which circulated as money. This scrip was of course illegal tender, but since Chicago bankers accepted it, it was usable in business transactions. Bankers' support of the scrip soon gave it the validity of real money, and Chicago's reputation as a commercially sound community spread. Nevertheless, disaster engulfed hundreds of citizens and everyone suffered. Land values dropped from a peak of over ten million dollars to about one and a quarter million. As one account described the consequences: 'The land resounded with the groans of ruined men and the sobs of defrauded women.'

But panic and depression could not halt the stream of land-hungry emigrants from the East heading towards the fertile farm lands to the west. Year by year the tide of homesteaders crept farther and farther west, crossing the Mississippi into Iowa and beyond. Chicago was the logical place to outfit before journeying on into the empty prairie. Chicagoans ruined by the collapse of the local boom some-times joined in the westward trek. Wagon shops, plow, scythe, and hoe factories, lumber yards and dry-goods stores could find business in supplying the home-steader bound for new country. As new farms began to produce, Chicago began to have surpluses to export. The first thirty-eight bags of wheat were shipped east from Chicago in 1838; three years later 212 bushels were shipped, and the next year 586,907 bushels. Thus while the dreary-looking little lake port watched travellers move on rather than settle in her muddy midst, she was laying the foundations of her future fame as a grain exporter.

At last, fortified by the promise of the grain trade, tenacity won the fight to re-finance the canal and push it through to completion. William B. Ogden, the city's first Mayor, a young man who had come reluctantly from New York in 1835 to watch over family real-estate investments, took an active part in negotiating a new loan and getting taxation authorized to secure the interest. As a Chicago real-estate broker, he had ample reason to wish to see the job finished. He was not alone. Merchants, lawyers, and local bankers subscribed to the loan, the necessary state legislation was passed, work resumed in 1845, and in April 1848 the Illinois and Michigan Canal was opened. It was not the deep cut originally planned, deep enough for lake steamers, but a much less costly, shallower channel fed by the Des Plaines and other small rivers. Only canal barges and small river boats, not lake steamships, could traverse it. Yet it was the tie to the farms of the interior whose products had hitherto reached Chicago's wharves only through seas of mud so thick as often to prevent transport altogether. Farmers who had been obliged to ship their crops *via* the Illinois and the Mississippi rivers to New Orleans now had the choice of Chicago as a market. In operation the canal would be a disappointment. A waterway wide and deep enough to be a commercial artery between the Great Lakes and the Mississippi would have to wait for more than fifty years. But the immediate effects upon Chicago were as heartening as if the canal were a Suez. A week after the first barges passed through, the *General Thornton* arrived from New Orleans with sugar for Buffalo; *via* the Illinois and Michigan Canal and Great Lakes the shipment reached Buffalo two weeks sooner than cargoes sent by sea to New York and thence west by the Erie Canal. St Louis, to which the state of Illinois had built its first good road from the capital in Springfield, was suddenly uneasy. St Louis merchants who had thought of the canal as merely giving them an outlet to the Great Lakes began to smell a new competitor in the city on the Onion river. In New Orleans De Bow's *Review*, half in envy, half in admiration, wrote:

> Whilst she [New Orleans] slept an enemy has sowed tares in her most prolific fields. Armed with energy, enterprise and an indomitable spirit, that enemy, by a system of bold, vigorous and sustained efforts, has succeeded in reversing the very laws of nature and of nature's God—rolled back the mighty tide of the Mississippi and its 10,000 tributary streams, until their mouth, practically and commercially, is more at New York or Boston than at New Orleans.

Long before the first Canal Bill had passed the state legislature, northern Illinois had given serious consideration to building a railroad to supplement a waterway connecting the lake region with the Illinois river and the Mississippi. In fact, before digging on the canal began, a group of men had obtained a charter for a railroad between Chicago and Galena, a town on the Mississippi river where lead mines were building up a thriving community. Hard times had discouraged promoters of the road—the American abbreviation for railroad. Not until 1846 did interest revive to the point of taking action. Early in 1846 a group of Chicago citizens, headed by William Ogden, bought the charter and land and prepared to raise the money needed to build the line. Eastern investors were not interested. A road wandering off through the prairie west of Chicago? How could that fill any Easterner's pockets? Consequently, though Boston capital had gone into the Michigan Central Railroad in hopes of diverting western farm products from other Atlantic ports to Boston, the Galena and Chicago Union Railroad had to get its money at home. Retailers within the city opposed the plan as likely to discourage farmers from coming to market in person. Ogden and his associates raised the needed funds by scouring the countryside along the route and persuading the farmers, or more often the farmers' wives, of what the railroad would mean to them. Most of the stock, purchased by monthly instalment payments, was subscribed for in very small lots, one share or two, rarely as many as ten. But funds sufficed. Construction began in the spring of 1848, and by November the tracks had reached the Des Plaines river, ten miles away. On 20 November, the first train of second-hand cars drawn by a second-hand locomotive brought a load of wheat into the city, and a week later Chicago learned with astonishment that another thirty loads were waiting at the Des Plaines terminal. In its first year of operation the road earned $2,000 a month. Thus Chicago's railroad career began.

Railroad building progressed rapidly in the next six years. The chartering of the Illinois Central Railroad to cut south toward the cotton region on the Gulf was the next triumph. A Congressional grant to the state of over two and a half million acres of land was turned over by the state to the company in return for a promised 7 per cent of gross earnings. This magnificent gift, if not a surety of success, at least guaranteed funds with which to start construction and, source of peculiar gratification to Chicago, promised to bring into Chicago markets downstate produce that would otherwise go to St Louis and down river to New Orleans. Chicagoans alluded gleefully to the road as the 'St Louis cut-off'. And so indeed it became. In 1852 the Michigan Southern and Michigan Central lines came into the city from the east. The cumulative result was that between 1850 and the end of 1853, Chicago's population increased from 30,000 to over 60,000.

Early in 1854 the Chicago and Rock Island completed its line from Chicago to the town of Rock Island on the Mississippi river. The story of the building of the Chicago and Rock Island, as told by the son of the Connecticut engineer who took charge, gives an idea of how men carried through such an undertaking. Henry Farnam had gained experience in canal building in New England. In 1850, at the invitation of the persuasive William Ogden, Farnam had journeyed west to study the work on the Galena and Chicago, then extended forty-two miles west

Chicago Lake Front, 1866

The tracks and the breakwater were constructed by the Illinois Central Railroad

from Chicago. Ogden succeeded in getting the state legislature to grant the Chicago and Rock Island a charter and a right of way through the canal lands, and early in 1851 Farnam and his partner, Joseph Sheffield, undertook a survey of the best possible route. That September Ogden and his associates contracted with Farnam and Sheffield to build the road, offering the engineers a block of stock in the company and a small sum of money with which to meet construction expenses. Setting to work in April 1852, Farnam's crews pushed the work at a feverish pace. On 22 February 1854, the first train ran the hundred miles from Chicago through to Rock Island. Farnam's *Memoir* notes that between July 1854 and January 1855 he made 'nine per cent' and that in December 1854 the road carried 168,825 passengers and 49,735. 80 tons of freight.

By 1855 Chicago had ten trunk lines into the city and eleven branch lines. Ninety-six trains a day puffed into and out of her depots where seven years before not a locomotive had existed and not a rail had been laid. She was the undisputed railroad center of Illinois, and Illinois, with 2,235 miles of track, led every state in the Union.

Jealous rivals contended that Chicago had contrived this miracle by 'bribery and corruption'. Doubtless a number of questionable deals took place. In so ambitious a city, men would not boggle over short-sighted or illegal promises. In 1850, for instance, the City Fathers, eager to have railroad depots built, sold to the Illinois Central Railroad at a token price the site of the old Fort Dearborn on the lake shore. Two years later, in order to save the city the expense of building a breakwater south along the lake where winter storms were eating away the shore, they turned over to the company the whole lake shore to the city's southern edge. Yet citizens bragged that railroad financing had come from outsiders who foresaw the brilliant future of the city. Certainly gifts like these were not the only incentive for investors. New harbor improvements made Chicago increasingly important as a port, whence wheat, corn, and meat could be shipped east inexpensively, and to which lumber from Michigan and Wisconsin forests could be readily brought. Railroad men could see for themselves the possibilities of the location. Chicago boosters were more vocal than ever they had been in the thirties. Chicago newspapers sang her praises endlessly. Visitors were conducted on tours of the city with self-appointed guides who called attention to her every glory as adroitly as they hurried over her too visible hell-holes. The very envy felt by St Louis and Cincinnati, Galena and Wisconsin's Milwaukee produced newspaper articles and talk that advertised Chicago further. Richard Cobden, influenced perhaps by the ceaseless propaganda, is reported to have advised

Goldwin Smith of Oxford as he set out for the United States: 'See two things in America, if nothing else—Niagara and Chicago.'

But hell-holes there were. The city was filthy with mud, offal, and sewage. Streets, barely above lake level, were unpaved. Sewage fed into the river and thence out into the lake, the source of the city's drinking water. Evil smells permeated everything. Typhoid, smallpox, and cholera struck yearly; tuberculosis was chronic. The city's death rate in 1855 exceeded New Orleans'. In summer the heat could be stifling; in winter bitter winds swept in across a thousand miles of prairie to cut through the flimsy boards of the hastily built huts and shanties that housed much of the city. Prostitutes, gamblers and card-sharpers, drunkards, confidence men, pickpockets, thieves, and murderers flourished in a community where everyone appeared to be too intent on getting ahead to be greatly concerned. There was vulgarity, vice, and violence, but there was also virtue, and always vitality. About the hot winds of summer and the icy blasts of winter the city could do nothing. About the crime and petty viciousness she did little beyond applauding an occasional police raid or voicing periodic protests over police laxity; Chicago's reputation as a 'Gehenna of Abominations' would endure for decades. But about the mud and the sewage and the water supply and public health, Chicago took action.

Built on land scarcely more than two feet above the lake level, the city had made futile attempts in the 1830's to escape the mud by laying planking over the streets. 'Water accumulates under the planking,' wrote a local newspaper man, 'streams up through every crack of the rotting boards, and poisons the town.' Engineers declared that the only solution was to raise the level of the streets twelve feet and fill twelve hundred acres of land. In 1855 the task was begun by dredging the river and using the tons of dirt scooped out for the fills. The deepened channel incidentally improved river navigation. New houses were for the first time built with cellars and the excavated earth was used to raise the elevation. For a decade, while work progressed at an uneven pace, sections of streets ran six feet or more above adjacent sections; steps went up and down from one level to the next. Still more difficult was the problem of raising buildings to the new street level. The proprietor of Chicago's finest hotel, the four-story brick Tremont House, was in despair as the street rose in front of it, leaving it as if sunk in the swamp. George M. Pullman, a New Yorker newly come to Chicago, announced that he had had experience in jacking up buildings along the Erie Canal and that he could raise the Tremont House without causing hotel guests a moment of discomfort. Engaging twelve hundred men, Pullman placed them in the hotel basement around five thousand jackscrews. At a given signal each man gave four jackscrews a half-turn. The building rose inch by inch while guests in the rooms above felt nothing. Other buildings were lifted by the same process. Pullman's reputation was made, and Chicago's fame for audacity spread.

With the streets well above lake level, the city began paving and now laid out a sewerage system, though a system adequate for a great metropolis had to wait thirty years till engineers could permanently reverse the flow of the Chicago river. When she discovered that the first municipal water supply was polluted because it was pumped from the lake too near shore, engineers tunnelled under the lake bottom to a point two miles out where they erected a crib over intake pipes connecting with the tunnel. Thereafter, with a good water supply and relatively clean paved streets, epidemics subsided, the Board of Health could function, and Chicago made herself into one of the most healthful cities in the United States. Moreover, genuine humanitarianism, coupled with civic pride, fostered undertakings to ease the lot of the helpless and needy—a Chicago Relief Society, ancestor of the United Charities, a city hospital, followed in the sixties by a number of church-supported hospitals, and, as time went on, a host of organizations, secular and religious, for helping the destitute. All through the nineteenth century this generosity went hand-in-hand with an obliviousness among business leaders to the underlying causes of economic and social distress.

While individuals and the city as a whole struggled to make Chicago a decent place to live in, the community, centered upon its business life, was making far-reaching adjustments. Before the coming of the railroad, Chicago had been a local retail marketing center. Farmers brought their produce into the city and made their purchases there on the spot. Now, as the produce of the countryside poured in by rail, the farmers ceased to come. How were local merchants to meet that problem? The answer had been indicated by Cyrus McCormick, the inventor of the McCormick reaper. In 1847 he had transferred his works from his farm in western Virginia to Chicago because he saw that his market lay in the farms of the open prairie, where horse-drawn reapers could operate easily. He also saw that he could not sell his reapers by waiting for buyers to walk into his new Chicago factory. He therefore sent salesmen out to the farms to explain how the reaper worked, to guarantee performance by promise of money refund to the dissatisfied purchaser, and to offer long-term credit on purchases. When wary farmers discovered that McCormick stood by his guarantees, sales jumped astoundingly. The McCormick salesmen set the pattern: in the late 1850's an army of travelling salesmen, 'drummers', began setting out from Chicago to sell a long list of Chicago wares to the shopkeepers in small towns all through Illinois, Wisconsin, and beyond the Mississippi. Chicago merchants found that wholesaling to the country retailer built up profits of proportions once undreamed of. In the sixties, led by the enterprising dry-goods and household furnishing store of Field, Leiter and Company, advertising circulars and catalogues distributed through the countryside brought in orders on the understanding that purchases were on approval, that the customer could return anything which upon examination proved unsatisfactory. At Marshall Field's, Gordon Selfridge received his training for his later London venture. In the 1870's the mail order house of Montgomery Ward and, a decade later, Sears Roebuck and Company carried this scheme several steps further by selling only by catalogue and mail order. Chicagoans early learned how to exploit their railroad ties with the backcountry, a lesson they have never forgotten.

Upon this vigorous, growing community of 109,000 inhabitants, the Civil War burst in 1861 with sharp effect. For a decade a center of anti-slavery agitation as deep-seated as Boston's and rather more violent, the city was nevertheless aghast at the disruptions war imposed upon her expanding commerce. Anger turned against Jefferson Davis, the engineer whose report to Congress had brought federal money for Chicago's harbor improvement, now the President of the Confederacy. Chicago was not cut off from her sources of export as was New Orleans, nor torn with internal dissensions as was St Louis in half-rebel Missouri, and was less hampered than Cincinnati by loss of southern markets, but for a time her commercial balance was upset. Then army contractors for foodstuffs, clothing, saddles, harness, and leather boots discovered that here was an ideal location for both manufacturing and distributing. Thereafter speculators in essential supplies swarmed in the city like flies. The livestock market boomed, and horses for the army were sold in thousands. Over the network of rails, corn-fattened hogs rolled into Chicago slaughter-houses to be packed and sent down the Illinois and Michigan Canal and the Mississippi river or the Illinois Central Railroad to the army of the West. Almost before she knew how it had happened, Chicago found herself the pork-packing center of the United States; Cincinnati was Porkopolis no more. Wheat, harvested by the McCormick reaper now that men and boys had been drawn off to the army, poured in to be shipped east by lake steamer or rail, and flour, milled in small settlements scattered through the wheat-belt of the Northwest, was distributed from Chicago in even greater quantity than wheat. Iron ore from Lake Superior landed in Chicago in ever-rising mountains, brought down Lake Michigan from the southern railhead of Michigan's upper peninsula at Escanaba. Using coal from southern Illinois or even from eastern fields, rolling mills that had opened in the late fifties now began to produce iron on a large scale. In 1865 a Chicago plant turned out the first steel rails made in America. Chicago emerged from the war commercially more powerful, financially stronger, and with a greater industrial future than her most braggart boosters could have foretold.

If newspaper circulation and newspaper influence be a gauge of urbanization, as one American scholar has contended, then Chicago by the end of the fifties was urban. Seven daily newspapers had appeared by 1853. The Chicago *Tribune* had not yet arrogated to itself the title of 'The World's Greatest Newspaper', but its power was already felt not only in Chicago but in all the rural area of the Northwest. The *Tribune* has frequently been credited with doing more to elect Abraham Lincoln to the Presidency in 1860 than any other single agency in the United States. The *Democrat*, the *Times*, and the *Herald* were also widely read and copied by small town papers of the region. Articles focused attention upon Chicago but served the broader purpose of bringing alike to local citizens and to farmers of the Northwest glimmerings of the intellectual developments in the world at large, some awareness of the fine arts, and a taste for things they could otherwise have known little of. Foreign language papers, magazines, and a great variety of trade journals published in Chicago added to her role as educational center of the prairies. The *Prairie Farmer*, a paper issued by one of Chicago's most ardent promoters, through its tremendous circulation put at the disposal of innumerable back-country farmers sound advice and information on agricultural problems which would have been otherwise unavailable to them. A hundred years later the *Prairie Farmer's* radio station would widen the paper's influence. Just as her railroads made Chicago the chief market of farm produce, so her press made her the principal distributor of ideas in a large area of the upper Mississippi valley.

The war prosperity and post-war growth were partly accident—sheer geographical advantage. But partly they derived from the capacity for co-operation that citizens showed again and again. When a St Louis editor wrote angrily of 'Chicago, the tool of the Philistines of the East who were jealous of the strength of St Louis', he failed to note what was generally acknowledged, that Chicago citizens relied upon themselves as well as upon eastern capitalists. The building of the Union Stockyards illustrated perfectly that ability of Chicagoans to act together energetically to introduce an improvement. The inconvenience and expense of switching cattle cars to pens located all over the city was manifestly clear as, during the war, the incoming carloads of hogs and beef-cattle increased in numbers. By joint agreement, railroads, butchers, and meat-packers bought an area on the southwest side of the city, drained and filled it, laid out water mains and sewer pipes, threaded it with rails and stockaded it with cattle pens, and open-

Union Stockyards, Chicago, 1866

ed the yards for use on Christmas Day, 1865. Cattle, one observer remarked, got better sanitation in Chicago than humans. The few packers who had hesitated about joining in this pooling of facilities were soon won over. The Union Stockyards became the meat-packing center of the world. Later, Kansas City and other western cities would take over some of this business, but Chicago had shown how co-operation among local competitors could build up a great enterprise. Ingenious utilization of the by-products of meat-packing, a system simplified by the concentration of the industry in one spot, early gave Chicago packers command of a wide field—oil, tallow, lard, glue, fertilizers, and leather. Wheat and corn built the city to begin with; lumber and steel built it stronger; the products of the Union Stockyards built it stronger still.

Commercial and industrial strength, however, was not synonymous with structural strength, as Mrs O'Leary's cow proved. Legend has so enshrined the story of the cow that kicked over the lantern that set the shed afire that started the great Chicago fire that the historian dare not discard the tale for mere want of verification. The blaze that October Sunday night in 1871 jumped from one tinder-dry shanty to another, and a high wind carried sparks quickly to buildings in the business area. Miles of lumber yards and sawmills along the river burned in a few hours. By Tuesday morning two-thirds of the city lay in ashes. The entire United States was shocked. Rival cities laid aside their jealousies and sent carloads of supplies. St Louis gave $500,000 within the first few days. Cincinnati had raised $160,000 before the fire was out. Citizens' committees organized wholesale relief and distributed with equity and efficiency the money and supplies that came in on every train from the rest of the country; the relief fund was even stretched over several years so that a backlog remained when the panic of 1873 occurred. English writers, inspired by Thomas Hughes, author of *Tom Brown's Schooldays*, sent books and Queen Victoria a contribution for a new public library. When the city was rebuilt, city ordinances stipulated only brick or stone buildings in the business district. Undaunted by staggering losses, Chicago business houses began again, and, though some companies were ruined, others by hook or crook tided over, advertising the city's resilience by the rapidity with which they recovered.

Chicago's confidence in her own prowess reached out in all directions. New railroads and extensions of old crept further into the trans-Mississippi West where they snatched trade from St Louis. Before the end of the sixties Chicago's railroads, a St Louis newspaper declared, having gobbled up the river city's commerce with all the upper Mississippi valley, were making matters progressively worse:

Not only is the trade of the Lower Mississippi in winter cut off by the same hand, using the Illinois Central Railway, but even the trade of the Ohio River at Pittsburgh is this day being clipped by the Fort Wayne and Chicago Railway.

The Chicago capitalists are bridging the Mississippi River at Quincy and even the Missouri River at Kansas City, and propose to draw off the trade not only of our Missouri Pacific Railroad, but also of the Southwest, even daringly striking at the center of our State.

In 1869 the first transcontinental railroad, the Union and Central Pacific, gave Chicago a direct line to San Francisco, while several other roads were nosing steadily westward until in the 1880's they would reach into Denver and beyond. Chicago's railroad empire indeed became seemingly self-enlarging. In the early seventies the Baltimore and Ohio, intent on competing with the Pennsylvania and the New York lines, extended its tracks into Chicago to capture a share of her growing traffic, just as small western and northwestern companies hastened to link themselves with lines into Chicago because there they could connect with any one of the five trunk lines from the eastern seaboard. The lake freighters, moreover, eight months of the year kept railroad rates lower than they were inland and tightened Chicago's commercial hold on the Mississippi valley and the Northwest. Realization that she dared not rest on past achievements kept her businessmen alert to abuses that might damage her reputation. In 1870 the Board of Trade instituted inspection and grading of meat at the stockyards. Sensing that Chicago's grain trade would have an ill-name if warehousemen were not obliged to follow grading regulations and give honest measure, the Board succeeded in 1871 in getting a state Warehousing Act passed. Paid inspectors, upheld by public opinion, were now able to enforce some degree of control over the unscrupulous.

When the panic of 1873 closed the doors of banks in almost every city in the country, Chicago bankers refused to weaken Chicago's credit by taking the same course. Their defiant stand was possible because the city's economic foundations rested on grain and hogs. The fire of 1871 had not reached the stockyards. However financially hard hit, people had to eat. European demand for Chicago pork packed in dry salt instead of the brine used elsewhere strengthened Chicago's position in the domestic market. Cities whose well-being depended upon products less essential than food suffered to an extent unknown here where processors, while selling at declining prices, could always find buyers. Chicago bankers could thus continue to pay out cash on depositors' demand until no financial crisis existed. One local booster, forgetting St Louis' generosity in 1871, rejoiced openly at her plight. Remarking upon the drop in hog-raising in Illinois,

Wisconsin, Iowa, and Missouri, he gloated over the fact that St Louis' loss in 1875 was double Chicago's and that his own city had gained in cattle shipments while St Louis lost some 24,000 head.

Nevertheless, Chicago did not emerge unscathed from the five years of depression. Many firms failed, and unemployment spread. Workmen who had come to rebuild the city after the fire added to the number of unemployed. Citizens took steps to make work by public employment paid in grocery orders and fuel, but the scheme was carried out on too small a scale to do more than scratch the surface of the city's needs. The city had nearly trebled in population between 1860 and 1870, rising from 109,000 to 299,000, and, so far from losing population, gained as a result of the fire. Wealth was concentrated in the hands of a few hundred men; several thousand others were 'comfortably fixed' in small retail businesses and the professions, but the rank and file were wage-earners dependent upon the stockyards, the grain elevators, McCormick's reaper works, the lumber yards and sawmills, the railroads, and building trades. Nearly 145,000 inhabitants in 1870 were foreign-born, and it was the newcomers, unfamiliar with the American scene, who made up the poorest element here, as in every American city. Chicago had more than 53,000 Germans, as well as 6,200 Bohemians, almost 40,000 Irish, 15,000 English, Scots, and Welsh, over 13,000 Scandinavians, and a sprinkling of other Europeans. From these came the bulk of the unskilled labor force. In the skilled occupations German craftsmen were in the lead. The large admixture of skilled German artisans—their leaders men of some education and convinced socialists—encouraged the rise of radical labor groups. In 1864 the Chicago Typographical Union had staged a strike against Chicago newspapers which indicated the strength of local labor organization. The union's fight for higher wages and the protest against using women as strikebreaking, 'scab', typesetters had failed, but it had forecast some of what was to come. Energy formerly directed at the destruction of Negro slavery now began to turn upon 'wage slavery'. In the depression of the 1870's native American workmen, left jobless and as hungry and helpless as foreign-born, joined forces with the foreign 'radicals'. Here was the first move within the city to make the melting-pot melt, and it was not welcomed by Chicago's well-to-do.

In the summer of 1877 resentment turned into action. In July a railroad workers' strike in Baltimore spread to Pittsburgh and a week later aroused Chicago switchmen. Pay had already been cut 15 per cent and a further slash was impending. When the switchmen walked out, other railroad employees followed. Within twenty-four hours every railroad yard in the city was paralysed. Lumbermen and other workers struck in sympathy. Business men screamed for suppression of the 'Commune'. Hysteria seized the city as hoodlums, 'idlers, thieves, and ragamuffins', as Carter H. Harrison described the mob, destroyed railroad property and engaged in street fighting. Harrison, later elected Mayor, was determined to make frightened employers realize that these were not acts of the strikers but of all the lawless elements in the city. Twenty thousand men, one account estimated, were under arms, and a score of people were killed before the strike collapsed. Whether it simply wore out or whether the appearance of two companies of the United States army, fresh back from Indian campaigns in the Northwest, frightened the mob when they paraded through the streets is uncertain. As the strikers returned to work, sanity returned to the city. Newspapers that had castigated the strikers began to temper their judgments, declaring it nonsense to deny that there were two sides to the question and pointing to the ruthless exploitation that railroad companies had indulged in—charging whatever rates they pleased, corrupting state legislatures, city councils, and Congress itself, milking their bondholders, and finally 'raiding not only upon the general public but their own employees'. But belated conciliatory words could not dispel wage-earners' anger and distrust. The *Working Man's Advocate*, an outspoken anti-capitalist sheet published locally since 1864, became one of the most influential labor papers in the country. Socialists and international anarchists found Chicago fertile soil for their teachings, for 1877 left a bitter taste, and social inequities were spread out for anyone with eyes and fair mind to see.

Despite this undercurrent of unrest, as the depression faded at the end of the seventies, Chicago had a new boom. She had proved to the world the soundness of her credit and the flexibility of her business methods. After the greatest fire in modern history she had rebuilt substantially and, depression notwithstanding, by 1875 showed no trace of the holocaust. She even turned that disaster to account: no other city could boast of a fire like that. European immigrants, discouraged Easterners, and Southerners, ready now at the end of the harsh regime of Reconstruction to try life in a Northern city, flooded into Chicago. Citizens no longer bothered about outdoing St Louis. The Missouri city, for all her growth during the late seventies, no longer rated as a serious competitor of the 'Queen of the Lakes'. The city of 30,000 in 1850 became before the end of the 1880's a city of a million inhabitants. The horse-drawn street railway system, started in 1859 and nursed by more than the usual amount of fraud and graft between traction magnates and city Councilmen, could not begin to meet transportation needs. Insufficient housing and a growing population created crowded slums huddled alongside the 'princely structures of marble' of the rich. Neighborhoods changed character almost overnight, making real estate speculation hazardous but diminishing it no whit. Poverty and wealth, Christian concern for the needy and heartless exploitation of the working man, apprehensive efforts to adjust to this hurlyburly and passionate determination to make Chicago bigger—contradictions were the essence of Chicago. Out of the welter of conflicting aspirations came fresh corruption, a Citizens' Association for clean municipal government, new charitable institutions, a great settlement house founded by Jane Addams, and a more vigorous labor movement.

Many substantial citizens found the truth about the condition of the working classes hard to perceive. This new doctrine of socialism must be a dangerous foreign importation brought from Europe by wild-eyed agitators who had not been privileged to grow up in the land of the free. Could not anyone with sense, diligence, and patience win his way up to economic comfort or even affluence? When in 1886 a strike was called at the McCormick works and picket lines formed along the 'Black Road', the cinder path leading to the Reaper plant, half of Chicago was frightened. Some were hopeful that issues would now come into the open and be settled fairly. The city administration was ready for strike action. The strike was more than two months old when police, attempting to disperse a gathering along the Black Road, fired into the crowd and killed six men. Labor leaders called a mass meeting. The Haymarket Riot that followed, the panic fear of social revolution that swept the city, and the brutal behavior of the city police force make a story as grim as any in American history. At that protest rally in the Haymarket, a bomb thrown into the crowd killed a policeman, wounded several others, and led to the arrest of eight anarchist leaders. Though no evidence could be adduced that they had had any direct connection with the bomb-throwing, and though all asserted their innocence, all eight were convicted of murder as men dangerous to society. One man committed suicide in prison. Four were hanged. The Governor of Illinois commuted the other sentences to life imprisonment. For a generation thereafter thousands of visitors to the city made pilgrimages to the cemetery where a monument to the executed men had been raised. It took nearly two generations to sift fact from frenzied fear and to reach a reasoned analysis of the riot. A British account in the 1911 edition of the *Britannica* reveals the extent and duration of misconceptions about this outburst. The barbarity of the punishment meted out to the anarchists did not prevent other conflicts in the years ahead. The riot set back the movement for organized labor reform for nearly a decade.

As the city regained equilibrium, sober citizens began to examine more carefully the foundations of this society that they had built and had been proud of. Men tell the story of a delegation of capitalists seeking out the Mayor to urge him to suppress free speech: Marshall Field, merchant prince and multi-millionaire, opened his argument with the statement that 'we represent great interests in Chicago'; Mayor Harrison cut him off with the retort that any poor man who owned his cottage had an equal interest. Informal meetings of public-spirited men held at the home of Lyman J. Gage, a leading banker in the city, turned into public sessions to discuss the ills that bred such violence. Jane Addams and her selfless associates at Hull House in a slum area peopled by foreigners collected facts about conditions in that section of the city that shocked self-satisfied Chicagoans. Churchmen stirred uneasily. Self-analysis killed much self-congratulation and substituted determination to make the hidden places of the city liveable.

And then John D. Rockefeller, the Standard Oil millionaire, was persuaded to donate first $600,000, a little later two million more, to found a university in Chicago. It was not the first; a Baptist university had been opened in the fifties, but had gradually withered away. The idea of a new University of Chicago captured the imagination of citizens of every creed and kind. Contributions poured in, a building went up and the first students enrolled in the fall of 1892. It is doubtful whether Rockefeller looked upon this as more than a Baptist institution. The brilliant young President, William Rainey Harper, on the other hand, saw two things clearly: his faculty must be scholars as well as teachers, and the university must keep itself a part of the city whose generosity and enthusiasm had helped build it. The men who joined that first faculty were learned, but they were also young, vigorous, and enthralled by the challenge of the great city about them. Sociologists and psychologists, political economists and historians, physiologists and chemists, philologists, literary critics, and theologians, they perceived their obligation and their opportunity. The university would thus become not only one of the world's great universities but a mighty, constructive force in the city, enriching Chicago's intellectual life while it studied her social structure and drove for intelligent, concerted civic action.

With all this new soul-searching and horrified discovery of her shortcomings, Chicago at the end of the eighties was still a community proud of her achievements and sure of her destiny. If corruption reigned in her municipal council chambers and municipal courts, if poverty and ignorance engulfed some of her citizens while wickedness and depravity infested others, if her schools were not too well taught and were ill-attended, if sanitation was sketchy and medical care scanty, she could still regard herself as no worse than other American cities and, because of her rapid growth, more worthy of acclaim. Unsolved problems she could cope with when she had time. She had crudities, but she also had culture. Important European visitors, ranging in distinction from the Prince of Wales and

Lord Bryce to continental counts seeking American heiresses for wives, included Chicago in their tours. One of Levi Leiter's daughters married Lord Curzon. Huge hotels gaudy with red velvet hangings and pseudo-Louis XVI furniture enticed the sightseer and served to house conventions. Theatres offered new plays, Shakespeare, burlesque, and old-style melodrama. The Art Institute's collection of paintings was growing. Citizens patronized the opera so enthusiastically that a company built an Auditorium in 1889 to seat the eager crowds. Adeline Patti 'opened' the Auditorium. People could hear symphony concerts weekly. Bookstores were multiplying. Though coal smoke cast a grimy film over lawns and shrubs, the city was planting trees and expanding a park system. Work was beginning on deepening the river and construction of the Sanitary Canal which, when finished in 1900, would make the Chicago river flow backward without the pumping that had been necessary when the lake level was low. What Chicago lacked today she would acquire tomorrow.

She had already developed a form of architecture as original as it was dignified, simple, and functional. After the fire, demand for housing had been so acute that local architects hit upon the apartment house as the answer. Its suitability to urban life inspired other cities to adopt the plan. To Chicago of the eighties and early nineties, Sigfried Giedion has attributed 'the greatest architectural vitality of the period'. William LeBaron Jenney, trained as an engineer, was the chief innovator. From him younger architects—William Holabird, Martin Roche, Louis Sullivan, and others—learned the principles of 'skeleton construction' and the use of the horizontal windows that characterized the Chicago school. Land values in the business district were high, and office space was hard to get. Jenney pointed the way to the solution of that problem when in 1885 he erected the first modern skyscraper. Built with steel girders hung with a curtain of light masonry to serve as outer walls, the ten-story office building with its bands of horizontally set windows was a new departure. Jenney used the new materials of the industrial age, structural steel and glass, to provide the primary needs of a city office building, maximum space and maximum light. Three years later, when his disciples William Holabird and Martin Roche erected the twelve-story Tacoma building, its occupants discovered that 'gain in renting area through use of skeleton rather than masonry construction was equivalent to the rent of an additional floor.' Skyscrapers rose higher and higher, to sixteen stories, then to twenty-one; part of the floor space in each was left unpartitioned, so that tenants could subdivide it to suit themselves. Chicago's sandy soil, some of it quicksand, necessitated new types of foundations, columns going down to bedrock and the floating foundation. In all Jenney's buildings and those of his followers, in office buildings, hotels,

Home Insurance Building, Chicago, 1897
This building (1885–1930) was the first skyscraper, designed by William LeBaron Jenney.
It stood at the corner of La Salle and Adams Streets

and apartment houses, skilful fenestration and starkly simple line did duty for ornamentation. New York in adopting the skyscraper abandoned that simplicity.

As the nineties rolled round and the United States saw fit to celebrate the four-hundredth anniversary of the discovery of America, Chicago bid fiercely for the privilege of staging the World's Columbian Exposition. She had her way. The importance of that World's Fair to the Middle West cannot be overstated. A site on the lake shore on the city's southern edge offered space, though it looked depressingly bleak and swampy when the citizen's committee chose it in January

1891. A well-known Chicago architect, made Director of Construction, laid his plans on a large scale. Seduced by Daniel Burnham's persuasiveness, Chicago men financing the fair agreed to let him engage the architects he considered the most distinguished in America, the most gifted sculptors, the most imaginative de-signers. Unfortunately perhaps, he chose mostly conventional New York archi-tects instead of Chicago innovators. The greatest landscape artist in the country undertook to lay out the grounds and arrange for the planting. Where, among all this talent, jealousies and clashes of artistic temperament might have been ex-pected, Burnham and his staff maintained harmony and enthusiastic co-operation. The Columbian Exposition opened formally on 1 May 1893.

Visitors flocked from every state in the Union, but the largest crowds came from the farms of the Middle West. The white plaster of the temporary buildings gave the fair grounds their name, the White City. Its copies of classical and Renais-sance architecture led Louis Sullivan, trained in Jenney's school, to declare that native American art had been put back fifty years by the passion for the imitative that the Exposition aroused. Yet the White City, brilliantly lighted by arc lights at night and by day gleaming in the summer sun, was a thing of dramatic beauty. The masterpieces of the world's painting, lent for the occasion, and the industrial exhibits opened the eyes of sophisticated people from the East and from Europe, but the effect upon the less worldly-wise of rural America was overwhelming. Chicagoans adopted the characteristically phrased slogan: 'Make Culture hum!' One foreigner proclaimed the fair a step toward 'municipalizing the prairies'. A farmer leaving the fair grounds was overheard saying to his wife, 'Well, Mother, it took the burial money, but it was worth it.' Upon Chicago herself the effect of the Exposition was greatest of all. Imagination and courage in the face of innumer-able obstacles had built the White City. It vanished in a year, leaving only the park along the lake front, the Midway Plaisance and the Art Building as a per-manent visible legacy to the city; the invisible legacy was beyond measurement. The sooty, sprawling city north of the Exposition grounds, ugly despite the dis-tinction of the buildings in the business district, could be similarly transformed. The dream of Chicago, 'the City Beautiful', took shape in men's minds that year.

The immediate triumph of the fair was short-lived. Panic had struck the busi-ness world and Chicago's prosperity was disappearing even while visitors con-tinued to throng the Exposition grounds. The rapidity with which the summer's gaiety and excitement gave way to a winter of bitter hard times and then to new violence was characteristic of this city of contrasts. The fair itself ended on a tragic note. An aggrieved office-seeker assassinated Mayor Harrison on the closing day.

Black-eyed, gray-bearded, powerfully built Carter H. Harrison, Kentucky-born, educated at Yale College, had typified the strength and the weaknesses of Chicago. A believer in the inescapability of some vices, he had never advocated Sunday closing of saloons or felt troubled over the open existence of brothels in the city. On the other hand, he had vigorously upheld free speech and had given support to the working man's cause by refusing to yield to the pressures brought to bear by the city's magnates. He was reprobated by some citizens for his laxity, loved by more for his generosity and his passionate devotion to his adopted city. He had taken infinite pride in the White City. The Black City to the north now entered upon a period of strife and anxiety greater than that of 1886.

Unemployed men that winter lined the streets. Soup kitchens opened in vacant stores, paid for by the contributions of a few business leaders and more largely by the gifts of humble people. Saloon-keepers fed thousands. A British editor visiting in the city harangued a group of prominent citizens with the accusation that poor men could now exist only in the saloons. 'You are gigantic in your virtues,' William Stead told them, 'and gigantic in your vices. I don't know in which you glory most.' The next year he published *If Christ Came to Chicago*; its pages spared no detail of the miseries that men who might have stopped them permitted in the city. The shock of his charges brought the Civic Federation into being, a carefully organized group with a central council of one hundred and branches in each of the city's thirty-four wards. Lyman J. Gage, the banker who had headed the similar, albeit smaller and abortive, movement in 1886, was its President; Mrs Potter Palmer, leader of Chicago's high society, its first Vice-President; Marshall Field, Cyrus McCormick, Jr, and other powerful business men served on committees along with Jane Addams of Hull House, social scientists of the University of Chicago, and labor union officials. Unable to create work for all the jobless or to remodel the city's economic structure, the Federation directed its first efforts at providing relief, at forcing the city Council to hire men to keep the streets clean and garbage properly collected, and at closing the city's gambling houses. The Civic Federation unhappily could not forestall the Pullman strike.

George M. Pullman, famous since his feat of 1855 in raising the Tremont House, had built up a company town at Chicago's southern edge where the Pullman Palace Car Company under his presidency ruled as lord of the manor over company employees. Pullman's paternalism had conceived of the town as a model from which 'all that is ugly, discordant, and demoralizing' would be eliminated. That concept did not prevent the company from charging high rentals to its men who built all the sleeping and dining cars for American rail-

KING DEBS.

'King Debs', 1894
Debs is seated on the swing bridge over the Chicago river

roads, nor did it inspire the company to lower rents when it cut wages. In the spring of 1894 workmen, their pay already reduced 30 per cent, protested, got no satisfaction, and walked out. A month later the American Railway Union held a convention in Chicago. Because of her large hotels, her central location, her far-flung business empire tied together by her railroad network, Chicago was the great convention city. The fact that the Railway Union happened to convene there that June of 1894 brought its members into closer association with the Pullman strikers than might otherwise have been the case. The Railway Union, after a fruitless attempt to negotiate with the Pullman Company officials, ordered a country-wide boycott against Pullman cars. From Chicago to San Francisco, Railway Union members 'cut out' the Pullmans from trains by running the sleepers and diners on to sidings. Railroads, under contract to handle Pullman cars, declared these acts unlawful and discharged men right and left. Members of other unions allied with the railway workers promptly went on strike. Stock-handlers in the Union Stockyards joined; a meat famine threatened Chicago's customers. Open war in Chicago spread until President Cleveland was persuaded that 'this hour of danger and public distress', as he wrote the Governor of the state, justified sending federal troops to the city. Governor John Altgeld angrily argued that Illinois could settle its own problems, but the United States Attorney-General contended that interference with the United States mails was federal business.

The presence of federal soldiers, so far from ending the trouble, heightened the anger of strikers, but, as was true in 1877, the burning of freight cars and shooting was the work of irresponsible and lawless hangers-on rather than workmen with a stake in getting equitable settlements of labor disputes. The blow that really ended the strike was the arrest of officers of the American Railway Union for dis-obeying a United States court injunction restraining them from compelling, or by threats inducing, railway employees to strike. The injunction had been issued under the authority of the Sherman Anti-Trust Act of 1890. The Judge of the Circuit Court, in finding Debs, President of the Union, and his associates guilty of contempt, ruled: 'Combinations are condemned, not only when they take the form of trusts, but in whatever form found, if they be in restraint of trade.' The United States Supreme Court upheld the decision though basing it upon broader grounds than the Anti-Trust Act. So ended not only the strike but also labor's hopes of enlisting any legal support for its cause in the United States courts. For the next thirty-nine years the labor injunction would be a formidable weapon in employers' hands.

Chicago was neither the only American city where wage-earners rebelled nor the immediate inspirer of strife elsewhere, but Chicago's boosters had so success-fully kept her achievements before the rest of the country that Chicago's doings were always news. Industrialists, bankers, railroad company directors, labor union officials, and workmen for years had watched to see what would happen next in the lake city. The Chicago *Tribune*, other daily newspapers, and the flood of weeklies and trade journals, published here and read regularly through a large part of the Middle West, carried the story of her ills as well as her successes. She had made herself, for good or evil, a key to the question of whether bloodshed and lawlessness or orderly, albeit slow, evolution would obtain in rapidly in-dustrializing America. That role would later pass to Seattle and the far North-west and in 1937 to Detroit, but at the end of the nineteenth century it was Chicago's. Fair-minded citizens were ashamed and appalled at this record of violence; self-seekers could see that business might suffer if the city henceforward could not keep order. Attempted suppression of wage-earners' campaigns for better pay, union shops, decent working conditions, and an eight-hour day had ended in further trouble. Some other answer must be found.

Yet even while the battles were waging, new hordes of immigrants were pouring into the city. By their labor they added to her wealth, but at the same time added to overcrowding, poverty, and disease. Upton Sinclair's *The Jungle* paints the picture of the poor early in the twentieth century, the conditions in the Union Stockyards—that monument to businessmen's co-operation and the symbol of tyranny to thousands of workers—the hunger, the squalor, the ineptness of well-meaning charity groups, the despair and the hope of new foreign-born citizens. His novel aided, though it did not originate, the movements to cut to the root of the evils everywhere visible. Civic conscience had already stirred. Carrying further the work begun by the Civic Federation in 1893, a dozen new organizations set themselves to the task. The Chicago Woman's Club forced the city to establish Juvenile Courts, a group at the University of Chicago opened and supported a settlement house near the Stockyards, social workers and laymen organized the United Charities, and, backed by the City Club, the Municipal Voters League appeared, to fight for honest city government. Men who had left city management to political bosses and ward 'heelers' began to run for public office. Though they were usually defeated, their electioneering brought abuses to light and occasionally impelled the Old Guard to take long-needed action. Good will, money-raising, group and individual effort could not reconstruct the city's economic foundations, but the humbleness of spirit and the intellectual honesty with which humanitarians faced the problem partly redeemed their failures and spurred them to renew the struggle. It continues today.

Literature dealing with social consciousness was still largely confined to serious, if impassioned, exposition. Yet Upton Sinclair was not alone in writing novels that revealed the hope and the shame of Chicago. Theodore Dreiser's *The Financier* portrayed the life of Charles T. Yerkes whose manipulation of Chicago utilities made him a fortune and the city his victim. Frank Norris' *The Pit* traced the demoralization of men entangled in Chicago grain speculation. Perhaps most effective of all in reminding the thoughtless that the city contained poor people as well as rich, helpless foreign-born as well as self-sufficient natives, greed as well as generosity, were the books of Finley Peter Dunne, 'Mr Dooley'. Mr Dooley, the Irish saloon keeper with his rich brogue and refreshing humor, made a series of penetrating observations on life and politics that his readers could not forget. Though the scene was not set in any one city, Dunne lived in Chicago and the

Chicago Lake Front, 1927

The 'Lief Ericson Drive', shown under construction in the foreground on filled land beyond the Illinois Central railway tracks, was a feature of the 'Chicago Beautiful' plan. Today it skirts the lake from the old World's Fair grounds at Jackson Park to the Chicago river

source of Mr Dooley's experience was unmistakable. Poking good-natured fun at Americans' 'Anglo-Saxon hurtage' and at efforts of the foreign-born to win recognition, Mr Dooley remarked:

> Th' Bohemians an' Pole Anglo-Saxons may be a little slow in wakin' up to what th' pa-apers calls our common hurtage, but ye may be sure they'll be all r-right whin they're called on. . . . I tell ye, whin th' Clan an' th' Sons of Sweden an' the Banana Club an' th' Circle Francaize an' th' Pollacky Benivolent Society an' th' Rooshian Sons of Dinnymite an' th' Benny Brith an' th' Coffee Clutch . . . an' th' Turrnd'yemind an' th' Holland Society an' th' Afro-Americans an' th' other Anglo-Saxons begin fer to raise their Anglo-Saxon battle-cry, it'll be all day with th' eight or nine people in th' wurruld that has th' misfortune iv not bein' brought up Anglo-Saxons.[1]

Open warfare in Chicago ended in the last years of the nineteenth century, but fights between Negroes and whites would occur, described in all their brutality in Richard Wright's *Native Son*. Dirt, wretchedness, crime, and poverty would persist, and brazen thievery dressed up with fine words about high finance would go on for years. Men, themselves law-abiding, would continue to find fascination in Chicago's wickedness. In the 1920's during the Prohibition era, the city would be, in the Holywood phrase, 'a gangster's Heaven'. The influence of the Chicago *Tribune* would widen steadily to spread the beliefs of its isolationist owner and to encourage in its million and more readers prejudices and hatreds against the rest of the world. Nevertheless, to men who had known the Chicago of the 1880's and 1890's her progress was heartening. Today, when twitted about her colorless present, her drab mediocrity, her lifeless middle age, these Chicagoans smile. The future, though different from the past, will, they believe, still be exciting.

Virtually every nation on earth had contributed to her population. Eastern cities had supplied some of her most vigorous citizens and money to build part of her railroad network. Men in newer cities could not resist investment in Chicago. The Atlantic seaports and, through them, Europe were her eager customers. While the farmers of the Middle West furnished the wheat and hogs, Texas and the open range the cattle, the forests of Michigan and Wisconsin the lumber, and the Upper Peninsula the iron and copper ore, Chicago did the processing, the wholesaling, and the trans-shipping of this material wealth. Through her stockyards she had shown how competition could be turned into co-operation. Her packers had developed new methods of handling and utilizing by-products. They introduced the refrigerator car that revolutionized American

[1] 'On the Anglo-Saxon' in *Mr. Dooley in Peace and War* (Boston, 1898), pp. 55–7.

diet. Selling non-perishables through 'drummers', by mail catalogue, and always 'on approval', Chicago merchants altered the purchasing habits of people living in remote places. New towns and newer cities springing up through the Middle West admired and imitated. Chicagoans firmly believed that they gave more than they had borrowed from older communities. Men born elsewhere quickly forgot earlier ties; no pride of ancestry equalled pride in Chicago. If she had produced no great painters and few distinguished men of letters, had her architects not introduced the well-lighted modern office building and the sky-scraper? Had her engineers not performed the miracle of reversing the flow of the river in order to make Chicago a model of sanitation? Had her university not scholars and scientists of utmost distinction? If she was sooty and ugly, was she not rebuilding with an eye to beauty, turning the lake shore into a forty-mile parkway? Chicago, her citizens say, is not finished. Less than one hundred and twenty-five years old, she has just begun.

# VI

# Cities of the Great Plains:
# Denver and Wichita

URBAN growth in the region east of the Mississippi was conditioned by climate, soil, and topography generally similar to western Europe's. The European traveller in the eastern United States found himself in a not unfamiliar setting in Boston or Charleston of mid-nineteenth century. He saw in exotic New Orleans a subtropical distortion of France, and though in Cincinnati, and even more in Chicago and St Louis, he detected a distinctively American flavor, he must still have sensed there some kinship with Europe. Had he visited the New England manufacturing cities, they would have shown him features of an expanding industrial society varying from that of English manufacturing communities more in degree than in kind. But when he crossed into the Great Plains of the trans-Mississippi west he would have been in a new world. Only if he knew the Russian steppes well, might he have felt somewhat at home. The settling of this vast stretch of the continent within a half-century, in itself an extraordinary feat, was accompanied by the relentless decimation of the plains Indians and, almost simultaneously, by the rise of cities. Of these cities, Denver, Colorado, represents one group of economic interests, Wichita, Kansas, another.

## DENVER

Many well-educated people in the eastern United States are prone to think of Denver as a mountain city, because Colorado is a mountain state. Colorado guide books are at pains to point out that it is the highest state in the Union; its western stretches include fifteen hundred peaks more than 10,000 feet high—fifty-one over 14,000—and the state capital in Denver is located exactly a mile above sea level. Yet the city lies ten miles from the first ridge of the Rockies. The traveller by train or car approaching Denver from the east is unaware of the long steady upward climb from the Mississippi river nine hundred miles away. Suddenly before him the city is there, rising out of the high plains in front of a curious unreal skyline where the wall of the Rockies stands like a cardboard stage backdrop. Look westward and mountain ranges, fold upon fold, stretch north and south, blocking off the world beyond. Along the base of the mountains the South Platte river runs north, fed by mountain streams and by a sandy little rivulet, Cherry creek,

DENVER IN 1859.

Cherry creek, in foreground, joins the South Platte river which runs parallel to the line of the mountains flowing west from the high plains to the southeast. Near Cherry creek's mouth stands Denver. In 1857 nothing was there but a cottonwood grove, the stream itself, plains and mountains, and, arching over all, a deep blue sky that dwarfed even mountains and plains. Today a third of the 1,300,000 people in all Colorado live in Denver.

The peopling of the Great Plains was a sequel to the settling of the far West. San Francisco had been a busy city for nearly ten years when the first cabins went up on Cherry creek, and for almost twenty years when the town of Wichita was settled in southern Kansas. For in the 1840's America's expansion ceased to be a matter of steady movement westward; upon discovery of gold in California, from a line roughly a hundred miles west of the Mississippi, settlement jumped two-thirds of the continent to the Pacific coast. The opportunities of the west coast, to be sure, were known long before 1849. The struggle to preempt the Oregon country, including British Columbia, had begun before 1844 and, epitomized in the American slogan '54-40 or fight', ended in 1846 in an agreement with Great Britain to draw the international boundary at the 49th parallel. The war with Mexico, bitterly characterized in parts of New England as the slave-owners' fight for a new slave-holding empire, had taken an American army into the Southwest and on to California. The treaty at the end of the war had ceded to the United States the territory north of the Gila river and all upper California, and recognized the accomplished fact of the annexation of the Republic of Texas. Most Americans rejoiced at this working of 'Manifest Destiny', that naively arrogant expression of faith in the United States' mission to control and to extend the blessings of its democracy to all the western hemisphere; but even the most visionary American expansionist had not conceived of settling the West in a generation.

The gold rush that took the Forty-niners to the west coast brought California into the Union in 1850 and made San Francisco the great city of the far West, but by-passed the Great Plains and the mountains, leaving an expanse of more than fifteen hundred miles between the populated areas just west of the Mississippi river and the California coast. The reason for the creation in mid-century of a double frontier, one some hundred miles west of the Mississippi, the other bounded on the east by the Sierra Nevada mountains of California, is not hard to explain. More than half of the Forty-niners went by sea round the Horn. A great many others, unwilling or unable to take that long sea voyage, tried a route across the Isthmus of Panama. The men who packed themselves overland direct across plains and mountains were a minority of those who reached the California gold fields. In that difficult journey by horse, mule, or ox-train, men had to guard against Indian attack, thirst, and hunger; the grisly story of the Donner party was already known, that caravan of families caught in the winter snows of the high Sierras and by spring dead of starvation, except for one man who, whispers said, had survived by cannibalism. The hardships of travelling the overland route discouraged all who could choose any other way. Consequently few newcomers in California knew much of the plains and high mountains lying between them and the eastern United States, and those who had traversed that country had little desire to know it better. Once landed in the temperate clime of the Pacific coast, new Californians had no wish themselves to turn eastward beyond the Sierra Nevadas, even though they welcomed any plan for better communication with the East. Even today the Californian considers an Easterner to be anyone who hails from this side of the Rockies, whether from Montana, Colorado, or Texas. Thus settlement eastward from the Pacific frontier after 1850 was slow, pushing up into the Sierras in search of more gold, later into Nevada for silver, and still later from the Northwest into the farming lands of the interior back of the Cascade range in Oregon and Washington. In large measure the peopling of the Great Plains and the mountain country east of the continental divide was done, not from the west, but from the east.

At about the 95th meridian and some seven hundred miles east of Denver's site the terrain begins to change in character. There the forests that covered most of what was the United States in 1800 give way to open grasslands. The grasslands, or prairie, to be sure, stretch eastward across Illinois in a wedge running into northern Ohio, but that land is well-watered and the climate is similar to that of the original northern states. Beyond the Mississippi the treeless plains rise gradually, the climate becoming more severe as one moves westward, the winds more violent, the atmosphere more arid, the rainfall lighter, vegetation sparser, and the soil seemingly unproductive. The well-watered lands just west of the river had attracted farmers by the 1830's, and before 1850 four states bordering on the Mississippi—Louisiana, Missouri, Arkansas, and Iowa—had populations large enough to warrant statehood, though their western sections were still thinly settled. The inhospitable plains beyond, where buffalo herds roamed, were hunting grounds of fierce plains Indians and, though fur traders ventured among them, before 1860 other white men rarely tarried in their country. Only in Texas had settlement made any progress.

Apart from the danger of intruding into the Indian country, homesteaders were convinced that the Great Plains were uninhabitable. The myth of the Great American Desert lying at the base of the Rocky mountains and extending far out over the plains had taken root early in the century. Neither Lewis and Clark nor later exploring parties had collected specific information about the southwestern stretches of the Louisiana Purchase, until in 1819 a party under the command of Major Stephen Long traversed the country from the Platte river south along the mountains to the Arkansas river, part of which formed a boundary between United States and Spanish territory. Long's reports were unenthusiastic. He described the region as desert where nothing would grow. Thus official maps for years thereafter marked out a great swatch of the West as the Great American Desert and, upheld by General John Pope's report of 1867, school geographies as late as 1869 labelled it 'utterly unproductive and uninhabitable by civilized man'. Perhaps the tradition would have endured even longer had the gold-seekers of 1859 not brought in their wake settlers who gradually destroyed the myth.

The Fifty-niners, with the canvas of their covered wagons carrying the motto 'Pike's Peak or Bust', were as picturesque as the Forty-niners, and many of them far more deluded. Yet ultimately they contributed as much to the consolidation of the nation. Trappers had long suspected that the Rocky mountains contained gold; occasionally Indians of the region had vaguely hinted as much. The gold poured into circulation from the new mines in California had contributed to the United States' economic imbalance that brought on the panic of 1857, but men ruined by that disaster were not deterred from seeking more gold. The inspiration to prospect along the eastern base of the mountains apparently came nearly simultaneously from several different sources: from mountain Indians who told convincing tales in a Kansas town to the eastward, from gold dust displayed by a traveller who got it from a teamster accompanying an army scouting party along the South Platte river, and from the experience of Green Russell of Georgia whose Cherokee Indian wife was believed to have given him a lead. Early in 1858, upon his return from the California gold-fields, Russell decided to renew a search along the mountain streams where he had 'raised color' on his way west nine years before. Two separate parties thus began prospecting along the base of the mountains that summer. Russell and his followers made camp near the mouth of Cherry creek where he had made his original find; the others prospected further south near Pike's Peak along the Sangre de Cristo creek. The thirteen men of Russell's party discovered pay dirt first. The amount of gold they panned was negligible, but exaggerated rumors spread quickly. By Christmas-time several hundred impatient fortune-hunters had arrived in the 'Kansas gold-fields' and settled down along Cherry creek to wait for spring to melt the deep snows in the mountain valleys. In March wagons began to come creaking in marked for Pike's Peak, the one landmark of the region known to everyone. The rush was on.

For the hundreds of men that the panic of 1857 had left unemployed in the East and the hundreds more with battered fortunes to repair, the gold to be dug in the Pike's Peak country seemed to promise new life. Miners who, like Russell himself, had abandoned prospecting in California joined in the new hunt. Some 40,000 reached Cherry creek in 1859. Many more had set out, only to turn back or to fall by the wayside. One account puts the total of newcomers in the entire region as high as 100,000. Of the thousands who arrived, 10,000 or fewer weathered the second winter in all the Pike's Peak country. Rich strikes had been made in the mountain gulches and valleys west of Cherry creek, but most of the veins of gold soon 'pinched' out or produced only ore so refractory that the gold could not be reclaimed by the crude method of washing. Though miners had panned enough gold to lead three or four men in 1860 to set up a private mint in the Cherry creek settlements, the rush by now was over—at least until ore-crushing machinery could be installed that would permit extraction of the pure metal.

But several towns had sprung up in that year and a half, and in them men had vested interests they were determined to maintain. Some of these settlements were scarcely more than mining camps and were doomed to disappear altogether. Others, such as Black Hawk, Central City, Golden, Pueblo, and, most important of all, the towns on Cherry creek, profiting by the demise of the weaker, endured. The cottonwood grove on Cherry creek had served as a base for the prospectors from the beginning. The cluster of mud-plastered huts built by Russell's party had become the nucleus around which new arrivals in the mining country gathered. As early as November 1858, some of the newcomers had formed a town company to sell lots and promote an organized community. Why along Cherry creek rather than in the mountains? Initially, probably because Russell had first found a little gold here along the South Platte; second, because the place was easier of access than locations farther west; third, because there was water, and the cottonwoods supplied lumber for building rough shacks quickly; and finally perhaps because the location was midway along the mountain wall between possible gold fields in the north and promising prospecting country to the south. Sooner or later most of the Fifty-niners came to the Cherry creek settlements, sometimes to take off almost at once to stake a claim and camp at one of the diggings west in the mountains, often to return when weeks of work had netted only disappointment, and then again to set out when news came of gold strikes in some new spot. But the community at Cherry creek remained, not as a mining camp, but as a supply center. For hard on the heels of the gold-seekers had come the real-estate speculators and the shopkeepers. These men were intent on keeping the town alive.

Of the town promoters the most eager and the most experienced was General William H. Larimer, one-time officer of the Pennsylvania militia whose checkered career had won and lost him a fortune in Pittsburgh and started him upon real-estate speculation in Kansas before he heard rumors of gold in the Pike's Peak country. When his small party drew into the Cherry creek settlement late in 1858 he was dismayed to find that earlier comers had already established a land company. Hastily, therefore, he staked a claim on the opposite bank of the creek and, to make the claim good, at once put up a log cabin as a center around which a rival town fostered by his company should grow. He named his settlement for James W. Denver, former Governor of the Territory of Kansas, within which the gold fields lay. Larimer, unaware that a new Governor had taken office, hoped by this gesture to enlist official support for the claims of the Denver City company to the lands along Cherry creek. The struggle between Auraria, the original settlement on the left bank, and the upstart town, Denver City, on the right bank shows how the urge in some men to control the real estate in a new town overrode interest in gold itself.

Neither town company had any legal basis; the land by federal treaty with the Arapahoe tribe was Indian property. But the 'squatters', so the story runs, bought off the Indians by staging a barbecue of three old oxen, and then the fight for overlordship of the settlements began in earnest. The stakes were high. 'Lots that would not have brought $5 per acre in May last,' wrote one observer in the fall of 1859, 'are now freely selling at from one to five hundred dollars.' The newspaper editor, newly come from Omaha, built his office on piling in the middle of the creek in order to sell his sheet in both towns. A letter from a Denver City man suggests the character of the rivalry: 'We have thirty-eight beautiful and substantial buildings in our town now while them contumacious villains has but eighty. We have named our city after Governor Denver, as fine a gentleman as ever set foot on the soil of Kansas, while them braggarts have gone to the poetry book for a name.' Who first extended the olive branch is not clear, but early in 1860 a gift of four lots in Auraria to General Larimer and similar distributions in Denver City to influential residents across the creek persuaded the competing companies to merge. In April Denver City and Auraria together became Denver.

Meanwhile shopkeepers had arrived, setting out their goods in the back of a wagon or in a tent until cabins could be built. Provisions were scarce; flour in the summer of 1859 sold at $16 a hundred pounds, more than ten times the price in Illinois. Over the barrel heads that served as counters the shopkeepers sold mixed wares—salt, sugar, picks and gold pans, coffee, nails, onions, and shoes. With the traders up from New Mexico came a villainous whiskey, Taos Lightning, which apparently neither killed nor cured. Log saloons, with or without gambling tables, cropped up by the dozen, though brothels, in the absence of white women, were lacking. Men carried six-shooters, or at the very least heavy knives, as naturally as they wore boots, and the frequent brawls often ended in shooting and sometimes in lynchings.

The Pike's Peak gold rush with its violence, its excitement, and its personal tragedies followed a universal pattern of mining booms. It resembled California's before it and was later repeated in mining camps all over the world, in Australia, in South Africa, and in the Klondike. The characteristically American feature of this stampede was the rapidity with which town and territorial organizations appeared, and politics, manipulated by votes, took over. Before the Cherry creek settlements were more than a few weeks old, men had elected county officials and a People's Court to administer a kind of home-made justice, while the mining camps in the mountains established Miners' Courts to enforce a self-evolved code to meet those local conditions. Notwithstanding the popular belief in the lawlessness of the mining country, law was respected, but it was a different law from that of older settlements to the east. Within six months men were drafting a constitution for the 'State of Jefferson' which was to include all of present-day Colorado, part of Nebraska, Wyoming, and Utah. Before the constitution was completed, a popular vote taken in every settlement in the mining region rejected the plan of a state in favor of a territorial government, and the self-created Territory of Jefferson then came into being. It functioned with duly elected officers, albeit with no recognition from the Congress of the United States and with uncertain relations with the Territory of Kansas, until, in February 1861, Congress established the Territory of Colorado.

The territory, and later the state, had no natural geographic boundaries. The gold-fields were taken as a center and a rectangle was marked off east, west, north, and south, including miles of the high plains to the east and mountains up to and over the continental divide on the west. Denver now had to obtain a new city charter, since the incorporation of 1860 was labelled illegal. For a city of 4,749 the array of elected officials was impressive: a Mayor, a Board of twelve Councilmen, a City Clerk, a Recorder, a Marshal, an Assessor, a Treasurer, a City Attorney, a City Engineer, and Street Commissioners. City officials and residents at once set themselves to the task of winning for Denver the honor of becoming the territorial capital. Colorado City was chosen in 1861 and Golden in 1862, but Denver, by constantly pushing her claims, succeeded in 1868.

Despite that postponement of political recognition, Denver's reputation for leadership in the territory was established early. It was well earned. A city directory published in January 1860 listed what Cherry creek had to offer: twelve retail and wholesale establishments, twenty-seven houses retailing groceries, clothing, and household goods, three 'commission and forwarding houses', four lumber yards, two express offices, nine real-estate and mining-claim agencies, eight hotels, nine boarding houses, eleven restaurants, twenty-three saloons, four billiard saloons, four ten-pin alleys, two theatres, one newspaper, seven surveyors and architects, fourteen lawyers, and fourteen doctors. Unlike towns in the mountain valleys, here wives and children soon came to join the men of the family, though women long remained few. Before 1859 was out, the Cherry creek settlement had a school with thirteen pupils and the next year a second school. The founder of the first, 'Professor' O. J. Goldrick, dressed in a broadcloth frock coat, a stove-pipe hat, and yellow kid gloves, drove into Denver City behind a team of oxen and, claiming to have a Bachelor's degree from Trinity College, Dublin, and a Master's from Columbia University, reeled out oaths in Latin and Greek with a glibness that won him the immediate and deep respect of the miners. They literally passed the hat and collected $250 for his salary. Through his efforts and those of his successors, teaching in the Denver schools was sound. Testimony to its quality was voiced twenty-odd years later when the superintendent of schools in Boston, where public schooling was considered to be of the best, inspected the Denver schools and reported them exceptionally good. Moreover, in country that in the spring of 1858 had scarcely been touched by white men, the *Rocky Mountain News* was appearing regularly in 1859. It is still published in Denver. Equally important were the churches that were organized the very first year. In June 1859 a Methodist preacher was drumming up trade in his own special frontier style: announcing by placard where he would preach, he then paraded the streets, like the Pied Piper drawing his congregation after him by the hymns he sang in his mellow voice, until townspeople remarked admiringly: 'Brother Adriance songs up his congregations.' A Sunday School opened that October. From the bishopric of Santa Fe came a Roman Catholic priest to found a parish, and Protestant pastors from the East arrived soon after, some of them to prospect for gold as well as for souls. An Episcopal church, St John's in the Wilderness, went up in 1862, and a Methodist church the next year. In 1864 a Methodist Seminary opened, sixteen years later transformed into the University of Denver.

Social amenities of sorts also appeared early—a Masonic lodge, a chess club, and a Reading Room Association, in 1859. Hard though it is to imagine how pianos could have been carted in over roads that were mostly deep-rutted tracks across the plains, every well-run gambling saloon had its orchestra of piano, banjo, and fiddle, and several private householders imported pianos of their own. After 1866 an Episcopal church choir and the Denver Musical Union provided other music. At the theatre, always a source of popular diversion in western frontier towns, barnstormers and amateurs staged everything from *Richard III* to a native dramatist's production, *Skatara, The Mountain Chieftain*. The *Rocky Mountain News* noted that the playing of the delirium tremens scene in *Skatara* was particularly fine. Society was raw, but the marvel is that anything that could be called a society at all came into being so quickly.

Indeed, within five years Denver, by frontier standards, looked like a city. Her streets were laid out in the conventional gridiron pattern. 'Instead of uncouth log structures,' wrote a chronicler in 1866, 'comely, and soon even elegant and stately frame houses were erected. Of late the brick era has also been inaugurated.' To safeguard against fire, the city dug a channel from the South Platte some miles upstream which diverted mountain water to the city, though not enough for general use. Pedlars hawked water through the streets down into the eighties, and even today, whenever a winter's snowfall in the mountains is light, water becomes a valuable commodity.

Food remained expensive throughout the sixties, for farmers in Colorado were few. When with the passage of the Homestead Act in 1862 the government abandoned the earlier system of selling federal lands, anyone with the courage to risk the hardships of life on the frontier could stake out a claim to a quarter-section of land and, by occupying and improving it, obtain title to his homestead at the end of five years. This scheme of settling the West eventually brought hundreds of newcomers into empty country, not as prospectors, like the Fifty-niners, but as farmers seeking permanent homes. But the persistence of belief in the Great American Desert and occasional Indian raids kept the flow of homesteaders into Colorado small before the 1870's. Only those better-informed or bolder than the rest in the 1860's settled upon bottom lands along the South Platte river and streams where irrigation was not difficult. The fertile soil, when well-watered, raised abundant crops saleable to gold prospectors at round prices. Denver, where miners outfitted and to which they returned at intervals, was the logical market center. Samuel Bowles, a Connecticut valley newspaper man who journeyed through Colorado in 1869, wrote: 'The irrigated gardens of the upper parts of Denver fairly riot in growth of fat vegetables, while the bottom lands of the neighboring valleys are at least equally productive without irrigation. Think of cabbages weighing from 50 to 60 pounds each! And potatoes from 5 to 6 pounds, onions 1 to 2 pounds, and beets 6 to 10! Yet here they grow, and as excellent as big.' Horace Greeley of the famous New York *Tribune* and Henry Villard, a comparatively little-known journalist, who had served the Cincinnati *Commercial*, were equally enthusiastic. Farming in Colorado awaited only advertising in the East and better transport facilities. Meanwhile cattle ranching, begun after 1866 when Texas drovers discovered that the high plains offered good grazing ranges, was bringing Denver some prosperity. Besides flour mills, slaughter houses grew up in the city and, along with these, shops and factories for supplying farmers and ranchers with harness, wagons, and a variety of household wares hard to obtain from the East. Thus Denver early achieved a diversification of interests which enabled her later to weather depressions more successfully than could other Colorado settlements.

In this remote world of mining camps, ranches, and isolated farms, Denver originally owed her primacy to being the center of communication with the East. The Leavenworth and Pike's Peak Express Company sent coaches regularly into Cherry creek in 1859. News of Abraham Lincoln's election to the Presidency eighteen months later took sixty-nine hours to come from Missouri by Pony Express, but in 1863 a telegraph wire strung across the six hundred odd miles of plains from western Missouri reached into the town. After the Civil War, when the first transcontinental railroad was under construction, citizens campaigned vigorously to have the route cut through the mountains west of Denver, but engineers chose passes to the north in Wyoming. Denver, having scarcely grown at all since 1860, realized that she could hope for little as long as mining machinery had to be dragged from the East by ox team and, for want of rail transport for their products, ranching and farming in the vicinity remained at a standstill. Local men therefore decided that since the Union Pacific Railroad would not come to Denver, they must go to it. In 1869 they organized a local company and built one hundred and six miles of railroad north into Cheyenne, Wyoming, there to connect with the Union Pacific tracks. The first train pulled into Denver in June 1870, less than twelve years after Green Russell's men raised their first log cabins on Cherry creek. In August the Kansas Pacific Railroad reached Denver, still a city of fewer than 4,800 people and 1,500 buildings.

Two railroads in one year would seem to be more than a beginning, but citizens were not satisfied. In 1871 Denver men, in the face of ridicule from many eastern financiers, enlisted the interest of Boston capitalists and began construction of a narrow gauge trunk line, the Denver and Rio Grande, a daringly conceived plan to tap all the Southwest, through the mountains along the course of the Rio Grande del Norte and on to Mexico City, two thousand miles south. By 1872 the road had reached Pueblo, one hundred and ten miles south, where rich coalfields lay. Now coal became easily available for driving railroad engines and

DEPARTURE OF A COLONY OF EMIGRANTS FOR COLORADO.

From a drawing in *Harper's Weekly*, 1870

feeding smelters in Denver to extract precious metals from Colorado ores. The original plan of running the road down into Mexico was abandoned before the end of the 1870's when prospectors discovered valuable deposits of silver in the high mountains near Leadville. Since improved processing now enabled men to extract the silver from the lead carbonate ores, the Denver and Rio Grande, re-named the Denver, Rio Grande and Western Railroad, ran tracks up into Lead-ville and brought back to Denver tons of ore to smelt and silver to mint. By 1883 the road reached over the continental divide into Ogden, Utah, and, with stand-ard gauge tracks laid from Denver to Ogden seven years later, became an integral part of several transcontinental railroad systems. Even before 1880, the railroad most eastern capitalists had derided as an absurdity was earning enormous divi-dends for its stockholders and bringing into Denver coal, gold, silver, and lead ores, as well as the produce of multiplying farms.

For the 1870's saw the long-awaited influx of farmers and ranchers. The rail-roads and vigorous, locally directed advertising campaigns by 1871 had brought some five thousand new settlers to the thinly populated territory. The Kansas Pacific Railroad Company, anxious to sell land along its route, flooded the East with pamphlets and sent an agent to Europe in search of homesteaders. A German philanthropist of Chicago, in an attempt to move his countrymen out of Chica-go's slums, organized a colonization society which, though a failure, inspired more successful endeavors. Town development companies in southern Colorado created Colorado Springs, South Pueblo, and Fort Collins. Samuel Bowles' prophecy of 1869 proved sound: 'The two things she [Colorado] lacketh chiefly now are appreciation at the East and women; what she has of both are excellent, but in short supply; but the Railroad will speedily fill the vacuums.' Denver claimed many of the newcomers, but a number turned to farming. Fed with water by irrigation ditches, the new farms were soon producing abundant crops, and a succession of seasons of unusually heavy rainfall induced some men to under-take 'dry farming' on the semi-arid plains. Only cattlemen and the ranchers now embarking on sheep-raising objected; farms and fences reduced the area of the open range.

Local enterprise thus overcame the nearly insuperable difficulty of tying Denver to the rest of the United States and of connecting her with the mining camps in the high mountains whence Colorado mineral wealth came. Colora-doans had not financed the railroads unaided, but Denver men had taken the all-important initial steps, and western gold and silver helped create considerable independence of Eastern financial centers. The United States mint, the original private establishment of 1860 bought by the federal Treasury, doubtless strengthened the city's financial position; no aspiring rival town could literally mint money. Freed of outside control, Denver ceased to be a frontier town in the mid-seventies. In 1876 Colorado was admitted to the Union, and Denver became the state capital.

The country-wide depression of the seventies slowed Denver's progress, but in 1879, with the opening of the silver mines in and about Leadville, her activities immediately quickened. Her bankers, seeing the potentialities of the mountain country, lent money for ventures few Eastern capitalists would touch, and these loans tightened Denver's hold over surrounding areas. Exploiting every possible advantage, by 1880 she had become the metropolis of a region much larger than Colorado. There was no other sizeable city for five hundred miles in any direction; and though in 1890 Denver's permanent population was still under 107,000, the whole of the mountain region and of the high plains was within her sphere of economic influence. Her hegemony showed that the city rather than the state was the key to development of new country.

Though this rise of urban power followed an established historical pattern, to Americans the declining significance of the states was surprising. Sovereign states had existed before the United States was created, and the Constitution declares that all powers not expressly granted to the federal government reside in the states. Americans who reached adulthood before the Civil War had thought of themselves first as citizens of South Carolina, or Massachusetts, or Ohio, or whatever their native state, and only secondly as citizens of the United States. While the Civil War heightened immeasurably men's consciousness of the United States as a nation, it was not the war alone that submerged the states. In the 1870's and 1880's men came to identify themselves first as Americans and second as Bostonians or Philadelphians or Cincinnatians, though Charlestonians and Chicagoans, it is true, had from the beginning marked themselves by their city.

Outwardly Denver in the eighties and early nineties grew in much the fashion of other prospering American cities, although with less authority over her own municipal government. For while Denver money and Denver initiative greatly influenced, when they did not direct, the development of all Colorado, the state legislature chose to run the state capital. The Governor appointed the Board of Public Works and the Police and Fire Boards, and these bodies exercised a power which, irritated Denverites grumbled, left the city the plaything of Colorado's mining and railroad barons. A number of these men were themselves citizens of Denver, and when she later won 'home rule', municipal politicians proved little better than state. 'Deals' between state or city officials and the magnates holding public utility franchises made Denver conspicuous even in a nation where, as Lord

Bryce observed, graft in municipal affairs was almost a matter of course. However excessive the cost to taxpayers, urban improvements nevertheless went forward. Sewers were laid, street paving was extended, and pipes from reservoirs built in the mountains replaced the old water main from the South Platte river. Because of the fire hazard, frame houses gave way to brick or stone, and, despite the preciousness of water, the city planted trees, and private householders nursed flower gardens. Isabella Bird, the English journalist, would hardly have recognized in 1890 the city she described in 1872 as 'spread out, brown and treeless, upon a brown and treeless plain which seems to nourish nothing but wormwood and Spanish bayonet'.

These external changes notwithstanding, the tone and temper of life in Denver changed less than in rapidly growing cities of the East and Middle West. The first reason was her relative isolation, which neither railroads nor the flow of visitors into and out of the city could alter. Even more important was the comparative homogeneity of her population. In 1890 only 23 per cent were foreign-born, a smaller proportion than in any other large American city except Kansas City and Indianapolis. Equally unusual, 52 per cent of her citizens were native-born of native parentage. Nor did that percentage shrink in the next decade. By 1900, of her 133,857 inhabitants, 28 per cent were native-born of foreign parentage, and over half of them were Colorado-born. Furthermore, well over a third of the 25,000 foreign-born were English-speaking. Hence the adjustments required elsewhere were needless in Denver. Finally, early attitudes of mind were perpetuated because householders who came to live here generally remained and, however many newcomers arrived, the city was thus still dominated by Denverites. Since many families remembered hard times, when drought, flash floods, or mining disasters had turned well-to-do people into poverty-stricken job-hunters, men kept alive the spirit of the mining camp days. Snobbery could not endure in such a setting, and the thought that 'there but for the Grace of God go I' bred generosity.

The career of H. A. W. Tabor dramatically illustrated the circle a man's fortune might make. A stonecutter from Vermont, Tabor arrived in the first days of the gold rush, working one claim after another at intervals for twenty years and between times running a store in one mining camp or another, until in 1878 a grub stake he reluctantly gave to two insistent starving prospectors in Leadville suddenly put him in possession of one of the richest silver mines in Colorado. Purchase of more mines and investment in a dozen grandiose and profitable schemes made him in two years' time a multi-millionaire. His diamond studs, his flashy horses and carriages, and the 'Italian villa' he built in Denver made him only less talked of than his meteoric rise in the world and his largesse. Having built an opera house in Leadville, when he moved to the metropolis he felt obliged to do as well for Denver. At the opening of the Tabor Grand Opera House in 1881, when he observed in the lobby a large oil painting and learned in response to a sharp question that it was a portrait of Shakespeare, Tabor exploded: 'What the hell has he ever done for Colorado! Take it down and put my picture up there.' Like all the 'bonanza kings', as miners who made rich strikes were called, Tabor soon developed political ambitions. Elected Lieutenant Governor of the state, he then aspired to be a United States senator. For a thirty-day substitute term he was. But upon his return from Washington several of the mines he had recklessly exploited began to run out. When the public discovered that some companies had been borrowing money to pay dividends, mining stock prices tumbled. Frantic endeavors to salvage part of his fortune stripped Tabor of one holding after another, until his every possession was sold at auction and he gratefully accepted a $3,500-a-year appointment as postmaster in Denver where a few years earlier he had spent that much in a single night. He died in 1899. His history, though more spectacular than most, was not unique in Colorado.

Denver had ample occasion to show generosity when the depression of the nineties set in. A three-year drought that cut the supply of water for irrigation caused all farmers severe hardship and utterly ruined homesteaders who had relied upon dry farming methods. Ranchers could not feed their cattle. In 1893 cancellation of the federal government's silver purchase policy plunged the mining districts into a long slump. Central City and Black Hawk turned into ghost towns, to be resurrected as tourist and summer theatre centers only fifty-odd years later. Banks closed, mine workers struck, lockouts followed, and in some mining towns bloodshed was halted only by recourse to martial law. Denver fared better than most of Colorado, since the city's varied business interests gave her some flexibility, but here too unemployment spread. The people from the towns and countryside roundabout who flocked in to look for jobs, charity, or the comfort of a change of scene added to Denver's problems of providing relief and keeping order among men driven to panic by their wants of the moment and the uncertainties of the future. Whether justified or not, Coloradoans apparently accepted as Gospel the motto inscribed upon the building of the Denver *Post*: 'O Justice, When Expelled from other Habitations, Make This Thy Dwelling Place.' The state legislature in a special session in 1893 passed an emergency relief act, and, doubtless an innovation unrelated to the depression, woman suffrage went into effect, making Colorado the second state in the Union in which women could vote. Though labor wars recurred in the mining towns, Denver recovered from the depression before the end of the century. Building of new irrigation reservoirs and water tunnels and the introduction of sugar beet raising in Colorado about 1898 revived farming and brought sugar refineries to the city. Early in the twentieth century the discovery of drought-resistant crops further assisted farmers and thus spelt new prosperity for Denver.

When times were good, money rained upon Denver gaming tables, and saloons and the more elegant hotels overflowed with open-handed patrons. Elaborate new houses for cattle barons and bonanza kings went up on new streets. 'The distinguishing charm of Denver's architecture,' wrote a visitor, 'is its endless variety. Everyone is ambitious to build a house unlike his neighbor, and is more ambitious that it shall have some novel feature than that it be surpassingly beautiful.' German castles, Swiss chalets, and Spanish villas might stand adjacent, separated by wide lawns dotted perhaps, like 'Haw' Tabor's, with cast iron dogs and deer. As the Romanesque Revival swept America, Denver architects built some fine examples of houses in that style. Interspersed among the new stood the older houses, marked by simplicity of line, economy of space, and lack of ornamentation. In this community of frequent change, old-established householders took the extravagances of the newly rich for granted.

While some aspects of nineteenth-century Denver verged on the ludicrous, no one laughed at her long. Inner unpretentiousness offset bad taste, and the kindly welcome extended to strangers made newcomers feel at home. When Oscar Wilde arrived on his American tour, Denver took to him with gusto and he to Denver. His idiosyncrasies of dress and behavior caused comment, but he was a foreign oddity in a city where native oddities abounded. Challenged to a drinking bout with a party of miners, he drank the mountain men under the table, and Denver roared approval. The vitality and good humor of the city delighted everyone. A visitor in Denver might be startled, but he would not be bored. The arts, though long considered merely a diversion, were not wholly neglected. However bizarre the domestic architecture, public buildings showed restraint, if not great originality of form. The most conspicuous building, the massive neoclassical Capitol with its gilded dome, was an adaptation of the national Capitol in Washington. The theatre continued to flourish; companies that refused to stop in more than two or three cities between Chicago and San Francisco usually chose to play in the lavishly equipped 'Tabor Grand' or in the newer theatres of the nineties. Writers found the community congenial. While few native sons wrote with distinction, their reminiscences and verses published in Denver newspapers or the *Colorado Magazine* of the Historical Society supplemented the observations of later comers like Hamlin Garland, Upton Sinclair and Willa Cather, and an

Denver in 1912

The photograph is taken from almost the same spot as the 1859 view, on p. 130. The domed building is the Colorado State Capitol

occasional volume, such as *Hands Up: A Pioneer Detective in Colorado*, written by the chief of Denver's police force, has become a collector's item. Painters enchanted with the mountain country also congregated here, though Colorado Springs at the base of Pike's Peak became the principal artists' colony in the state.

In the twentieth century Denver again changed course. From moving steadily toward an industrial complex, she veered in a new direction after 1903 when a state-wide strike of mine, mill, and smelter hands closed her great Omaha-Grant smelter. Ore reduction thereafter ceased in the city and, apart from manufacture of mining machinery, operation of the United States mint, and banking, Denver's association with Colorado mining gradually disappeared. With it went the excitement and swashbuckling of earlier years, elements vanishing also in the mining towns themselves, as big impersonal corporations, their stock widely held, took control of most Colorado mines. Such industries as remained in Denver revolved around the stockyards, the leather boot and shoe factories and the beet sugar refineries. Russians, German sugar-mill workers, Italians who manned the railroad equipment repair shops, and Mexican field hands, imported to work on the sugar beet farms of the surrounding countryside and who wintered in Denver, gave to sections of the city a new heterogeneity. Although over the years the percentage of foreign-born in the entire population shrank, their numbers came to be the more striking because they now lived in separate colonies. In this city set amid endless space, tenement houses and slums like those of older cities never developed, but streets once thronged with the patrons of the brightly lighted gambling saloons and elaborately decorated bordellos became a colorless succession of second-hand shops and drab little houses occupied by Negroes and the foreign-born.

While run-down areas thus appeared in sections of the city where bonanza kings, ranchers, and railroad promoters had swaggered in the nineties, Denver in the era after the first World War spread out in a widening circle threaded by boulevards planted with trees and lined with the modern houses of the growing host of twentieth-century white-collar workers. For the boom town of mining-camp days turned little by little into a city of business and administrative offices. As she lost her 'wild west' aura, she gained in stability. Financial center of the mountain region, terminus of half a dozen railroads, and the trans-shipping point for the agricultural products of the high plains, Denver in the 1930's became also the western headquarters of a series of bureaus and departments of the federal government—the Reclamation Service, the regional office of the United States Forestry Service, the Bureau of Internal Revenue, the Veterans' Administration and a number of others. But even these were of less importance to the city than the tourist trade.

Before the end of the nineteenth century, Denver had come to be known as a place good for tuberculosis patients. The clear air was tonic. Brilliant sunshine the year round killed germs, and severe dry cold in winter kept the city healthy. Only pneumonia spelled danger for the unwary or ill-housed. And then the mountain country came into its own as a playground for city dwellers of the East where streams teeming with trout, forests filled with game, and sheer empty space were no longer within easy reach. As the fame of Estes Park spread, hundreds of campers poured into Denver every summer to outfit for the weeks of holiday in the mountains beyond. Colorado Springs at the foot of Pike's Peak became a center of 'permanent tourists', wealthy temporary visitors who found themselves lingering month after month and even year after year, but to Denver fell the business of supplying the transients.

Multiplying automobiles and a network of national and state highways have increased this yearly flood of tourists. Along the spokes of the wheel whose hub is Denver, the highways today are lined with 'motels', the American answer to the motorist's needs. Frame and stuccoed cabins, supplied with running water and heat for the chilly evenings are set side by side, with space between for each visitor's car. Proprietors, learning that a well-kept appearance is the best possible bait, vie with each other to grow shrubs and turf which can withstand the aridity of the climate. On either side of the roads stretch the brown plains, with the wall of the Rockies on the western skyline. As the motorist, after hours of driving through the dusty plains to the east, south or north, at last enters Denver, he is struck at once with her green beauty. He rarely sees the shabby areas in the old part of the city, and, as an American, he takes for granted the sprawling ugliness of the industrial outskirts. Despite the sandpapering of the yearly dust storms, buildings in the heart of the city look trim, and the trees bordering the streets, the public parks, the tenderly kept lawns, and the gardens create a freshness as astonishing as it is lovely. Denver, at the threshold of the Rockies, has become the tourist's symbol of the gateway to the mountains.

## WICHITA

Some four hundred and fifty miles east and south of Denver and six hundred miles west and south of Chicago lies Wichita, Kansas, at very nearly the central point of the United States. The city stands on the flat banks of the Arkansas river about half-way along its two-thousand-mile course from its source in the high mountains near Leadville, Colorado, to its confluence with the Mississippi.

This largest western affluent of the Missouri–Mississippi system swings sharply southward at Wichita's site and, though here enlarged by the waters of the Little Arkansas flowing from the north, no longer runs swiftly. The main stream from time immemorial provided a water route inland, although never easily navigable because of the frequent, dangerous shifts of channel. More important for settlers of the region, the Arkansas supplied that most treasured of commodities in western and southern Kansas, water, and along the banks grew cottonwood trees, their rattling gray-green leaves breaking the prairie winds and their silvery trunks offering lumber for the cutting. The Wichita Indians knew the advantages of the location; driven south earlier by the fierce Osage tribe, they had returned in 1864, and in 1865 Wichita, meaning 'Many Lodges', became their tribal village perched on the table lands near the mouth of the Little Arkansas. Yet, while the rivers originally attracted both red men and white, it was not so much the waterways as the coming of a railroad in the 1870's that encouraged the development of the white man's town.

Kansas had been admitted to the Union in 1861 on the eve of the Civil War, but the population of the new state was concentrated along its eastern edge on the Missouri border. Before the end of the war few settlers had moved into central Kansas, for though geographers and map-makers had not included that country in the 'Great American Desert', men could buy good arable land nearer eastern markets, and Indian tribes still occupied much of the region. Between the mining towns in the Rockies and the communities of eastern Kansas stretched the unbroken expanse of treeless plains, their grasses still providing grazing for several million buffalo. Swayed by the arguments of Western senators, the United States government had long planned to induce the Indians of Kansas to move south into the area just above Texas which was marked off as the Indian Territory, but not until 1866 were negotiations successful. Meanwhile, the movement of farmers westward, halted by the Civil War, had resumed with new force, encouraged by the free land obtainable under the Homestead Act and by the need of war-weary, ruined men to start life anew. As white men with ploughs intruded further and further into the plains, the buffalo herds retreated, and Indians, tribe after tribe, gave ground. Their withdrawal was hastened by railroad construction in Kansas. From Kansas City on the Missouri border in 1866 men were laying rails out into the plains, and from the state capital, Topeka, in 1868 a venturesome company, believing settlement would follow, began building a railroad southwestward toward Santa Fe across miles of empty country. Railroads, eager to sell the lands with which they had been endowed to settlers who would supply freight to their lines, advertised the country vigorously both in the East and in

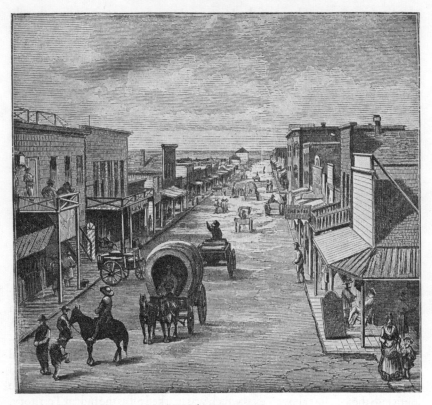

Wichita in 1874
From a drawing in *Harper's Weekly*, 1874

Europe. By 1868, few red men remained in southern Kansas, and the Wichita village of grass huts had disappeared.

In 1865, while the Wichitas still occupied their lands on the Arkansas, the accidental marking of the Chisholm trail and the first 'long drive' of Texas cattle to northern markets combined to create the opportunity that white men would seize later to transform the deserted Indian village into one of the busiest towns in Kansas. James Mead, a white trader among the Wichitas, unknowingly contributed to the 'blazing' of the famous trail which would make the name of his half-breed Cherokee assistant, Jesse Chisholm, familiar to three generations of Americans who never heard of Mead himself. At the close of the Civil War, Mead had dispatched Chisholm, who knew the country well, down into Texas to bring back a cartload of buffalo hides. On the return trip, a prolonged rain storm struck, so saturating the tough sod of the grasslands that, since Chisholm doggedly chose to press on, the wheels of the heavily laden wagon cut deep ruts in the earth reaching across the plains of Texas, through the eastern stretches of the Indian Territory into southern Kansas. Meanwhile, a Texas rancher, seeking a more profitable market than New Orleans, was driving his cattle north over the open plains, letting the steers graze and fatten as they went, until, arrived at the railroad running into a town in central Missouri, he sold his herd at $40 a head, more than six times the price on the range. Word of this feat spread quickly, inspiring other cattlemen to risk the long drive north. Thus opened that most picturesque brief era in American history, the thirty years of the Cattle Kingdom on the open ranges. And from its beginning, there stretched the Chisholm trail to guide cowboys over the empty spaces of the Great Plains by a direct route into Kansas. Before 1867 was gone, Texas drovers and thousands of cattle had beaten the trail still farther north, nearer the railheads leading to Kansas City and thence on to Chicago's stockyards.

The land speculators who laid plans for a new Wichita in 1868 foresaw the future importance of the Chisholm trail to the town, although the nearest railroad was still some eighty miles to the north. A circular, printed in Topeka and addressed to 'Drovers and Dealers in Southern Cattle', declared that a market on the Arkansas would so shorten the long drive that cowboys could make two trips a year, and buyers would have a choice of cattle still in their prime. Without a railroad into Wichita, the argument was as futile as it was fallacious. Nevertheless, as a way-station on the trail, the location had unmistakable promise, and Mead's trading post made a nucleus around which to build. By 1869 four shops, a blacksmithy, a saddlery, and a saloon had opened, and twenty families had put up crude board houses, some of them roofed with prairie sod. In the summer of 1870, a hopeful Presbyterian minister, turned editor, began publishing the Wichita *Vidette*, in which he announced: 'There is no use talking, we need money here now. Wichita has enough brains, she's gorged with them. We wish we could influence some capitalist who has plenty of the needful to emigrate our way, he need not know enough to tend to his own business, there are plenty here who will do that for him.' While the blacksmiths, the harness-makers, and the saloonkeeper prospered by meeting the wants of the Texas drovers, other townspeople made only a meagre living until the extension of the Atchison, Topeka, and Santa Fe Railroad and the energy of Joseph G. McCoy, an Illinois cattleman, brought the cattle market to Wichita.

In 1867, McCoy had seen that if the long drive from Texas could wind up at a western town into which a railroad ran, then the problem of shipping steers to the slaughter houses in eastern cities would be answered; without refrigeration facilities, large-scale butchering and beef-packing on the plains was not practical, and, though barb-wire fencing was still unknown, driving tens of thousands of Texas long-horns across land under cultivation in Missouri and eastern Kansas was out of the question. The drive must end west of the farming country. As McCoy tells his story, when he perceived that Abilene, Kansas, in 1867 the western terminus of the Kansas Pacific Railroad, could be made the principal market for Texas cattle, he sought out railroad officials to explain his plan; after repeated rebuffs he finally elicited from an underling a half-hearted promise of co-operation. With that slim encouragement, McCoy built cow pens to accommodate three thousand cattle—and soon after many more—and then so widely advertised Abilene's advantages that within a matter of months the town became, and for the next four years remained, the chief 'cow town' of the plains.

Not all Abilene was pleased. Some townspeople abhorred the drovers, for the cowboy, beloved in fiction and in the cinema, in real life was often a very 'tough customer', particularly at the end of the long drive with his season's job done and money in his pocket to spend in the saloons and whore-houses. Furthermore, by 1871 homesteaders were beginning to farm parts of the township, and incoming droves of cattle trampled down crops. Consequently, in February 1872 a few Abilene citizens conspired to send out notice through the local press that thereafter cattlemen had better go elsewhere. McCoy, incensed and alarmed, acted quickly. Wichita still had no rail connections, but, thanks to the persuasiveness of James Mead and a $200,000 county bond issue, the Santa Fe Railroad was building a branch line into the town, and construction was nearing completion. Wichita was therefore a logical successor to Abilene, and Wichita, like Barkis, was not only willing but eager to be wed to any new enterprise. McCoy immediately sent an agent down along the lower stretches of the trail to intercept the drovers and tell them that Wichita would give them the welcome Abilene denied, while McCoy himself waylaid the cattle buyers to explain that their best market had moved eighty-odd miles south. The first train came into Wichita in May 1872. On 8 June, eighteen carloads of cattle were shipped out for Chicago, and, before the end of the year, a total of 3,530 carloads, or nearly 350,000 steers. Wichita's career as a cow town was launched. Abilene shrank into insignificance and eighty years later would be largely known as the boyhood home of a new President, Dwight D. Eisenhower.

As the railroads pushed farther out over the plains, Wichita had to share the cattle trade with towns farther west, but in the mid-seventies she had all she could manage. Like Abilene, she soon discovered that being a cow capital, as Kansans called it, was not an unmixed blessing. Townspeople who might have voiced objections were apparently silenced by observing the rapid decline of Abilene, and farmers moving into the neighborhood were stricken in 1874 by swarms of grasshoppers that stripped the fields and left homesteaders grateful for the livelihood the cattle drives made possible in the town. Yet in the summer heat the overpowering stench of the cattle pens blanketed the town day and night. Sanitation was primitive or non-existent. The flimsy wooden buildings lining the dirty sun-baked streets were gray with the dust stirred by cattle hooves. Human beings, thronging in yearly when the cattle market opened, frequently brought trouble with them. Cowboys rode in, chanting perhaps verses of 'The Old Chisholm Trail', with its lilting chorus 'Come ti yi youpy, youpy yea', while they herded their cattle into the stockades and prepared to celebrate the end of the long drive. Saloons and dance halls, cafés and shops were hastily built and fully patronized. Buyers from 'back East in Kansas City' and from Chicago, drovers, homesteaders, Mexican ranchers, scouts, Indians, and gamblers made the most of the town's hospitality. Signs posted at the outskirts announced: 'Anything goes in Wichita. Leave your revolvers at police headquarters and get a check. Carrying concealed weapons is strictly forbidden.' The sheriff was kept busy in this 'wildest and wickedest place in the West', where, in addition to committing more serious offenses, cowboys regarded it as legitimate sport to ride through the streets at breakneck speed shooting their revolvers into the air.

Newcomers flocked in to share in the prosperity and hectic festivity, and, though no census recorded the number who stayed to swell the permanent population, the total soon sufficed to entitle the town to incorporation under Kansas law as a 'third-class city', with an elected Mayor and Councilmen. The inevitable land boom set in, the federal government established a land office, prices soared, merchants profited. The godly were troubled, and one preacher, carrying his fiddle in hand, occasionally made the rounds of the bar rooms to sing first ballads, then hymns, in vain hopes of persuading sinners to listen to the Gospel. As usual in a boom town in the United States, locally published daily newspapers appeared, the Wichita *Eagle* to represent one political view, the Wichita *Beacon* another, and both dedicated to reporting on the all-important topic, the cattle trade.

The end of the cattle kingdom of the open ranges was in sight in the early eighties. Drought, unprecedented blizzards, and overgrazing of the arid grasslands were to bring sharp disaster in 1885 and 1886 to ranchers and cowmen all through the West. Thereafter the cattle industry took new form. In southern Kansas the change came somewhat earlier. During the late seventies farmers had been moving steadily into the area, taking up homesteads and fencing off greater and greater slices of the range. The federal land office had done its work well. By 1880 the Chisholm trail from the border of the Indian Territory to Wichita was crisscrossed with barb wire which cattle could not break through. The drovers therefore turned west to follow trails into towns beyond the homesteaders' zone, beyond it at least for another brief span of time. Without cattle Wichita could not be a cow town. The gamblers, the real-estate speculators, and the saloon-keepers followed the cowboys to the new cow capitals immediately and some shop-keepers not long after. Wichita faced a decline. A few herds were still driven into her cattle pens, since the refrigerator car, perfected by Chicago packers and after 1880 in general use in the West, enabled local butchers to slaughter and ship some beef east; but without a huge outlay of capital, competition with the big Chicago, St Louis, and Kansas City firms was impossible, and the business nearer home was small. As the country about Wichita turned into farm land, the little city served as a market center, but until farmers learned how to combat recurrent drought, insect pests, and the soil erosion that frequently followed the ploughing under of the centuries-old, deep-rooted prairie grasses, the agricultural products of the region were meagre, and people had little money to spend.

A partial solution of farmers' problems came early. By the mid-eighties the farmers of the region had found a crop well-suited to southwestern Kansas. The soil of the level or slightly rolling terrain was fertile and could produce mighty harvests of any drought-resistant grain, but the kinds grown in the eastern United States matured so late in the year that the fierce July and August suns of Kansas burned the fields brown before they could be cut. Who first introduced the hard winter wheat which, planted in the fall, ripens in early summer, is a matter of some controversy. The man chiefly responsible for forcing the cattle drovers out of Abilene claimed to have been experimenting in 1872 with 'Turkey Red' wheat, but whether at that date he could have obtained seed is doubtful. Probably Ukrainians first grew it successfully here. Certainly Russian Mennonites who settled in Kansas in 1874 brought some seed with them, and some was smuggled out of Russia by German-Ukrainians who emigrated to the United States after Czar Alexander III withdrew their special privileges in 1883. Kansans tell a tale of a Ukrainian leader sent by his people to select a new home for them and his choice of Kansas because of the similarity of its soil and climate to that of the land they were leaving. In the new country their crops were so abundant that other farmers planted hard winter wheat as soon as they could buy the seed.

Before 1890 the fields about Wichita were waving with miles of winter wheat ready for harvesting in June or early July. Today to pass at that season across the plains of Kansas is to see a sight of beauty as breath-taking as snow-capped mountains. As far as eye can reach spreads an unbroken sweep of golden grain.

Wichita was less concerned with the beauty of the wheatfields than with the profits they brought her. In the late 1880's at harvest time heavily laden wagons lined her streets while farmers waited as long as thirty-six hours to have their loads weighed. Grain elevators arose at the city's outer rim whence the wheat could be shipped out by rail. Manufacture of farm tools began. Flour mills multiplied. Within four decades Wichita would be the fourth largest milling center in the United States and the sixth most important grain center. Meanwhile, the city was developing other resources. By 1888 fifteen lumber yards, six planing mills, four sash and door factories, and two carriage works were supplying customers in western Kansas where wood was at a premium. Clay in the neighborhood, coal in southeastern Kansas and the constant fear of fire inspired other Wichitans to open brick yards. Factories to make household wares arose, and the manufacture of stoves would remain a stable industry for the next forty years. Railroad systems expanding into the Southwest brought four additional lines into the little city and gave her competitive freight rates.

The greatest force, however, in keeping Wichita alive during her first years of adversity was the determined campaigning of her citizens. Ceaseless advertising had increased Chicago's stature; advertising could help a Kansas town. Marshall M. Murdock, editor of the Wichita *Eagle*, took the lead. His paper daily pointed to the city's virtues and prophesied glories destined shortly to come to the 'Bride of Fortune'. Merchants, picking up the theme, organized a Board of Trade which paid 'boomers' to spread far and wide glowing stories of Wichita's future. Since Denver had pre-empted the title 'Queen City of the Plains', the smaller city, forced down a bracket of royalty, became the 'Peerless Princess of the Plains'. And the advertising, fortified by the mounting prosperity of southern Kansas, worked. The community of scarcely 5,000 souls in 1880 grew to a city of 24,000 in a decade. Yet the exaggerations of her promoters were blatant. An illustrated folder of 1888, after announcing that population had reached 40,000 and the railroads entering the city ten, labelled Wichita 'the largest city in Kansas, a city of fine Educational Institutions, Magnificent Business Blocks, Elegant Residences and Extensive Manufactures, with more Railroads, more Wholesale Trade, More Manufacturing, More Enterprise than any city in the Southwest'.

The success of the advertising revived real-estate speculation and encouraged building. The city paved streets, laid sewers, built bridges across the rivers, and erected an auditorium where travelling companies of actors could stage their road shows. Horse-drawn trams ran out to the city's edge where the grain elevators shared space with the shanties of the poor. Well-to-do householders built roomy frame or brick houses with Mansard roofs and 'gingerbread' trim and fenced their lawns with wooden pickets or iron palings, while in the business district the 'false fronters' of the seventies, one-story buildings with a facing toward the street to make them look two-storied, gave way to substantial brick structures. Congregations built churches, and new public schools arose, including a large high school. For more startling than the wealth and the outer changes it brought were the shifts in social attitudes. The reasons underlying the growth of these new points of view bear examination.

From the moment settlers began to push into western Kansas, the state had been divided into two groups. Eastern Kansas, since the troubled fifties when free-soilers and slavery men were contending for control of the new territory, had had a large number of New Englanders in her population. New Englanders, whether they migrated direct or moved into 'bleeding Kansas' after a sojourn in Ohio or a newer northern state, brought with them their code of behavior still tinged strongly with Puritanism. Much of eastern Kansas today is more rigidly Puritan than New England has been for more than a century. Through political pressures brought to bear by this element, and supported by the 'Women's Crusade', a state law was enacted in 1881 prohibiting the sale of liquor in Kansas; later cigarettes were similarly banned. Western Kansas, on the other hand, was occupied by men ready to take a chance, the 'go-getters'. Wichita, on the border between these two groups, was influenced by both. In the days of the cattle drives the sober Puritan had little say in the town, but when milling and shipping farm produce became her mainstay, the atmosphere changed. The gamblers now shared power with churchgoers and conservatives. Saloons, though illegal, did not disappear: in 1900 Carrie Nation, a militant of the Women's Christian Temperance Union, strode into a Wichita bar-room, smashed all the bottles in sight and threw rocks at 'Cleopatra at the Bath', a large painting over the bar which she described as 'the life-sized picture of a naked woman'. Nevertheless, the community had largely settled into law-abiding ways before the end of the eighties. A characteristic local summary stated: 'Where cattle had built dance halls and gambling houses, wheat built churches and schools.' The churches—Presbyterian, Methodist, and Baptist, Congregational, Episcopal, and Roman Catholic, and even a small body of Friends—were at once the center of most social life and the source of civil conscience. While promoters advertised the city's material strength, the churches stressed her needs and educational opportunities, although the two groups, symbolic of western and eastern Kansas, tended to merge and usually combined forces.

Everyone took pride in the city's hospital, her seven public schools, her private academy, and, even more gratifying, the four church universities projected between 1885 and 1888. For in that brief period of prosperity Lutherans, Roman Catholics, Friends, and Presbyterians all chose Wichita as the most promising site for new colleges, institutions which would draw students from the entire Southwest, spread the Gospel, and, Wichitans believed, turn the city into 'the new Athens' of the West. While the Catholic diocese proceeded warily and Kansas Quakers laid plans for John Bright University, Lutherans in 1886 opened Wichita University and Presbyterians Garfield University. Although the central governing body of each denomination gave some financial support, local churchmen carried the banner. When Garfield University reported 750 students enrolled and a faculty of 37 members, citizens, never doubting the university's permanence and scholarly distinction, poured out money to assist the trustees in financing a huge building on the city's outskirts.

Unhappily, the prosperity on which good works chiefly depended vanished in the nineties. The drought that ruined Colorado farmers hurt Kansas wheatgrowers also, and the depression of 1893 curtailed farm credit throughout the country. Moreover, in 1889 the United States government had opened the 'Cherokee Strip' in the Indian Territory to settlement, and the rush of people to take up land there, in the words of a contemporary, 'drained the country tributary to Wichita of men'. Reports from the Boston headquarters of the Congregational Education Society, which was concerned with its recent investment in a small Congregational academy in Wichita, spoke of 'the disastrous boom from which the city has been suffering for many years' and later added with more truth than sympathy: 'During the boom, the business men of the city subscribed large bonuses to stockyards, factories, and colleges, most of which ventures proved disappointing.' The Lutheran university went out of existence, the cellar hole dug for the John Bright University building remained a cellar hole, and the Catholics abandoned their plans for a college. Garfield University closed its doors in 1894, leaving its great building to the prairie winds. The city, however, though seeing her business shrink severely, was determined amid the collapse of the universities to preserve the Congregational academy. Fairmount, in 1892 a school of fourteen students and two teachers, in 1896 enrolled 147 students and became Fairmount College. Intent upon strengthening Wichita's reputation for civic-mindedness, business men now raised $10,000 for Fairmount's current expenses, and though the faculty, the Congregational Education Society reported ruefully, at times went months without pay and even suffered hunger, the college survived and expanded. Then in 1898, when business was beginning to recover, Quakers in Kansas announced that they had funds to purchase the vacant building of the defunct Garfield University. Aided by the contribution of a St Louis Quaker who had made a modest fortune selling stereoscopes to American farmers, Friends' University opened that autumn. On the fourth of July, the city, rejoicing in the turn of her fortune, celebrated by opening her first public park, located on the tongue of land between the rivers.

The twentieth century brought rapid changes. As credit eased at the end of the depression, farmers could buy the machinery that enabled them to plant and harvest hundreds of acres in the flat open plains and produce bumper crops. With the development of the internal combustion engine and the rise of the automobile industry, mechanized drills, harrows, and reapers came into use. Wichita opened farm-machinery factories, fostered new sales agencies, and widened her banking interests. As a result, between 1900 and 1910 population doubled. Of her 52,000 inhabitants in 1910, 77 per cent were native-born of native parentage. These included some 2,500 Negroes whose poverty and limited cultural background created a special problem in the city. Most of them presumably were 'exodusters' or their children, Southern Negroes who had migrated into Kansas at the end of the seventies under the illusion that here they would be given 'forty acres and a mule', as promised in the Civil War chanty:

> Every nigger's gwine to own a mule,
> An' live like Adam in de Golden Rule,
> An' send his chillun to de white-folks' school
> In de year of Jubilo!

Negroes, like white men, could stake out homesteads, but, lacking farm tools and draft animals, most black families had gradually drifted into the towns and cities.

In Wichita, the eight hundred Germans, the seven hundred English and Canadians, the three hundred and fifty Mexicans, and the handful of Irish and Russian families made up an exceptionally small proportion of the inhabitants of a growing American city of this era, when immigration into the United States reached its all-time peak—1,285,000 in 1907 alone. Wichita lay over fifteen hundred miles from the nearest port of entry and, in addition, was considered a farmers' city, as, in fact, she primarily was. Railroad companies were no longer combing Europe to find settlers for lands along their routes, for though parts of the Great Plains were still unoccupied, homesteaders had by now taken up most of the sections along the railroads. Foreigners who migrated to this city in the heart of America usually came because of relatives and friends in the vicinity. Thus spared many of the problems confronting larger communities where peoples of a dozen nationalities, however eager to become Americans, remained alien, Wichita was better able to keep pace with her growth than could cities like New York and Boston in the East, San Francisco and Seattle on the Pacific coast, or Chicago and St Louis inland. Here housing lagged very little behind the arrival of new householders; in 1910 there were 11,293 dwellings for 12,671 families. A still greater achievement, the city kept illiteracy to an astonishingly low figure, 1·3 per cent. Negroes were allowed to send their 'chillun to de white-folks' school', though later, avowedly in the interest of improving Negro education, the city inaugurated separate schools. Meanwhile, in 1909 citizens, dissatisfied with the running of the city, voted to adopt the City Manager plan, an experiment in concentrating responsibility which a small Virginia city had first tried out the year before. The Mayor and two other elected officials formed a Board to select the Manager and to give him counsel.

Increasing wealth created new social disparities, although, since acute poverty was rare, class distinctions were not hard and fast. Money flowed into the hands of the men who controlled the farm-machinery plants, flour mills, and grain elevators, while, if they had shrewdly grasped opportunities, the local bankers, the real-estate speculators, and people who had simply clung to their property within the city during her earlier slumps were frequently only less well-to-do. Even before the outbreak of war in Europe in 1914 and the consequent agricultural boom, Wichita's 'first families' were sending their sons east to college at Harvard, Yale, or Princeton and their daughters to expensive eastern schools to learn more of the world than they could see on the plains of Kansas. A visitor from Baltimore, expecting to find in 1912 a raw and simple community, discovered her Paris gowns matched in elegance by her hostesses' wardrobes, her friends' automobiles the latest models from Detroit, and a dinner party of eighteen served by a butler no great novelty to Wichita's social leaders. Cincinnati and Chicago could do no better. Radio broadcasts and Hollywood films had not yet established a standard of behavior which, no matter how vulgar, most middle-class Americans would accept as fitting, whether they lived in Massachusetts or Maryland, Ohio or Kansas. But long before 1912 Americans with money had ceased to find distance a barrier that could prevent Wichita millionaires from behaving like Baltimore's or interfere with wealthy Easterners' discovery that moneyed Kansans were cast in a mould outwardly similar to their own. Humbler Wichitans, as formerly, found diversion in picnics, church sociables, and whist parties, or in meetings of

Wichita, looking north, with grain elevators in background, 1953

the fraternal organizations that had arisen during the nineties. Ladies' clubs still held afternoon sessions to discuss the history of Europe in the nineteenth century or more homely problems, such as gardening. The coming of the automobile had destroyed interest in the Cycle Club but encouraged use of two golf courses on the city's outskirts, and the Wichita 'Eagles' still played the rival baseball nines of neighboring towns.

The rise in wheat prices during the first World War brought Wichita still greater prosperity, heightened by a novel war industry, manufacture of aircraft for the army and navy. The city, proud of her growing importance, erected a large public library, and an Exposition Building to house civic and industrial exhibits, concerts, and road shows that overflowed the Auditorium. In exclusive new residential districts, expensive houses arose, many of them built in the Georgian style then reviving in popularity in America, while semi-public buildings went up, displaying the architectural variety found in most American cities

—Gothic in the large Presbyterian church with its tiers of stained glass windows, Renaissance in the Roman Catholic cathedral, its copper dome copied from the twin churches in Rome's Piazza del Popolo, neo-classical in the Fairmount College library. Stark functional beauty was confined to the columned simplicity of the grain elevators.

Yet wheat and airplanes seemed almost unimportant when, at the end of the war, oil was discovered practically within the city limits. In the 1850's men had skimmed oil from the surface of Kansas streams, and after 1860 wells in the region south of Kansas City had produced some petroleum, but not until 1915 did the opening of the far richer fields northeast of Wichita suggest that oil might underlie the entire area. Wichita's 'door-step' pool, if not unlooked for, nevertheless carried several steps further the transformation under way before the war. The city, begun as a cow town, turned into a farmer's market, and then into an agricultural processing and farm-machinery center, was becoming also an industrial city with a national demand for her products. The incongruous sight of the large Georgian houses erected on the eastern edge of the city now flanked by the steel girders of the oil derricks that punctuated the sky-line soon became familiar and, because of the money it represented, welcome.

Much of that money went back into the community for oil refineries, palatial houses for the new millionaires, and, in the business district, large office buildings that gave Wichita as metropolitan an air as that of her only remaining rival in the state, the older, bigger Kansas City. Experience gained in developing the local wells, moreover, together with ready local capital, enabled citizens to make Wichita a headquarters for firms specializing in exploratory surveys and in financing new oil fields in the Southwest. In addition to the oil industry, airplane manufacture boomed during the twenties. Promoters fastened upon the facts that the open plains offered ideal testing grounds free from fog and that Wichita was located in the heart of the United States. Probably more essential were the skilled mechanics in the neighborhood, men trained in the plants making tractors and other farm machinery or simply schooled on the farms where mechanized equipment must be kept in running order. Before 1926, citizens fired with ambition to see Wichita the 'Air Capital of the United States' had built fifteen aircraft factories, and by 1928 these were producing some 1,500 planes a year, one fourth the total output of commercial craft in the country. Under the spur of this industrial growth, population increased to 110,000, and the city spread out in an ever-widening circle.

More remarkable, the sense of civic responsibility, weakened in many American communities by the undreamed-of wealth accumulating in the twenties, strengthened here. Anxiety about the future of Wichita Negroes, in 1924 numbering about 5,000, led the Council of Churches and the American Social Hygiene Association to hold a two-day conference on race relations, in which Negro leaders and white participated equally. Careful advance canvassing of householders prepared the way for the crowded meetings that followed. Perhaps the principal achievement was the discussions held between Negro and white women, where both groups discovered that they shared common problems, and mutual respect grew as they faced them together. The final report of the conference listed the measures best calculated to lessen the handicaps of the city's black families. The consensus of opinion was general that the separate Negro school system, contrary to the expectations of some, had proved itself wise, for here well-trained Negro teachers handled situations all too familiar to people of their race but which white teachers, outsiders in a Negro community, found nearly uncontrollable. The development of musical talent in the Negro schools had made notable gains. On the other hand, the community badly needed a colored truancy officer, a Negro social case worker, and more Negro visiting nurses. Competent Negro nurses would discourage the still-prevailing custom of using midwives and, while enabling the city to keep accurate vital statistics, would check infant mortality in the Negro sections of the city. A Negro case worker could get to the bottom of problems no colored family would discuss freely with a white person, just as a Negro truancy officer could exercise an authority impossible for white. The conference members urged upon employers a policy of equal rights for both races and commended the local press for its refusal to stress Negro crime. To doubters within the city, the report appealed on the basis of ultimate economy in saving the public the expense of heavy costs for poor relief and prosecution of crime. Two years later the city voted to take over Fairmount College as a municipal university, where educators then introduced courses to train police officers properly. If the city failed to carry out the program of civic improvement in its entirety, citizens at least knew what waited to be done.

With the economic collapse of 1929, Wichita's aircraft industry all but fell apart; older enterprises suffered only less. Eleven of the fifteen airplane companies went out of business. The local oil wells continued to operate, but new drilling was kept to a minimum. With the drop in commodity prices, farmers could no longer buy machinery or, in many cases, meet their notes at the banks. In this situation, repeated in one form or another through most of the western world, Wichita's troubles were lessened, first, by the diversity of her business interests and, second, by the character of her citizens. Small companies had grown up in the decades preceding, enterprises that were allied with milling or meat-packing, aircraft manufacture or oil-drilling, but, because not entirely dependent upon those major industries, able to keep their plants running. Yet without courage and a strong sense of community feeling, neither the men who composed these companies nor the bigger concerns that survived could have helped the city through the blackest months. The magic in Wichita was the public spirit of her leading citizens. Here men were still living who remembered the crisis when the cattle drives turned westward and the later hard times of the nineties. Families tempered by earlier adversity set the example, giving outright what they could and keeping employees on their payrolls after strict business efficiency would have closed shops down. In 1933, when the federal government, under the leadership of President Franklin D. Roosevelt, instituted that series of measures soon known as the 'New Deal' legislation, Wichita had already weathered the worst of the storm. Still she was grateful for the help given by the Civilian Conservation Corps, that federal agency which gathered together young men and employed them as civilian troops to fight insect pests, improve roads, and carry out a host of other public projects; for the assistance of the Public Works Administration which supplied most of the money for building the Wichita Art Museum and thus increased employment and enabled the city to satisfy a long-felt want; and for the opportunities offered by the Works Progress Administration. In every state in the Union the 'WPA' employed thousands of men and women unsuited to hard physical labor who now earned a living at congenial and creative tasks, such as preparing state guide books under the aegis of the Federal Writers' Project or in working with the Federal Theatre Project. Testimony, however, to the solid foundations that citizens had laid in Wichita was the unbroken peace in labor relations within the community. In 1937 when most American cities were torn by strikes, Wichita factories were untouched. As the outbreak of war in Europe brought an end to unemployment in American industry and to the troubles of American agriculture, Wichita was ready to make the most of her opportunity.

Industry, particularly airplane manufacture, leapt to new life, and the population grew from the 114,000 of 1940 to over 166,000 before 1950, to make Wichita the largest city in Kansas. During the war her companies turned out some 30,000 aircraft. Housing inevitably lagged; some workmen in the aircraft plants reportedly commuted daily as much as two hundred miles, a lesser feat, to be sure, over the straight roads of Kansas than it would have been in the East. Yet by 1950 more than 20,000 dwellings, including apartment houses, had been added to the 40,222 of 1940, and manufacturing concerns had increased from the 200 companies of 1939 to over 500. Because natural gas is abundant in the region and in-

Wichita, looking northeast, 1952

dustrial plants consequently used gas instead of coal for fuel, the city escaped the grimy appearance of most American industrial communities. Wichita, no longer content to be known as the 'Air Capital of the United States', took to herself the title 'Air Capital of the World', an international port. 'Airplanes, wheat, live-stock, and oil,' an American business journal reported in 1950, 'are keeping Wichita stepping. . . The secret of the town's prosperity is an unusual balance between industry and agriculture.'

If, as Americans are wont to do, the observer gauges urban distinction by size, he will consider Wichita insignificant unless he gives weight to her potential for future growth. Measured by other standards, she ranks high among the urban communities of the United States. Amid the confusions and excitements of war-time expansion, Wichitans kept in mind the well-being of the community as a whole. Unhappily, some signs now point to a mounting pre-occupation with material things and sacrifice of the emphasis upon human values that marked her earlier career. Nevertheless, parks and playgrounds have multiplied, public schools have increased in number, and illiteracy has virtually disappeared. Evidence of public concern with civic affairs occurred before the end of the 1940's when the commissioners responsible for the appointment of the City Manager dismissed one incumbent and installed a more competent man. In less mundane realms, the city's ambitions remain unfulfilled. Europeans or Americans accustomed to the life of cities whose traditions reach far back into history may be struck by the naïveté of so young a community in aspiring to become a center of the creative arts. Not so unsophisticated that she contends, as the popular song puts it, 'Anything you can do I can do better,' Wichita nevertheless believes that by effort she can attain a cultural level equal to that of older cities. The hope of the eighties of becoming the 'new Athens', if no longer so phrased, burns brighter today than ever before. Citizens attend concerts and lectures, frequent the Art Museum and encourage local talent. In addition to its collections of Indian art and some of the old masters, the municipal Art Museum gives space to several marine paintings of a native Wichitan, John Noble, who first won local fame when Carrie Nation spoiled his 'Cleopatra at the Bath'. Wichita University and the Friends' University, in spite of Quaker teachings of austerity, lay stress on the quality of their courses in literature and music. Though the background of most of her citizens is provincial and though the setting of this rapidly growing commercial and industrial city is rural Kansas—even in this age of air travel still remote from the large cultural centers of the United States—who dare say that in time to come she may not achieve her artistic ambitions? Up to the present, her creative work has been the building of an enlightened, responsible community.

The mining town of the high plains and the cow town of Kansas have both changed beyond recognition since their pioneer days. Each added to the bridging of the double frontier of mid-nineteenth century, and, in the process, suffered periods of hardship when only men's stubborn faith in themselves enabled their communities to survive and strengthen. The success of their determined efforts to build cities in the wilderness, a wilderness of prairie grasses and treeless space, fostered the rise of other towns and cities in a region deemed uninhabitable a century ago. Certainly without closing the gap between East and West the United States could scarcely have become a united nation; even with railroads crossing the 'Great American Desert', divisive tendencies, growing out of sectional differences, might well have created two countries instead of one. Cities to serve as local markets and regional centers for the settlers of the wide expanses of the Great Plains were the cause as well as the result of the peopling of the region. Although the urban civilization in which both Denver and Wichita take pride is less individual today than in earlier years, some of its features are still distinctive and bear witness to the travail by which it was born.

# VII

## Seattle, City of the Northwest

OF all the large cities of the United States, Seattle has the most magnificent natural setting. She lies amid hills and lakes on an arm of the sea with high mountains on her eastern and western skyline. Puget Sound, like a narrow fjord cutting south from the Juan de Fuca Strait and the Pacific Ocean, forms her western boundary. Across the Sound, five miles wide at Seattle's site, the Olympic Peninsula stretches west to the sea, a hundred miles distant, and the serrated ridges and eight-thousand-foot, snow-clad peaks of the Olympic mountains break the ocean winds and lessen fogs over the city. Some thirty miles to the east rise the Cascade mountains, blue-green with firs in summer, white in the winter snows. Between the Canadian border and California the ten-thousand-foot range is pierced only by the Columbia river and acts as a barrier between the well-watered coastal region and the arid country to the east. On Seattle's southeastern horizon looms Mt Rainier, an extinct volcano 14,400 feet high, its upper slopes snow-covered the year round. To the northeast Mt Baker rises to more than 10,000 feet. Within the city, Lake Union, a half-mile from the Sound, feeds into the salt water, while further inland the twenty-five-mile length of Lake Washington spreads out at the city's eastern edge.

Before the city filled the tidal flats, thirty-five of Seattle's one hundred and four square miles were water. Much of the business district has been levelled to make municipal service easier, but inland from the waterfront, hills rise precipitously between deep wooded ravines. Houses cling to hillsides sometimes so steep that householders park their cars on the roofs of the dwellings on the street below. Bridges span the ravines, the lakes, and the deep waterway cut from Lake Washington to Lake Union and out to the Sound. Flowers, watered by as much as 160 inches of rainfall a year, grow luxuriantly, and in this climate where temperatures rarely drop below 30° in winter or rise above 70° in summer, gardens are a mass of color nine months of the year. Parks and boulevards, houseboats and ferries, wharves and warehouses, factories and skyscrapers, fine residences and humble, pawnshops and 'flop houses' make up modern Seattle. At once ugly and beautiful, the city herself can never destroy the enchantment of the land and sea at her doorstep.

Seattle's history divides into two parts, nearly equal in time, very different in character. The first period encompasses the pioneers' struggles and gradual success, culminating in a literally golden burst of triumph with the Alaska gold rush at the end of the nineteenth century. In the second fifty years the focus shifts. Conflict ceases to be Seattle against the railroads and the indifferent East and becomes loggers and cannery and waterfront workers of the whole Northwest against lumber companies, bankers, and all the big employers of the region. Economic and class distinctions replace the single-mindedness of the community that once turned a solid front to the world. The early days make a story with a satisfyingly pleasant ending. Twentieth-century history is more complex, more disturbing, and still uncertain of outcome.

The double frontier created in the 1840's made it logical that the Puget Sound region should be settled before the Great Plains. The pioneers who founded Seattle arrived seven years before the Pike's Peak gold rush and sixteen before land speculators marked out Wichita. Yet the missionaries and farmers, who had pushed into the Northwest before and immediately after British recognition of American claims to Oregon, had occupied lands only along the three-hundred-mile course of the lower Columbia river and its tributaries. Before 1851, settlement had scarcely begun north of the Columbia between Walla Walla on a tributary near the base of the Rockies, Portland, two hundred miles farther west on the Willamette, and Astoria, once John Jacob Astor's trading post at the great river's mouth. In the arid region along the upper Columbia, where it flows southward from Canada before swinging sharply westward near Walla Walla, sagebrush, scrub pine, and rocks covered the countryside. West of the Cascades along Puget Sound stood virgin forests broken only by clearings at Tumwater and Olympia, insignificant huddles of houses at the southern end of the Sound, and by a few logging camps nearby. Above the international boundary, across the Juan de Fuca Strait on Vancouver Island, the Hudson's Bay Company maintained its western headquarters and supervised its stations on the mainland. Between these Canadian outposts and Olympia stretched the hunting and fishing grounds of Indian tribes who knew white men as trappers and traders, not as settlers. But in 1851, men who had recently made the long journey overland to the lower Columbia were beginning to be bitten with the 'North Oregon fever', that obsession to carve out for themselves a slice of the wilderness in the forests to the north. The best lands in the Walla Walla and Willamette valleys seemed to be already occupied; northern Oregon was still empty—save for a few thousand red men—and stories in Portland told of the fertility of the Puget Sound region, where firs grew to a height of two and three hundred feet and to a girth of twenty-five feet and more. Consequently in September 1851, several farm families, newly arrived in Portland from Illinois, decided to settle farther north. Seven months later the town of Seattle began to arise on the shores of Elliott Bay, sixty miles above Olympia.

Two young men, sent in advance to explore the country for the best possible location, first chose a site on the open Sound below the southern headland that marked the entrance to Elliott Bay. Here at Alki, Chinook jargon for 'by and by', they began clearing land and building a log cabin before one of them set out on foot for Portland to carry the news that they had found an ideal spot. Two months later boats from the schooner *Exact*, after a six-day run from the lower Columbia, deposited on the gravelly shore the five families who had been waiting in Portland. In the cold November rain, the five women of the little party, with twelve children under nine years of age, must have looked with sinking hearts at the still roofless cabin, the pine-clad slope and the nearly naked, curiosity-ridden Indians who swarmed about them. The Indians, friendly in spite of their annoying inquisitiveness, quickly proved helpful; they traded salmon and venison for ship's bread and showed the new settlers how to split cedar logs easily to build cabins. But the drawbacks of the location soon became evident. In December, when the captain of the brig *Leonesa*, in search of piles for San Francisco's wharves, sailed up the Sound and, having caught sight of the cabins at Alki, contracted with its settlers for a shipload of logs, the inexperienced woodsmen, lacking oxen or horses, discovered the difficulty of dragging logs to the beach and there, because the land shelved gradually into deep water, of loading the vessel anchored well off-shore. The householders also discovered that in the winter storms every wind swept down Sound upon their exposed little cabins. Convinced that the Sound, gouged by glaciers of the ice age to a depth of 900 feet along much of its length, offered better anchorage than Alki, three men of the settlement when spring came set out by Indian dugout to locate a protected site where deep water ran close in-shore. Armed with a length of clothes-line and a horseshoe to take soundings, they found on the northern side of Elliott Bay more than two hundred feet of water near high yellow gravel bluffs that tapered eastward to less precipitous slopes. Here a few men could easily roll or drag heavy logs down the hillsides to deep water, and here the headlands cut off the storms of the open Sound. In April 1852, four of the five families at Alki moved to Elliott Bay.

From the first, the new settlers saw that the forests must supply their livelihood. In San Francisco, encircled by barren hills, demand for lumber was mounting daily, and schooners loaded on Puget Sound could readily make the 800-mile run down the coast to California's 'Golden Gate' and bring back supplies needed in the logging camps to the north. Yet people of a later generation must be struck by the temerity of men bred on the Illinois prairie who ventured into this northern wilderness. The mild climate, the heavy rainfall, and the fertile soil of Puget Sound shores, when cleared of trees, held promise that here foodstuffs would grow abundantly, but Illinois farmers whose crops had depended upon the long hot nights of the corn belt must have realized that the coastal region of the Pacific Northwest could not become farmland of the kind that they had known. Arthur Denny's memoirs written at the end of his life made clear that he and his associates were impelled neither by a spirit of rash adventure nor by missionary zeal in seeking homes here, but solely by belief that exploitation of the virgin country of Puget Sound would quickly make them 'capitalists'. If they knew nothing about logging, they could learn, and when they had thinned the forests, other resources of the region would nurture a vigorous town. Who came first would have first choice of land. In the early 1850's before the slavery conflict reached the intensity that, as the decade wore on, would absorb the chief energies of men in the East, prospects looked bright for rapid settlement of the far Northwest. The year 1852, indeed, saw a mighty migration into Oregon Territory, and by 1853 northern Oregon claimed enough inhabitants to permit creation of the separate Territory of Washington.

In the summer of 1852 Dr David Maynard, physician, adventurer, and jack of all trades, had swept into Elliott Bay in an Indian dugout paddled by Chief Seattle and some of his tribesmen. Maynard was seeking a location for a fish-packing shop. The earlier comers, eager to see their still-unnamed settlement grow, welcomed him warmly, helped him built a cabin and agreed to his insistent proposal that they name the place for his friend, Seattle. The wise old chief, who from the days of the Hudson's Bay Company's rule had seen the futility of fighting the white men, objected to having the place take his name, since his people believed that when his spirit departed it would be troubled whenever his earthly name was spoken. Nevertheless, Seattle became the official name of the town when in 1853 the territorial legislature accepted the town plat, or survey. Although the territory extended from the high mountains of what is today Montana west to the Pacific and included all the country between the lower Columbia and Canada, settlers barely numbered the 5,000 required for separate territorial government. Of these Seattle contributed several more than the original twenty-four at Alki, principally because Henry Yesler, once of Baltimore and then of Portland, in the fall of 1852 had established a steam sawmill on Elliott Bay. Maynard's salmon-packing enterprise proved a failure, since the fish, improperly cured, spoiled on the long voyage to San Francisco's markets. Lumber did not spoil. Seattle's original settlers had realized that a steam sawmill would be a boon, and, having assisted in erecting the building and running a small wharf out into deep water, they cleared a path down the hillside above so that logs dragged to the road by oxen could be skidded direct to the saws at the mill. 'Skid Road', today lined with waterfront saloons and pawnshops, in 1853 was Seattle's main street.

That year 1853, a cargo of ship spars for China marked the opening of a trade with the Orient which forty years later would assume major proportions. Though one must wonder today how men avoided a series of frightful accidents when the saws ran at night lighted only by fish oil lamps, pine flares, or bonfires, nevertheless the power-driven mill was soon operating twenty-four hours a day to feed piling and sawn lumber to ships putting in from California. Boston merchants' prefabricated frame houses sent around the Horn could not begin to meet San Francisco's needs. Newcomers, drawn by the activity at Yesler's mill, began to arrive. From a Sound schooner, an Illinois shopkeeper drove ashore behind the team that had carried him and his four little girls overland from the Mississippi; the town now had horses to help in lumbering and a wagon for lighter cartage. Dexter Horton opened his 'general store' and began accepting money for safe-keeping from the trappers, loggers, and sailors who came to pick up supplies. Out of the coffee-filled barrel that Horton used as his 'safety-deposit' came Seattle's first bank. By mid-1854 town lots were selling at $250. A Methodist minister had organized a church and his wife taught school in their cabin. The mill cookhouse served as social center, town hall, and church. Fulfilment of Arthur Denny's capitalist aspirations seemed imminent.

In 1855 Indian uprisings halted this promising growth. Chief Seattle and the Duwamish Indians had maintained friendship with the white men settling along the Sound, but hostility to the intruders had mounted steadily among other tribes. In 1853 the Governor of Washington Territory had persuaded them to agree to a reservation plan whereby they accepted certain parts of the territory for their own and $180,000 in money as payment for relinquishing to the 'White Father' in Washington millions of acres of their former hunting grounds. Later, evidence showed that the red men believed that the Governor had promised them an annual payment of $180,000, a yearly sum that would have still constituted a bargain for the white men. As the Indians discovered that they had sold their birthright for a mess of pottage, their anger increased, and in the fall of 1854 they began raiding and tomahawking settlers living in isolated localities. Families in Seattle had some warning that they might be attacked in turn and hastily converted one of the larger houses near the shore into a block house. The opportune arrival of a United States sloop-of-war in Elliott Bay late in December strengthened the town's defense, and when the savages attacked some days later, the guns of the sloop and the muskets of townsmen repulsed the Indians in two days of fighting. Only two white men were killed, but Seattle's brief boom was ended. New families moving into the territory looked upon Elliott Bay as still beset with danger. Though in 1858 a rumor of gold found along the Fraser river in British Columbia brought northward-bound prospectors into the town, only a handful of miners returned to Seattle. A blacksmithy, a foundry, a hardware shop, a saloon, and a dancehall appeared, but in 1860 the town still numbered only 182 inhabitants.

Primitive and remote though the place was, in 1861 plans were afoot to make Seattle the seat of a territorial university. In the territorial capital at Olympia, lobbying among the representatives of rival towns proceeded vigorously. The federal Congress in creating Washington Territory had set aside two townships, that is, seventy-two square miles of land, to support an institution of higher learning. When Henry Yesler bought some of the government land to feed lumber to his mill and other townspeople gave ten acres within Seattle for a campus, the territorial legislature accepted the offer. Before competitors could persuade the legislature to change its mind, Seattle men hastily cleared the land and erected a modest Ionic-columned building, fenced about with pickets, in order, one local wit declared, 'to keep the stumps from getting out of the yard'. For students had to be cajoled into enrolling. Asa Mercer, the university's president and one-man faculty, set out by canoe and in a four-hundred-mile journey canvassed every logging camp along the Sound. By promising to pay $1.50 a cord for split wood as credit toward their expenses, he succeeded in persuading twelve men to enter the first class. Since only one of the group had had a high school education, the university in its first years was more academy than college, but it gave Seattle prestige and foreshadowed her future growth.

The frontier settlement of the early sixties was made up largely of men, two-thirds of them bachelors. An enterprising San Franciscan had opened a bordello supplied with well-scrubbed Indian women, but Seattle promoters had no wish to father a village of half-breeds. Yet there was scarcely an unmarried white woman in all the territory. Migration of families into the far Northwest had dwindled when the Kansas–Nebraska Act of 1854 had pitted Northerners against Southerners in the race to settle Kansas and thereby claim the territory as free soil or slave. With the outbreak of the Civil War, the caravans of householders moving into the Northwest had ceased altogether. No single woman could venture alone into the remote Territory of Washington. In 1864, Asa Mercer, himself a bachelor, saw a solution. Realizing that the Civil War was making widows and orphans in every city of the East, he hit upon the scheme of importing young women to Seattle where lonely men would turn husbands with alacrity. Encouraged by some of his neighbors, he abandoned his duties at the university and took himself East to execute his plan. In New England, people listened to his proposal with approval. Several hundred women of good family agreed to risk the long voyage around the Horn and the matrimonial uncertainties ahead, provided that he supply transportation. Mercer had no money to charter a ship, but he felt sure that the United States government, perceiving the virtues of his plan, would offer him the use of a ship. After months of seeking interviews with officials in Washington, D.C., who, in the fashion of government administrators in wartime, shunted him from office to office, in the spring of 1865 he obtained a promise of help. A few nights later, the assassination of President Lincoln threw the capital and every supporter of the Union into mourning. No one in Washington could bother with the strange young man from Seattle or his plan of transporting future wives to that unknown spot. Mercer, returned to New York to await a more felicitous moment to remind the government of his need, grew desperate as the weeks went by. At length, he began to dicker with private steamship lines, only to find their prices exorbitant. And then a newspaper reporter, seeking a sensational story, heard of Mercer's problem. When the lurid tale of the white slaver caught in his own iniquitous toils appeared in the New York papers, indignant letters poured in upon Mercer. Women who had been eager to take ship with him denounced him. Left with a list of only twenty who still believed in his good faith, he hastily contracted to pay for their passage out of his own pocket. Arrived in San Francisco with practically no money, he was helpless to prevent some of his protégées from remaining there. Nevertheless, when the ship carrying the remaining eleven 'Mercer girls' at last hove around the headland into Elliott Bay, Seattle's bachelors, 'looking like grizzlies in store clothes and their hair slicked down like sea otters', lined the wharf. In 1866 Mercer persuaded a second group of women to come. The Mercer girls became the mothers of Seattle's foremost families. In marrying a Mercer girl himself, Asa, no doubt, reaped his reward.

Despite some natural increase in population and the occasional arrival of a new householder, Seattle saw that she could not develop unless she could improve communication with the rest of the world. Townspeople's delight in the country and faith in its future did not automatically bring capital to exploit its resources. Eighteen years had seen a community of twenty grow to one of 1,100. In 1870, a year after the territorial legislature had incorporated the town, she had a telegraph line, a newspaper, a school and a university, two churches, a hospital, and a bank; several shops, the sawmill, the blacksmithy, and some few other enterprises supplied immediate local wants or provided exports. Deep water close in-shore permitted the large ships of the seventies to anchor where logs and lumber could still be virtually rolled on to their decks. Prospectors had found coal a few miles inland. But a road east over the Cascades was still little more than a foot trail, and steamships called in only at irregular intervals. A railroad would end this isolation. In 1870, the Northern Pacific Railway was pushing its tracks westward at an encouraging rate. If Seattle could become its western terminus, townspeople knew her future would be assured. At this moment, to the sharp disappointment of men of western Washington, the directors of the railroad decided to abandon their original plan of running tracks over Skagit Pass direct to Puget Sound and chose instead to follow a route through the eastern sections of the territory to the Columbia, where river-boats could pick up passengers and freight for the coastal towns; a spur line north from near Portland to Puget Sound would meet the charter requirement for tracks to the west coast. Men of an obscure town of the far Northwest could not force the powerful Northern Pacific to reverse its decision. They could only bid for the privilege of having Seattle made the terminus of the branch line. To win this advantage, they offered the railroad builders every conceivable bait: valuable land, half the town's waterfront wharfage, and a quarter-million dollars in cash and bonds. But in the summer of 1873 the Northern Pacific announced that it had chosen Tacoma, some thirty miles south. Tacoma, Seattle bitterly believed, because the settlement there was tiny and the railroad men could build it into a company town. Seattle seemed doomed to remain remote and inaccessible.

Yet a community of 1,100 people who could offer some $700,000 for the privilege of a railroad was not to be thwarted by the greed and whims of the Northern Pacific. Within a week townspeople reached a decision: they would build a railroad themselves, not all the way across the continent, but across the Cascades into the rich farming country about Walla Walla. The wheat of south-eastern Washington would then pour into Seattle and the grain fleet would call at Elliott Bay. In two months' time, while a local lawyer was hurrying the necessary authorization through the territorial legislature, Seattle raised enough money to make the plan look feasible. In September, the banking house of Jay Cooke, financial backer of the Northern Pacific, failed and brought work on the transcontinental railroad to a stop. The collapse of the famous house brought about other failures and launched the panic of 1873. Seattle's assets shrank with those of her customers, and since she had been unable to obtain a government land grant for her railroad, she must abandon the plan or find other resources than cash.

The other resources were the determination and the brawn of her citizens. If they could not raise money to hire labor, they would do the job with their own hands. On May Day 1874, every man, woman, and child in the little town set off to the outskirts, there to begin construction on the Seattle Walla Walla Railroad. Following a picnic lunch came a series of speeches, ended abruptly by Henry Yesler's seven-word address: 'Let's quit fooling and get to work.' Thereupon men and boys turned to with picks and shovels, and throughout that summer, as their other jobs permitted, they worked at clearing and grading. Oregon newspapers jeeringly estimated that at the then rate of progress Seattlites would take two hundred years to build their road into Walla Walla. But the story made good copy, and Eastern newspapers picked it up. Men the country over talked of the little town that refused to acknowledge defeat. Ambitious Easterners with careers to make concluded that here was a place to use their talents; through the unsought publicity Seattle acquired a number of able new citizens. San Francisco steamship lines inaugurated regular service to and from the town suddenly become famous. The gratuitous advertising, moreover, helped raise the money to pay labor to carry on construction of the railroad after volunteers had completed four miles of track. A year later, in 1877, the rails reached into Newcastle twelve miles inland where coal mines produced paying traffic. A money-making railroad interested Henry Villard, in the 1860's a little-known newspaper man, in 1877 president of the Northern Pacific. Villard bought the mines, ran a coal fleet into Seattle and purchased the home-made railroad for a quarter of a million dollars. At the end of the seventies, though the town still had no direct link with eastern Washington or, save by steamship, with the lower Columbia valley, she had established herself as a seaport of some importance. The coal and lumber barges and the regular steamship runs to and from San Francisco gave her a definite place in the expanding commerce of the west coast.

But her struggle with the Northern Pacific was by no means ended. Villard had promised to extend Seattle's road south to Tacoma, but bankruptcy threw the Northern Pacific into other hands and cancelled the plan. In 1884, to be sure, tracks from Tacoma into Seattle were completed, but for some obscure reason the company ran no trains over them. Consequently, Seattle again determined to act for herself. North of the border the Canadian Pacific was nearing Vancouver. If a road were built to connect with that, Seattle would at last have rail connections with the East. Local business men sent a persuasive representative to New York to enlist capital, while at home they mapped out their route and arranged preliminaries. When word came that New York bankers would invest a half-million dollars in the projected Seattle, Lake Shore, and Eastern Railroad, construction began at once. The Northern Pacific, seeing its transport monopoly imperilled, created every obstacle lawyers and money could contrive to prevent the Lake Shore and Eastern's progress, but in 1891 officials of the more powerful company capitulated, bought the unfinished road, built it through to tie into the Northern Pacific system and gave adequate service over the line from Tacoma. In this way Seattle won her twenty-year fight for a transcontinental railroad into the city. Two years later the Great Northern Railroad came into Seattle, and in 1909 the Chicago, Milwaukee, and Puget Sound.

Meanwhile, Seattle had shed her primitive air. A gas company, using the coal of the region, introduced gas lighting in the seventies and installed street lights. The town laid sewers, built board walks along the principal streets and opened additional schools. An opera company from San Francisco received such an ovation in 1877 that not one, but two, opera houses went up. A population of 3,500 inhabitants in 1880 entitled her to the status of a 'third class' city, with Mayor and Council, Board of Health, and other elected officials. In 1883 a horse-drawn street railway went into operation, and in 1889, before New York, Philadelphia, or Chicago had shifted from horse-cars, Seattle boasted an electric tramway. Electric lighting for public and private buildings also appeared. In 1889 a devastating fire wiped out the entire business section of the city, but re-building began at once, this time with brick and iron. The fire, however, called citizens' attention to the inadequacy of their water supply, and in 1890 the city purchased the property of the private water company that had installed hol-lowed log pipes in 1881. In 1891 citizens approved a plan for a gravity water system with water piped from a mountain stream some twenty miles east in the foothills of the Cascades. By the turn of the century Seattle would have a com-plete, municipally owned water supply. In the interim, the $10,000,000 spent on reconstruction along the waterfront built not only substantial business blocks but sixty new wharves and warehouses and a greatly improved sewerage system. In spite of the disaster, by 1890 population had reached nearly 43,000, a twelve-fold increase in ten years.

The growth of the eighties was partly the result of the increasing demand for the lumber of the Northwest, as the forests about the upper Great Lakes ap-proached exhaustion. The giant firs of Washington kept sawmills in Seattle sup-plied with a seemingly endless quantity of large straight-grained logs. A shingle mill had begun operation before 1880. Soon after, a machine shop and a foundry opened to produce equipment for the sawmills, logging camps, and docks. As the canning industry developed in the United States, fish canneries multiplied in the city. Puget Sound salmon, long a local staple of diet, no longer spoiled *en route* to

California markets, and canned salmon became a delicacy to be found on grocers' shelves in every large city of the country. Seattle's prosperity attracted people from the East and the Middle West, from Europe and Asia. Coolies, imported to build the railroads, formed a China town until mounting anti-Chinese sentiment turned into violence and only ten days of martial law averted a race riot. When passions cooled, city officials deported some of the unwanted; the others were gradually absorbed into the growing industrial life of the city. Welcome newcomers from Scandinavia and Finland arrived to work in the lumber yards or on fishing smacks, Englishmen moved in from Canada, Germans opened small shops, and Irishmen came on construction jobs to build new business blocks, new houses, hotels, and saloons. Growing population here and elsewhere brought Washington into the Union in 1889. Old residents and new believed that here they might well make a fortune and could certainly enjoy a comfortable future.

The country-wide depression of the 1890's shook that confidence. Puget Sound lumber and shipping industries slumped badly, and Seattle workmen faced months of unemployment. In 1896 when the Nippon Yusen Kaisha steamship line began running its ships between Japanese ports and Seattle, business revived somewhat, and then on a July morning in 1897 the steamship *Portland* hove into dock with $800,000 worth of gold from the Yukon district in Alaska. The news spread like wildfire. Every city on the Pacific coast hastened to outfit miners, but Seattle had a headstart, and she was the nearest big city to Alaska. In a matter of weeks gold-hunters flooded in upon her. By the early months of 1898 hotel managers were putting cots along the corridors, and livery stables were turning into dormitories to provide sleeping space for the prospectors waiting to ship north.

Seattle's Chamber of Commerce, sensing the importance of making the city the permanent center for equipping miners, organized an elaborate advertising campaign. A skilled booster—in present-day American jargon, a 'public relations expert'—prepared a statement of Seattle's peculiar advantages as an outfitting point: her hardware firms built Yukon stoves adapted to use in the Klondike; her shoeshops made a special miners' boot; her woolen mill wove the most serviceable blankets; grocers could provide the most suitable canned goods; from her wharves, ships as comfortable as a Hudson river boat could steam up the inner water route to Alaska without putting out into the storms and fog of the open ocean; and finally and perhaps most telling of all, she had opened a public Bureau of Information from which the inexperienced could learn all that the prospector needed to know. Copies of this enticing literature then went out to the 70,000 postmasters in the United States, to 4,000 city mayors, and to 600

'Bird's Eye View of the City of Seattle, W. T., Puget Sound. County Seat of King's County, 1884'
The inset at lower left shows Mount Rainier on the skyline

public libraries, with several thousand more copies, for good measure, to the railroads to distribute. To ensure that successful gold-seekers would return to Seattle, the city persuaded the United States government to open an assay office here. Under the impact of ceaseless advertising, Seattle became in fact what her promoters claimed for her: the gateway to Alaska. The pioneer era had ended. Seattle was a city of national importance.

In the next thirty years individual citizens, civic organizations, and newspapers kept the publicity rolling out. Seattle was soon calling herself the 'Queen City of the Pacific', and although copywriters no longer used the whole gamut of extravagant phrases the nineteenth-century Chicagoan reserved for his city, they heralded daily the Seattle Spirit, always in capital letters. Seattle's braggadocio, boring to the reader of a later generation, was so convincing to contemporaries that in the 1920's it would bring hundreds of unemployables and shiftless people to make demands upon the community where, advertisers had insisted, jobs and well being awaited everyone. Families would sell their every possession, pile into their 'tin lizzies' and in those battered Ford cars drive to Seattle to demand their share of the fortunes promised.

Up to the end of the first World War, however, Seattle, in continuing to grow, outwardly prospered. By 1910 her population reached some 250,000. Shipyards to supply the Alaska trade multiplied. The government assay office handled millions of dollars of gold. The Great Northern Steamship Company, a subsidiary of the Great Northern Railroad, ran a fleet into and out of the port, until in 1906 the United States Supreme Court, acting in President Theodore Roosevelt's anti-trust campaign, decreed the railroad-steamship combination an illegal restraint of trade and ordered the monopoly dissolved. Steamship lines from the Orient brought in silks, curios, and tea, in return for American manufactures or lumber, and local promoters never failed to point out that Seattle was two days' voyage nearer the ports of the Far East than was San Francisco. In 1912 Seattle surpassed New Orleans in value of imports and exports and took rank as the fifth port of the continent. Manufactures of a wide variety added to the city's wealth. Pulp mills appeared and factories for processing the delectable fruits and vegetables grown in the irrigated sections of eastern Washington and on the farms near Puget Sound. Seattle was at once distributor and producer. To display her versatility she organized the Alaska-Yukon Pacific Exposition in 1909 and made money on it.

Nor were her achievements all purely material. Good sanitary engineering, abetted by a mild climate, put the death rate lower than that of any other city in the world—in 1913 just over eight per thousand. Infant mortality was infinitesimal. Public playgrounds were scattered through the city. Fishermen could catch black bass in Lake Union at any time of day at any season. Ten cents in car-fare took the sportsman to boathouses on Lake Washington where, for another few cents, he could rent boat or canoe and paddle himself off out of sight and sound of the city. Citizens eager to hear music founded a symphony orchestra. People could see plays in any one of several theatres. Thousands of readers regularly patronized the public library. Into the well-taught public schools the Superintendent of Schools introduced the innovation of promoting pupils as soon as they showed themselves ready for more advanced work. Other cities copied the plan. Besides sixty-five elementary schools and seven high schools, the city supported night schools which 6,000 adults attended. At the University of Washington, in the 1890's moved from its downtown location to a magnificent site on the shores of Lake Washington, several hundred young men and women enrolled yearly. The faculty included a number of gifted professors. While Seattle boasted, she felt she had reason.

The vaunted Seattle Spirit, defined as the impulse to think 'nothing is good enough; everything must be made better,' inspired civic undertakings of considerable magnitude before World War I broke out. In 1900, a journalist wrote, the city looked like a small boy who had outgrown his clothes. The Alaska gold rush had over-extended her and she needed new trappings. Unlike most fifty-year-old females, she needed to have her face lowered, not lifted. Hundred-foot hills in the center of the business area, inadequate wharfage and a landlocked, undeveloped inner harbor all called for action. To level the hills near the waterfront, the city leased the pumping system, formerly used by one of the private water companies, to an engineering concern that employed a novel method: powerful sluicing hoses washed the earth away. The tonnage thus removed, estimates figured, equalled two-thirds that excavated for the Panama Canal. On the levelled expanses new business buildings went up quickly, while the dirt sluiced off the hills filled in some hundreds of acres of tidal flats along the southeastern shore line and thereby created additional factory sites. The city met the harbor problem with equal skill. With the help of federal and state money, work began on a Sound-to-Lake-Washington ship canal, deep enough to take ocean-going vessels through locks into fresh water harborage. Wharves and dry-docks now lined Lake Union, a change that grieved fishermen who had caught black bass in its clear waters, but a blessing to the shipping interests. When the eight-mile canal opened in 1917, Seattle's harbor could accommodate all the fleets of the world at one time. Meanwhile the city engineer had prevailed upon the city fathers to approve his plan for piping additional water into the city and of using the power generated by the water's fall for a municipal electric lighting plant.

Sluicing down Seattle's hills, 1907

Seattle business men believed nothing could stop her. As the day approached for the opening of the Panama Canal, newspapers prophesied what the canal would mean to the Northwest. Eastern ports, one man wrote, face Europe and a quarter of the earth's population; Seattle faces Asia and half the peoples of the world. As the Orient discovered the bounties of western civilization, millions of buyers of American goods would arise there. Seattle would ship to these hungry markets and thereby confer benefits on Asia and gain wealth and distinction for herself. By 1925, he concluded, Seattle might expect to have a million inhabitants.

In actuality, the ties with the Far East took visible form a generation later when the city fell heir to one of the finest collections of oriental art in the western world. But that was the result of private philanthropy, not Seattle's trade.

The first World War shifted emphasis from commerce to industry. For a time Seattle profited from the closing of the Suez Canal and the threat of submarines in the Atlantic, but when the United States entered the war, shipbuilding over-shadowed commercial interests. Twenty shipyards, with 40,000 men, turned out hundreds of ships; 8,000-ton vessels were brought from keel to launching in three weeks. Government orders for airplanes introduced a new industry. At lumber yards and sawmills operations ran round the clock. Prices soared. The inunda-tion of war labor crowded rooming-houses and led to the hasty construction of makeshift quarters. Families lived on craft in the harbor or on houseboats in Lake Union. When power for the new industrial plants threatened to be in-sufficient, the city acquired control of the upper reaches of the Skagit river and pre-pared to develop its hydro-electric potential. Prospects seemed bright for a bigger Seattle, more influential in the nation's affairs than most older cities in the country.

The end of the war pricked the bubble: war industries closed down and in 1920 business recession set in. The lumber market collapsed and prices for agri-cultural produce dropped. As the Northwest had expanded industrially more suddenly than other parts of the United States, so the region and its business capital suffered more acutely. Investors were troubled, but the small shopkeepers and the wage-earners, as always, bore the brunt of this reverse of fortune. Little businesses, where the owner hired one or two helpers, had multiplied in the years preceding the war. Even today newspapers characterize Seattle as the home of the small business man. While these people undoubtedly suffered, the wage-earners were in worse case. The story of labor in the Pacific Northwest has been sometimes tragic, often melodramatic, rarely comic. It is, in fact, the core of Seattle's history of the last fifty years.

The roots of the labor struggle go back into the 1880's. As long as Seattle was a frontier settlement, any hard-working frugal person could be as well off as his neighbors. The men who staked the original claims to the choicest sites along the waterfront, in the course of years as shipping grew in volume, benefited from the rise in real-estate values, but the later comer who bought his lot and built his house or shop inland was only less 'well fixed'. Though loggers and fishermen drifted in and out, many of them dying, as they had lived, without worldly possessions, it seems fair to surmise that some, perhaps most of them, had deliberately chosen the unencumbered outdoor life. When sharp differentiations of wealth first began to crop up cannot be pinpointed; some time during the years of the city's rapid growth presumably marks the moment. The Knights of Labor local lodge began publication of a labor newspaper in 1889. Yet even then and well into the 1890's economic opportunity awaited most men. The avaricious with useful political connections, to be sure, were seizing every chance to acquire by devious ways vast stretches of forest land. Railroad magnates connived at intrigues that extracted from the federal government grants to priceless timber and mineral lands. Although without these grants probably few men would have risked money in building the railroads that permitted the Northwest to develop rapidly, a later generation frequently called this system 'the plundering of the public domain' and belatedly held it up to obloquy.

How pronounced the effects of growing concentrations of wealth were upon working men in Seattle before 1900 is uncertain. A few locals of American Federation of Labor international unions had appeared, but it was in the logging camps, not in any city, that organization took powerful hold early in the twentieth century. Exploitation of lumbermen had spelled low wages, bad food, overcrowded shacks, long hours of work during the season, no jobs at all in off seasons, arbitrary dismissal of men who complained and blacklisting which prevented their getting work elsewhere. Out of these intolerable conditions arose in 1905 the International Workers of the World, the IWW. Thirty years before the Congress of Industrial Organization broke with the American Federation of Labor on the issue of industry-wide instead of craft unions, the IWW preached the doctrine that workers of the world, regardless of craft, must stand together. Equally distinctive and more widely publicized over the country was their use of violence, on the principle: fight fire with fire. Lumber companies, backed by all the support money and influence could buy, shrewd corporation lawyers, venal state officials, county sheriffs, and lumber-camp foremen tried vigorously to destroy the IWW, but angry, sometimes desperate, men accustomed to the rigors of the outdoors of the Northwest were not intimidated easily. Roving delegates canvassing the logging camps spread the word that by acting together the lumberjacks could wield power. The Wobblies, as IWW members were nicknamed, grew in strength and stirred unrest in the more conservative ranks of labor. New locals of American Federation of Labor international brotherhoods formed, with membership mounting yearly. In 1913 anti-unionists raided the IWW headquarters on Skid Road. That year the labor vote in the state forced through the legislature an eight-hour law, which the state Supreme Court declared unconstitutional. Well before the first World War, strikes were investing Seattle's industrial career with characteristics that conservative citizens denounced as the result of Wobbly teachings.

After the Armistice of 1918 layoffs of workmen and wage cuts gave the signal for a full showdown. In February 1919 Seattle labor unions called a general strike in protest against the refusal of shipyard owners to maintain the wage rates of semi-skilled workers. Seattle was paralysed with sheer astonishment; no city in America had ever before faced a general strike. The 65,000 union members participating were perfectly disciplined; no disorder occurred; the strike committee kept control. The strike, at its beginning set to run for five days, was an extraordinary performance. The committee approved milk deliveries to households with small children, laundry service to the city's hospitals, operation of the municipal lighting plant, delivery of the United States mail and running of the federal Customs House. Otherwise all services within the city stopped. The committee admitted Japanese workers to its counsels, an unheard-of liberality in this region of enduring anti-oriental feeling. For 25 cents a meal, improvised union restaurants fed the families of men who held union cards. Though the Wobblies sneered at the strike as a meaningless gesture, they too could eat at the union restaurants. As proof of their fairness to their fellow citizens, the strikers suspended publication of their own union paper when they closed down the presses of the commercial dailies, but not before the Seattle *Union Record* had printed an editorial entitled 'They Can't Understand'. It opened:

> What Scares them most is
> That NOTHING HAPPENS
> They are ready
> For Disturbance
> They have machine guns
> And soldiers
> But this SMILING SILENCE
> Is Uncanny
> The business men
> don't understand that sort of weapon.

At the end of five days, the strikers returned to work. They had made no demands. Their avowed purpose had been to show the solidarity of Seattle's organized labor and the power it could exercise. The AF of L unions, despite the opposition of the Wobblies, believed they had won their point. Rejoicing in the labor camp, however, was premature, for the witch hunt against 'bolsheviki' which swept the United States between 1919 and 1921 weakened unions throughout the country. Employers formed counter-organizations to enforce the open shop and a return generally to the *status quo ante*. While all labor unions suffered, panic over the success of the Russian revolution lent bitter zeal to persecution of the Wobblies. Consequently, the IWW faded out in the Northwest about 1923, but the seeds it had sown, though dormant till the thirties, did not die. In the interim, strikes almost ceased; labor lay quiescent.

As the post-war agitations subsided, Seattle business men gradually recovered their faith in their prowess. Shipbuilding failed to resume, but lumbering and the building trades prospered and food-processing plants expanded. While other cities in Washington were claiming a larger share of the state's growing commerce and industry, Seattle succceeded in keeping her lead. Even Olympia, the state capital, played second fiddle. Catering to the 700,000 tourists and new-comers who arrived in Seattle between 1921 and 1924 became a major business. In addition to reaping some benefits from the more than $300,000 that the Chamber of Commerce spent on national advertising, the city profited from the publicity attending the election of a woman Mayor in 1925. Here, rumor said, must be a vigorous community unimpeded by the conventions that obstructed civic progress in the East. In 1929 William Boeing opened his aircraft factory. No great affair to begin with, Boeing's enterprise was nevertheless important because of the highly skilled workmen he employed and because of the cordial relations he maintained with his men. Seattle welcomed the company without fully recognizing the prestige it would bring her. Yet industrial growth notwith-standing, so far from reaching the million population mark prophesied before the war, Seattle in 1930 claimed few more than 365,000 inhabitants.

The depression of the 1930's checked industrial development everywhere; for wage-earners it spelled sheer disaster. Unemployment reached a peak Seattle had never before known. Relief rolls created a staggering burden on the city budget, a burden heightened by the number of incompetents and ailing who had thronged into Seattle during the lush twenties when local promoters were promising all things to all comers. While industrial employment shrank, the de-cline of the lumber industry in Washington affected Seattle tradesmen by reduc-ing their business with shoppers in all the outlying towns.

In the midst of this general misery, in 1934 the labor battle began again. It opened when the marine unions, which had recruited thousands of new members, organized a coastwise strike that tied up all the ports from the Canadian border to Mexico. Indignant citizens in Seattle formed a 'Committee of 500' to move cargo in defiance of the unions, while police guards protected paid strike-breakers and volunteers. When the strike ended, labor emerged victorious on the main issues in dispute. Contracts with employers recognized the unions and their right to hire halls for meetings, increased wages, and reduced longshoremen's hours to six a day. But the struggle was not over. Two years later waterfront employers refused to renew the contracts and the Maritime Federation called another strike. It lasted four months. The unions staunchly refused to settle separately, and, having learned the value of public opinion, conducted a skilful campaign for public support. Employers gave in. Meanwhile lumber workers of the entire Northwest, loggers, sawmill and lumber yard hands, mill-work and pulp-mill employees, had taken united strike action. The Wobblies had taught them how to fight. Seattle escaped the bloodshed and arson that occurred in some parts of the state, but here also tension ran high. Though widespread accusations of Communist influence damaged the strikers' cause, settlement at length awarded the lumbermen better working conditions and higher pay.

At this juncture, during a convention of the American Federation of Labor in Chicago, a group known as the Committee of Industrial Organization withdrew to form the CIO, in protest at the conservatism of the parent AF of L. In 1935 the federal Congress passed the National Labor Relations Act which gave labor new legal status. CIO unions, heirs of the IWW in accepting industry rather than a craft as an organizational basis, now enlisted huge memberships in the lumbering, maritime, mining, cannery, and fishing industries of the Northwest. White-collar workers also unionized. At the *Seattle Post-Intelligencer*, one of the oldest and most influential newspapers of the region, striking newsroom workers in 1936 closed the plant for three months and forced recognition of the American Newspaper Guild. Seattle emerged as a stronghold of unionized labor. The individualism that had characterized pioneer days at last gave way before the drive for collective bargaining.

While these revolutionary changes were coming about, another shift was quietly taking place. In 1934 when public attention was focused on the strike at the waterfront, David W. Beck, head of the AF of L teamsters' union, persuaded the brewery workers to join the teamsters. The Brotherhood of Teamsters then refused to let dealers in the city obtain a single bottle of beer or hard liquor until they had come to terms with Beck. A mere detail of the labor picture at the moment, the arrangement set the pattern. In the next ten years, the teamsters' union extended its jurisdiction over bakery, laundry, milk-wagon, and taxicab drivers, over department store clerks, garagemen, cannery workers, and employees of all Seattle's dyeing and cleaning establishments. But in the 1930's Seattle business men, concerned with the activities of what they regarded as the radical unions of the CIO, paid scant attention to the AF of L teamsters.

Business, moreover, began to revive about 1936. Seattle's waterborne commerce jumped to a value of more than 900 million dollars and gave promise of further increase. Industrial expansion looked imminent as the great federal

power project, Bonneville Dam on the lower Columbia river, neared completion. When in 1937 the dam and power plant were finished, electric transmission
lines could take cheap power into a wide area. At the Grand Coulee falls of the
upper Columbia in central Washington work was beginning upon a second
federal power development. Private investors, awakened to the potentialities of
the region, organized new private power enterprises. Seattle extended her own
municipal power plant. Drawing upon these hydro-electric resources, the
Northwest saw itself destined to become the industrial center of the nation.
Seattle saw herself as its industrial and commercial capital. Only the fish saw
things otherwise. Polluted rivers were destroying fish and great dams were
cutting off the salmon from their upstream spawning pools. Though government engineers constructed fish ladders at Bonneville to help the salmon leap
pool by pool up the falls to spawn where they were born, few of the little fish
hatched got back to the sea, because they were sucked into the sluices of the
generators at the dam. Dwindling schools of salmon threatened the extinction of
Seattle's fishing and canning industries. Ichthyologists, conservation experts, and
cannery owners believed for a time that the answer to this problem lay in transporting the salmon eggs to hatch in pools whence the fingerlings could swim unimpeded out to sea. Experiments soon dispelled that hope. Scientists discovered
that the newly hatched salmon apparently depends for survival upon absorbing
the oils deposited by his forebears in the waters up which they swam to spawn.
While partial suspension of fishing during the second World War has permitted
some increase in salmon, the problem of the fisheries is not yet solved.

Before 1939 was well advanced, other industrial prospects were diverting
Seattle's attention from the plight of the fisheries. Orders from Europe and then
from the United States government set the Boeing aircraft plant humming
months before war broke out. Soon after, shipbuilding, long suspended, came
to life and machine shops were swamped with work. The boom, started in 1939
and 1940, assumed major proportions in 1941. After Pearl Harbor, the great port
city that once had rejoiced in her nearness to the Orient shivered in apprehension
but turned her resources to defeating the nation whose trade she had recently
courted. Well-informed estimates place the increase of the working force of the
state of Washington at 47 per cent between 1940 and 1950. Seattle, with nearly
463,000 inhabitants by 1950, got her full share. New factories and additions to old
went up wherever space was available. The Boeing Company built a second plant
within the city and a third some miles out. The Bremerton shipyards expanded
again and again. In spite of citizens' personal anxieties, prosperity brought a new
gaiety to the community whose business and labor troubles had absorbed men's

Seattle with Mt Rainier

energies in the decade preceding. Strikes during the war were few. Production, profits, payrolls, and taxes rose to new peaks.

The post-war reaction, though not proportionate to war-time expansion, was nevertheless sharp. Company after company undertook drastic reductions in force. Labor grievances, consideration of which workmen and employers had agreed to postpone for the duration, now came to the fore. Were war-time labor gains to be permanent? Some Seattle employers, like employers elsewhere, hoped not; all wanted stability in labor relations. Though no one believed that the Northwest could return to the open shop, many employers still wished to see union strength curtailed. An odd turn of fate centered Seattle's labor controversies at the Boeing aircraft plants where relations between company and employees had been exceptionally good during the twenty-five years of William Boeing's and Phil Johnson's presidencies. Boeing, though an arch-conservative, had entered into a contract with Local 751 of the International Association of Machinists in 1932, a year when few companies in the United States saw fit to have any dealings whatsoever with organized labor. He had advocated unions as expedient. His successor, on the other hand, Phil Johnson, one-time college professor, was a liberal by conviction, an expert technician and a person of driving force—altogether an unusual man. Local 751 was also unusual. Organized in 1897, it had drawn its membership from workmen in the small machine shops scattered through the city. Its agents were honest and had had long experience. Their competence had enabled them after 1937 to include the Boeing truckers and teamsters in the machinists' union, in the face of the growing strength of Dave Beck. Boeing teamsters got higher wages than Beck had been able to obtain for his men. Labor relations at the Boeing plants remained untroubled until the death of Johnson in 1945. The new management, unfamiliar with local conditions and inexperienced in dealing with unions, veered away from Boeing's and Johnson's enlightened policies. In 1946 when Local 751 attempted to renew the war-time contract with minor modifications, difficulties arose. At the end of nearly two years of futile negotiation, in April 1948 the men walked out on strike.

At this point Dave Beck took the center of the stage. Beck, in the early thirties simply a labor leader, had built up the teamsters' local in Seattle little by little, while he participated in organizing activities elsewhere in Washington, in Oregon and in California. Probably he felt he had done the brewery workers a favor in adding them to the Brotherhood of Teamsters. He might have believed coercive measures against other unions justified by the advantages that would accrue to all labor from having a few powerful unions instead of many small weaker ones. Use of violence against strikebreakers and intimidation of employers had been successful weapons for the laboring man. A strong leader could adapt the technique to inducing other unions to join the teamsters. The teamsters supported Beck devotedly if only because captive unions paid handsomely for the unwanted privilege of being allied. When the war boom began, Beck's task became easier. Employers found labor hard to recruit and harder to keep. Beck could supply it. Always presentable in appearance and manner, he could talk persuasively to employers. He guaranteed them workers and got contracts for his unions. At the end of the war, as social pressures against Communism increased, almost any skilful person could use the Communist label to undermine competitors: the longshoremen under Harry Bridges were 'all communists'; CIO unions in general were suspect. A safely conservative union like the teamsters' seemed reliable, all-American, democratic. Beck convinced industrialists that his men were sound. 'The tough conservative Mr Beck', wrote the *Wall Street Journal*, 'who enjoys being called a friend of business' by 1948 had become a big business man himself. The commodity he handled was labor.

So it was the teamsters who broke the machinists' strike at Boeing. A technicality had caused the courts to declare the strike illegal, and Local 751 was without legal recourse. Professing to have jurisdiction over 5,000 of the 14,000 Boeing machinists, the teamsters nibbled away at the strikers' strength and, by driving scabs—that is, strikebreakers—past the picketers at the factory gates morning and evening, enabled the company to maintain partial production. At the end of five months the machinists accepted defeat. To reclaim their jobs the strikers had to pay dues to the Brotherhood of Teamsters and acquiesce in its representing all labor in the aircraft plant.

Liberal opinion in Seattle was shocked at Beck's treatment of the machinists. Union men elsewhere in the country who had looked on Seattle in the mid-thirties as the hard core of the American labor movement now crossed off the city as a source of strength. Conversely, employers found Beck satisfactory to deal with; he 'delivered the goods'. His career illuminates weirdly some aspects of the city's development. Where John L. Lewis, czar of the United Mineworkers of America, is universally feared, and even hated by some employers, Beck of the teamsters whom other unions fear and distrust has consolidated his position in high places. Leaders of the community that in the 1870's and 1880's fought the great railroad interests have accepted a man whose power and methods are autocratic. If the success of the machinists in reestablishing their own union at the Boeing plants in late 1950 suggested that Beck's empire in Seattle might have begun to disintegrate, expectations of his downfall receded in 1953 when the AF of L put him on the Central Executive Committee, and the President of the United States singled him out for the honor of dining at the White House.

To explain fully how present attitudes took shape in Seattle would require careful analysis of the social history of the whole Northwest. The historian, the sociologist, the ecologist cannot view the city apart from the region; Seattle's history of the last fifty years is inextricably interwoven with that of the lumber camps and waterfront conflicts of towns up and down the coast. The militance of labor was a response to the frightful exploitation of earlier years. Labor violence led to savage retaliation by employers' associations. As industrialism is newer in the Northwest than in most of the country, so time to make adjustments has been shorter. Pride in Seattle's industrial growth has inspired in business men ambition to see it still greater. Yet before the recent growth of native fascism in America, belief in the perpetuation of a one-man rule seemed inconceivable in a city where rival unions have had an honorable record.

Apart from regional influences, Seattle's insularity and non-intellectual interests have conditioned her social attitudes. The contributing causes are easy to perceive. Living in a setting of great natural beauty with all outdoors within easy reach, people cannot bear to contemplate living anywhere else. No opportunity outside Seattle has any appeal; they have little interest in other places and the ideas of other communities. They are not only indifferent to other communities; they are absorbed in the affairs of their own particular small groups within the city. Family life looms large. People outside the inner circle scarcely matter. Most householders own their own homes. Seattlites look clean, healthy, and generally satisfied, and if, despite the undercurrent of anger in the ranks of labor, citizens appear to be more pleased with themselves than stirred with the 'divine discontent' of genius, they represent, nevertheless, that rarity in the modern world, essentially happy people. Their diversions are largely outdoors—fishing, hunting, skiing, mountain-climbing, boating, or gardening. Householders are more likely to concern themselves with their rosebeds than with impersonal civic affairs, and with buying new cars than with examining the meaning of Seattle's labor history. Their pride in their city strikes the outlander as uncritical.

In widening Seattle's intellectual horizons the University of Washington has contributed less than might have been expected. Thanks to valuable downtown real-estate holdings, the university is one of the richest in America, but, though it is now over ninety years old, it has failed to do for Seattle what the younger University of Chicago has done for Chicago. As a state university, the University of Washington has always been subject to political influences. Charges of communism brought by a politically ambitious state legislator in 1949 and 1950 led to the dismissal of three members of the faculty at a time when Senator McCarthy was still feeling his way. Political pressures have long hampered the university's professors. Responsible to a President and Board of Trustees appointed by the Governor, they have affected social points of view in Seattle relatively little.

Another curious feature of the city is the age of her population. Birth rates and death rates have been extraordinarily low for many years. Couples marry at the age of eighteen, nineteen, or twenty, and wives go to work to enlarge the family income or because their friends take jobs. Presumably this circumstance has contributed to keeping the birth rate low. Whatever the cause, the mean age of the population is creeping steadily higher. And the world has always recognized conservatism as an attribute of age. The combination of this elderly conservatism and the radicalism of labor is startling. It makes the future of this old young city unpredictable.

The significance of Seattle in national history is somewhat beclouded by her anomalous position in recent years. In mid-nineteenth century she represented the farthest outpost of American civilization, the geographic 'jumping-off place'. Farther west in the United States no one could go, and even after Americans discovered the resources of the Great Plains, Seattle remained the symbol of the United States' last frontier. Today, amid the imposing modernity of her business district and the ugliness of the run-down sections of her waterfront, the visitor will find little to remind him of the pioneer spirit that built Seattle in the wilderness. Her early contribution to the development of the Northwest and hence to the strength of the nation grew out of the tenacity of her citizens in obtaining railroad connections with the East. In forcing the Northern Pacific to alter its plans, Seattle not only won railroad service for the lower reaches of the Puget Sound area, but she showed Americans the country over that they need not tolerate the dictatorship of railroad monopolies. Men remembering her successful fight were the readier a dozen years later to support President Theodore Roosevelt's anti-trust campaign. Her working people in the twentieth century taught laboring men of other cities that concerted action could prove effective. Yet Seattle of the 1950's, dismissing those episodes of her past, claims distinction rather as a city that lavishes thought and money on her public school system and that dominates the commerce and industry of the Pacific Northwest. Other cities, however, also have good schools and, in view of the vast natural wealth of the region, it seems reasonable to believe that, had Seattle not seized the business leadership of the region, some neighboring city would have assumed that role and made at least equally good, perhaps more generous, use of her power. Nevertheless, as in any composite, Seattle possesses elements of good as well as evil and includes upright men and women who deplore her supine attitudes of the present.

# VIII

# Detroit, a Biological Sport

TO an American 'f.o.b. Detroit' has become so familiar a phrase that few people recall that in 1900 the purchaser of a horseless carriage would have been more likely to turn to some small shop in New England or New York State than to Detroit. Detroit at the opening of the twentieth century was a city of 285,000 inhabitants, but not a city comparable in size or importance to the great seaports or the inland distributing points like Chicago and St Louis. Cleveland and Buffalo on Lake Erie, outlets for the Lake Superior ores and the fish and lumber shipped from the upper Great Lakes, were larger, busier commercial centers than Detroit. Detroit had easy access by rail to western Ontario: Michigan Central railroad cars had only to run aboard the train ferry and be carried across the Detroit river to Windsor. Railroads fanning out into Michigan brought into this largest and oldest city in the state the products of the lower peninsula, the area enclosed by Lake Michigan and Lake Huron, while ships, come through the Sault Ste Marie from Lake Superior, fed Detroit the copper and iron of the upper peninsula. But in 1900 not Henry Ford himself could have envisaged the city as the future motor center of the world. She had no grave disadvantages of situation to overcome, but neither had she any unique or exceptional fitness for automobile manufacture save one: here was the home of Henry Ford and of other pioneers of the industry. That fact, not geography, transformed Detroit in a single lifetime into a city renowned the world over wherever trucks and automobiles run. Had Cincinnati investors received Henry Ford's early overtures kindly, had Cleveland attracted Ransom Olds, Detroit today might be basically different.

Yet Detroit was more than two centuries old when the Ford Motor Company was organized. She has, in fact, a longer uninterruptedly significant history than any settlement in the United States between the Atlantic seaboard and New Mexico. In 1701, seventeen years before French traders founded New Orleans and fifty-odd before that fateful French force penetrated the trans-Alleghany country to build Fort Du Quesne at the source of the Ohio and thereby open the French and Indian war, Antoine de la Mothe Cadillac established a stockaded community, Fort Pontchartrain, at 'la place du détroit', the strait. While Robert Livingston, the secretary of the Board of Indian Commissioners in New York,

'Fort Pontchartrain, 1705'

was urging the English government to erect a fort there, the Frenchman acted. With unerring eye he chose these narrows as a key to the interior of the continent. Who held the Detroit river could control the vast area about the upper Great Lakes. For though the river is little more than a half-mile wide, some thirty feet deep, and, carrying hourly 637,000 million cubic feet of water, only moderately swift-running, it is the outlet for the waters of Lake Superior, Lake Michigan, and Lake Huron and links those inland seas with the lower lakes, Erie and Ontario, and thence with the St Lawrence. Cadillac located the fort on the one high stretch of land along the Detroit river's eighteen-mile course. At this point, the river, fed from Lake Huron above through the small Lake St Clair, swings westward for a few miles before turning south through swampy land to empty into Lake Erie. Above and below Detroit's site, good-sized islands lay off-shore, but here view of the river and approaching bateaux was unimpeded. To the north of Cadillac's fort stretched the forests of pine which a century later would supply the livelihood of settlers in Michigan. Within and outside the stockade, the French built a few houses to accommodate traders and their stores, while nearby some 6,000 Indians set up villages in order to make the most of fur trading with men at the fort. Within a decade the settlement had become one of the most important inland trading posts on the continent. Before mid-century habitants were farming the land adjacent, each man tilling a ribbon-like strip running down to the river, and by 1750, in addition to a garrison of a hundred soldiers, Detroit had nearly a thousand inhabitants.

When New France fell to the British in 1763, most of the French settlers at Detroit remained. Artisans and traders, they maintained the French customs and speech that would prevail for the next half-century, although a few Dutch, English, and Scottish families who settled here during the decade preceding the American Revolution gave the village a less purely French air than formerly. The Indians also lingered in the vicinity to profit from the beaver trade and, during the Revolution, from the prices paid for rebel scalps brought to the British commandant at the fort. At the end of the war, British troops continued to hold Detroit, treaty terms notwithstanding, until in 1796 a second treaty strengthened by an American victory over the war-like tribes of the region brought about surrender of the post. Seven years before the American flag rose over Detroit, the Continental Congress had ratified the Ordinance of 1787 creating the Northwest Territory from which the Territory of Michigan would be carved in 1805. But in 1802, Detroit had petitioned for and been granted local self-government. Women as well as men, many still French-speaking, voted at the first town meeting. After one hundred years of intermittent French, British, and American military rule the community at last had a civil administration of its own choosing.

Unhappily, self-government in Detroit was short-lived. Michigan's first territorial officials arrived in the summer of 1805, a few days after a fire had razed nearly every building in Detroit. While villagers prepared to rebuild, the new Governor and three judges of the territory set themselves to reorganizing local administration. None of them was familiar with the French customs of the village and all of them were intent upon making the community conform closely to American ways. Their first step was to abrogate the charter of 1802 and impose a government of their own which largely eliminated citizen participation. Governor and judges took charge of verifying land titles and grants in a fashion that slowed house building for a year. The most arrogant and opinionated of the officials, Judge Augustus Woodward, insisted that the frontier village be rebuilt upon his plan patterned on the national capital, with spokes radiating north, east, and west from two centers near the river bank. He named one of the two main thoroughfares for himself. Measure followed measure to heighten confusion. Attempts to introduce a banking and monetary system to supplant the beaver skins current as money created financial havoc. The climax of calamities came in the first weeks of the war of 1812 when the Governor of the territory meekly surrendered Detroit to the British. The American naval victory on Lake Erie in 1813 restored Detroit to the United States and brought a new Governor to Michigan, the able Lewis Cass.

Cass set about vigorously to repair the damage of the preceding years. In this difficult task, Father Gabriel Richard, the priest of Ste Anne's parish in the city, lent assistance by encouraging his parishioners, still incensed at their former treatment, to forget the past and co-operate as citizens. Father Richard had long been a force in Detroit. Early in the century he had published two issues of a newspaper, and in 1804 he had opened a 'young ladies' academy' and a school for young men. Judge Woodward also, stubborn, self-important, and quarrelsome though he was, lent his influence to promoting public education. In 1817 Woodward's imagination conceived a plan for higher education in the territory which, with characteristic pomposity, he entitled the 'Catholepistemiad, or University of Michigania'. Enacted into law, the Catholepistemiad included thirteen 'didaxum or professorships' covering mathematics, the natural sciences, philosophy, literature, and languages. Funds to support the institution were to come from a 15 per cent tax increase in the territory, the money to be set aside as a separate university fund. The Presbyterian minister of Detroit, John Monteith, a man of culture and wisdom, accepted seven of the professorships, Father Richard the other six. However preposterously high-sounding, the Catholepistemiad was the true forerunner of the University of Michigan, opened in 1837 when Michigan became a state. Woodward's plan thus inaugurated the system of state-supported higher education which other midwestern states would copy. More immediately significant in the history of Detroit was the union of Roman Catholic priest and Presbyterian minister to make the Catholepistemiad work. Their wise and harmonious labors welded the community together. In 1823 the people of Michigan elected Father Richard territorial representative to Congress, the first and last Catholic priest to hold Congressional office. Though the Governor and territorial judges largely controlled Detroit until 1824, that year a new city charter, creating an elected Common Council, restored local self-government.

Yet before 1830 Detroit failed to grow. For just as the westward movement down the Ohio left northern Illinois and the Chicago area untouched till the 1830's, so this Ohio river traffic by-passed the Territory of Michigan and its capital Detroit. In 1818 a first lake steamer, *Walk-in-the-Water*, began trips between Lake Erie ports and Detroit, but the great westward migration passed many miles south, leaving Detroit a frontier town long after Cincinnati, Louisville, and St Louis were thriving inland cities. Furthermore, a widely-circulated official report of the surveyor-general of the United States Land Office describing Michigan as a waste of swamp and sand discouraged homeseekers who knew of the fertility of lands along the Ohio. Despite the disasters that had attended the earlier experiment in banking, Governor Cass, perceiving that sound finances would aid territorial development, in 1817 incorporated the Bank of Michigan in Detroit. About the same time, the Detroit *Gazette*, Michigan's first newspaper, began publication. But neither bank nor newspaper succeeded in bringing settlers. In and about Detroit, poor roads, a morass of mud during months of the year, and the closing of the Great Lakes to navigation every winter kept the place isolated. Even after a public stage coach began to run in 1822, and after a larger steamboat replaced *Walk-in-the-Water*, new settlers in Michigan were rare.

Everyday life in Detroit during these years was uneventful. While skilled artisans, whose forebears perhaps had come in Cadillac's train, turned out articles for barter with the farmers nearby, other men earned a livelihood by fishing, by carrying on the beaver trade and by sawing the woods of Michigan's forests. The first Protestant Evangelistic Society, formed in 1817, included Presbyterians, Congregationalists, Methodists, and Episcopalians, but in the 1820's the denominations divided to organize separate churches. Nevertheless, during Father Richard's life-time, the French Catholic parish continued to dominate much of the community, and Catholic feast days constituted its holidays. Festivities were necessarily simple and diversions few. As long as soldiers were garrisoned in the city, they staged theatricals occasionally, and when the river froze, usually in early December, men enjoyed racing their ponies on the ice. Hunting and fishing were primarily business occupations rather than sport. Existence, if monotonous, was pleasant enough, but it held out little hope of affluence for either French- or English-speaking residents.

The opening of the Erie Canal in 1825 introduced the first change in Michigan's economic prospects. Canal boats brought newcomers and their household goods to the shore of Lake Erie and thence lake steamers could carry them comfortably farther west. Yet it took another ten years to convince Easterners that earlier surveys of Michigan had been misleading. Then by canal boat and wagon, by windjammer and lake steamer, the influx began. As southern Michigan farmlands proved fertile and the white pine forests covering most of the territory promised inexhaustible supplies of lumber, Detroit, the first port of entry to this newly discovered paradise, began to grow. In 1837 Congress admitted Michigan to the Union. Detroit, capital of the territory, continued as capital of the state until 1847 when the legislature chose a more central location at Lansing, but Detroit remained the chief commercial city of Michigan. In 1837 during the seven months when navigation was open on the Great Lakes, 200,000 people had landed at Detroit. Though most of them moved on, and though the belated effects of the panic of 1837 checked prosperity, by 1840 the city had a permanent population of over 9,000. Thereafter growth was steady. In spite of local interest in the Cathol-epistemiad and generous federal land grants to support public schools, the conservatism that long marked Detroit, the number of well-run private schools, and French Catholic preference for parochial institutions delayed adequate provision for free elementary education in the city. A survey of 1838 showed that three-quarters of the city's children were attending no school whatsoever and led to the organization of an elected Board of Education empowered to direct the building and staffing of schools in every ward of the city. In 1842 the imposition of a direct local school tax supplied the funds to make this machinery effective, although, as elsewhere, no truancy laws appeared for another generation. Meanwhile, business men promoting the Michigan boom chartered railroads and, with financial backing from Boston, hurried on construction. Discovery of copper and iron in the upper peninsula again interested Boston capitalists who, determined to tie Michigan's resources to the Bay State, provided much of the capital to dig the Sault Ste Marie shipping canal along the St Mary's river connecting Lake Superior with Lake Huron. Upon the opening of the 'Soo' in 1855 the long procession of ore boats began down the lakes, a procession that grew with every year. Not all ships stopped in Detroit, unless they needed repairs or fuel, but a large enough number docked to heighten the city's prosperity. When the Civil War broke out, Detroit ranked as an important lake port and, with three railroads entering, a railroad center as well.

The next forty years of Detroit's history repeats in general form the pattern of growth of most northern cities in the United States of that era. While Charleston lay crippled and New Orleans shrank in importance, northern manufacturing cities expanded, commerce jumped in volume and value, and money poured out into new ventures in the West. Detroit never touched Chicago's record of growth and failed to overtake in size and influence the Lake Erie ports that shipped coal and produce north as well as receiving Lake Superior ores. Nevertheless, she more than doubled her population between 1860 and 1880 and had nearly 206,000 residents within her limits by 1890. The rape of Michigan's forest brought her great wealth. Though Chicago, to which western Michigan shipped, became the chief lumber market of the country, Detroit was the metropolis of Michigan. Detroit banks financed many a lumber company, and Michigan men, with fortunes made, were prone to build homes in Detroit and make the city their headquarters. When lumbermen discovered in the mid-eighties that Michigan's despoliation was nearly complete, the more ambitious moved their operations to Wisconsin and Minnesota and later still to the Pacific Northwest. But Detroit remained the business center of what was left in Michigan.

Industry based on lumber continued in the manufacture of varnish, furniture, ships, railroad cars, and wagons. Carriage-making firms established a reputation for fine buggies which would be an asset when the twentieth-century companies turned to building automobile bodies. Diversification through manufacture of bicycles, tobacco products, and pharmaceuticals gained headway. Stove-making, begun in the 1850's when the first barrels of sample iron ores from Lake Superior landed on the city's wharves, grew in importance. Before the end of the century 'Jewel' stoves were warming thousands of farmhouses in the Middle West. Ironmongers could readily purchase coal shipped in from the Pennsylvania and Ohio fields, and iron ore came down the river by nearly every freighter from Lake Superior. Though steel furnaces would not appear until the 1930's, in the eighties and nineties smelters and manufacture of varied iron wares were multiplying. Still more important for the future, the demands of lake shipping created marine engine shops and a force of skilled workmen to man them. Some of these men had doubtless gained their experience in Cincinnati or St Louis machine shops building engines for river steamboats and, with the decline of the river trade, moved to the Great Lakes area where water transport was still increasing in volume. Some men, schooled in precision manufacture in the eastern shops that had produced firearms during the Civil War, naturally turned westward when that business contracted.

Civic attitudes also adhered to the American norm. Although early in the century citizens had awaited the return of self-government eagerly, when Detroit began to expand, men lost much of their former interest. Before the mid-eighties four new city charters had modified the provisions of 1824, each change designed to adapt municipal administration to a growing community, but each in fact complicating matters by a multiplication of elected officers and a diffusion of responsibilities. The city had built underground sewers and public water works in the 1830's, but after the Civil War Mayor and Council had let franchises to private companies to install gas lighting and a street railway system. Beyond investing in these enterprises, leading business men paid scant heed to local politics as long as lumbering and other industry flourished. Why spend energy on running the city when developing Michigan's resources promised fortunes to the bold? With the apathy characteristic of prospering nineteenth-century Americans, Detroit's well-to-do left city government to petty crooks who, for what they could get out of it, were willing to organize 'ward heelers' and carry on the time-consuming task of maintaining a political machine. Only when Detroit's prosperity declined did citizens feel the time ripe for reform. In the late eighties, they elected a capable, conscientious Mayor and Board of Aldermen. Mayor Pingree's battle against the public utility monopolies reduced gas rates and brought street lighting under municipal control. When the panic of 1893 started the long business depression, the Mayor ordered vacant lots in the city cleared for planting, furnished seed, and encouraged families of the unemployed to raise potatoes and vegetables. While the horrified well-to-do cried 'Socialism' at Pingree's 'potato patch' relief, the scheme helped feed hundreds of hungry families and lightened the city's tax burden.

As business conditions improved towards the end of the century, Detroiters could look about them with satisfaction. City government was now cleaner than in most American cities. If slums extended along the wharves on the lower east side where dirty unschooled children roamed the streets, in much larger areas of the city comfortable houses flanked avenues shaded by fine trees. Public schools were available to vagrants as well as to children of established householders. Belle Island, the island in the river upstream from the city's center, was a large public park where a zoo, bathing houses, boats to rent, and picnic tables set in groves of trees made a playground used by rich and poor alike. A hospital given to the city years before by an obscure philanthropist had developed into a well-equipped medical institution. A city library supplied books without charge, the Detroit Museum of Art maintained a permanent exhibition of paintings and a theatre brought travelling companies from Broadway to perform the most popular plays of each season. For the immigrants within the city, in 1900 well over a third of the total population, living was not easy, but neither was it untroubled for them elsewhere. For the older residents, life tended to be slow-moving, dignified, agreeable. Ships' bells and freighters' whistles echoed through the downtown city at all hours; trains puffed into the railroad station noisily; drays and heavy wagons creaked on the streets about the river front and railroad yards; hooves of carriage horses clattered on the cobblestones or clumped on the asphalt paving along residential streets. A brawl might occasionally disturb the peace briefly in the district known as the Potomac, so named in a word-play on a Civil War song, because all was *not* 'quiet on the Potomac tonight'. Nevertheless, Detroit at the turn of the century was generally orderly.

The horseless carriage was no new invention in 1900. Europeans had done the basic work. Daimler had driven a first model through the streets of Paris in 1886. In the United States, Charles Duryea had built a successfully running gasoline-engined automobile and in 1895 had opened a factory in Springfield, Massachusetts. In 1889 the gifted Ransom Olds had organized a company in Detroit to make cars of his design. Letting out contracts for transmissions to Henry Leland, precision machinist and maker of marine engines, contracts for bodies to a small firm of carriage-builders, for the motors to the Dodge brothers, well trained in metal-working in their father's machine shop, and himself undertaking only assembly in his Detroit plant, Olds in 1900 was making the finest cars built in America. Olds, not Ford, introduced mass-production methods into automobile manufacture. Olds' plant was the training school from which the leaders of the industry emerged in the next two decades—all, that is, except Henry Ford. Henry Leland, not Ford, perfected the application of precision manufacture to automobile parts, so that interchangeability was as sure in the car parts Leland turned out as in components of the fire-arms he had learned to produce years before at the government Armory in Springfield, Massachusetts. The technological skills of these men made possible the revolution in the life of twentieth-century Detroit. Nevertheless, it was Henry Ford more than any other one individual who, though himself neither true inventor nor organizing genius, brought into being the new Detroit. Ford's decision to build a car priced within the purse of every farmer in America changed the automobile business from a manufacture of a luxury article into an essential industry. The Ford Model T altered the face of America and many of America's basic social concepts. In the process of its production, it transformed Detroit.

If Ford was no genius, he had nonetheless unusual qualities and qualifications indispensable for the role he almost unwittingly assumed. He had great native shrewdness, patience, an iron will, an all-consuming interest in machines—a passion that had grown steadily stronger within him from his boyhood on a Michigan farm onward—and considerable mechanical experience acquired in nine years at the Edison Illuminating Company. He possessed also a kind of idealism, warped in later life by his overwhelming power, but as late as 1916 expressed in chartering and sending his 'Peace Ship' to Europe to bring the war there to an end. In 1898 when he succeeded in building a two-cylinder engine that drove a bicycle-tired buggy down Detroit's back streets, it was a triumph of persistence. A shed behind the little house where he lived was his workshop, in which, for lack of money and the necessary power-driven tools, he shaped by hand some parts of his engine. His refusal to be bested by circumstances that would have beaten most men showed a force of character that marked him through life.

Men at the end of the nineties were beginning to be as excited over the possibilities of the self-propelled buggy as their sons would be twenty years later over the airplane and then over the radio. Consequently, a group of men in 1899 sought out Henry Ford with an offer to build his car commercially, give him an interest in the company, and the post of chief engineer. The arrangement lasted less than two years. Ford left the firm and out of the company Henry Leland later formed the Cadillac Motor Company which in 1909 became part of the General Motors Corporation, by then Ford's principal competitor. Following his dismissal, Ford turned to building a second and improved model of his own and in 1903 found financial backers to organize the Ford Motor Company. The company's first cars sold immediately and netted stockholders at the end of the first fifteen months 100 per cent in dividends on the initial investment. In the next two years Ford succeeded in buying out the interest of two stockholders and thereby acquired control of the company. Many other men as years went on would contribute brains and energy to the business, but Ford's decisions alone would count. For weal or woe, he would direct the course of the enterprise that set the pace for the entire automobile industry during the next twenty years.

In 1906 Detroit's automobile manufacturers were producing luxurious cars that cost so much that only wealthy people could buy them. In aping this scheme for a time, Ford Motor Company profits shrank. Ford made up his mind quickly. He had a farm background and had for years ruminated over what mechanization of farming and easy transportation would do for the farmer. In the face of initial opposition from his associates he reversed company policy; the Ford Company henceforward would make the cheapest cars that could be built sound and it would make only one model. At that moment Henry Ford touched greatness. Demand for the Model T was instantaneous. Sales grossed nearly a million and a half dollars in the first year and four times that sum the next. In 1908 the company built a new plant on the outskirts of the city in Highland Park where improved machines soon ran production up to a thousand cars a day. By the end of 1913, according to estimates, Ford Company profits totalled about $15,000,000 a year. The secrets of this staggering success are generally reduced to a few simple principles: a single product of uncomplicated design, unvaried from year to year save for occasional improvements, cash sales, and, in manufacturing, use of every conceivable time- and material-saving device. Though competitors could not afford to admit it, an added factor was Ford's employment of the most competent men the United States' industrial civilization could produce. In the fall of 1913 when the company's output was falling far short of its orders, ingenious engineers devised a system of travelling cranes and overhead tracks to convey the work from one group of workmen to the next, each with a particular job to do. The result was an enormous speed-up of the work. The modern assembly-line was born.

Automobile manufacture did not become a dominant industry in the United States until after the first World War, but in the earlier years of the century effects upon Detroit were already pronounced. As early as 1908 twenty companies were turning out cars, and even then Detroit had established a reputation as the country's automobile center. Young men poured into the city from every part of the earth. First they came from the farms of Michigan's lower peninsula, deforested lands, where sandy, stump-speckled fields offered meagre agricultural returns. From across the river in Ontario and Quebec Province came French-Canadians and English. And then the flood was swelled by men and boys from other American cities, from rural areas of the Midwest, from the Kentucky and Tennesee mountains, from European villages and even Asia. Detroit in a decade became as polyglot as New York or Chicago. Even before the introduction of conveyors in the factories to bring work to the operator at a set inexorable rate with which he must keep pace, American labor realized that work in the automobile plants was a job for young men. So it was that most of the newcomers were young men who brought to the city the vigor and ambitions of youth. The slow-moving tempo of 1900 quickened. But the very traits of character which brought these men to Detroit bred in them dissatisfactions with what they found. The city was soon crackling with the tensions created by labor-employer conflicts.

Though men in the first decade of the automobile industry's growth preferred work at the Ford plant to any other, in 1913 affairs there were troubled. The experiments with the conveyors and the constant speed-up of work caused widespread discontent and were producing a high monthly labor turnover. Throughout the city, labor was beginning to organize more solid phalanxes than had existed among the rather feeble craft unions of the nineteenth century. The IWW, launched in 1905 and growing in strength in the Northwest, saw the opportunity among the automobile workers. Nine hours of hard and exacting work a day at no very high wage provided common cause; the despotic power of shop foremen over hiring, firing, and handling of grievances added to unrest. The Wobblies sent organizers to circulate among the automobile workers not only at Ford's but at other plants also. Agents who spoke the many languages of the foreign-born employees obtained a wider hearing than unionizers ever had before. Ford scarcely knew how to proceed. Without workmen his shops could not produce eleven hundred cars a day. James Couzens, Ford's right-hand man and a stockholder in the company, came up with the answer: offer a $5 'basic' wage for an eight-hour day, announce this measure as designed solely to promote employees' self-respect and well-being, and thus skim the cream of Detroit's labor market. The plan worked. The day after the company published the new pay rate, appli-

cants for jobs at the Ford Company ran to about 10,000 people. Talk of unionization subsided. Ford, the humane individualist, disapproved of unions, groups
which submerged individuals. Ford became the new Messiah, an industrialist
moved by altruism. Many Americans saw nothing incongruous in his 'Peace
Ship' of 1916 by which he expected to bring warring Europeans to their senses.
Nobody in Detroit or elsewhere publicized the fact that in his shops the workload
per man increased steadily, that foremen demoted skilled men to semi-skilled
jobs and that Ford mercilessly hounded his key executives for ever greater production. Couzens had resigned in 1915, and in 1919 Ford bought out the minority
stockholders. Sixteen years after Henry Ford's associates had invested their
capital in a venture to which he himself contributed his mechanical skill but very
little cash, he organized a new Ford Company capitalized at $100,000,000 and
composed of himself, his wife, and his only son, Edsel, whom he was destined to
outlive.

Meanwhile the influx of workers into Detroit pushed the building of houses
and apartments. The city spread out north, east, and west. Judge Woodward's
cobweb of streets and boulevards was lost in a confusion of new sections superimposed upon the original. In widening the streets to accommodate the increasing traffic, the Commissioner of Public Works cut down Detroit's maples and
elms. The quiet charm of the city of 1900 gave way before expanding industrialism. Detroit had no need to advertise herself. Her problem was rather how to
accommodate the incoming throng. Men compensated for the discomforts
this sudden growth created by making slogans: 'Dynamic Detroit', 'City of
Destiny'. The street railway system could not carry the crowds. At the Ford plant
alone 15,000 employees daily streamed in and out of the gates.

The war boom increased wages and numbers of wage-earners throughout the
automobile industry, as demand for cars, army trucks, tracked vehicles, and
finally airplane engines strained Detroit's productive capacity. Frantic recruit-
ment of labor led to the importation of Negroes from the deep South; Chicago's
factories and stockyards had taken the same course in an endeavor to find men for
the heavy unskilled work white men were reluctant to perform. Detroit had had
some Negro population for a century. The city, lying directly across the river
from Canada, had been an important station on the Underground Railway in
pre-Civil War days, and thereafter some Negroes had gravitated toward
'Kentucky', Detroit's Negro quarter.

If the 2,000 Negroes of 1900 had been no major problem, the case was otherwise with 40,000 out of a total population of less than a million in 1920. All could
not live in 'Kentucky' or the new satirically named 'Paradise Valley' area with-

out such overcrowding as to menace the health of the entire city. Yet prejudices, non-existent or dormant among whites when Negroes were few, now appeared. Property-holders feared a lowering in real-estate values if Negroes were to move into areas hitherto occupied only by whites. Law could not force white men to sell to black. The inevitable consequences were that 20,000 Negroes crowded into substandard dwellings originally built to house about 3,000 people. Faulty sanitation, or none, bred disease and a high death rate in all the black belts of the city, while lack of recreational facilities in colored neighborhoods fostered juvenile delinquents. In the course of the next twenty years Detroit's Negro population more than tripled, in spite of the obvious drawbacks for the race in this northern industrial community. The Negro, regardless of his capabilities, always got the unskilled job and lower pay than a white man. Some Negroes established shops and businesses, relying upon black patronage, though not always receiving it because business inexperience plus inability to purchase in quantity forced most Negro owners to charge high prices. The National Association for the Advancement of Colored People gave Detroit such help as it could, and an active local chapter of the Urban League worked diligently to promote better understanding between the races and thereby to open opportunities to black people. But the problem remained of having a large group of citizens who, because considered biologically unassimilable, were difficult to assimilate socially.

While white prejudice and Negro poverty combined to segregate Negroes, the foreign-born usually chose to live in colonies, each nationality in a particular section of the city. Most distinctive of these special localities was—and is—Hamtramck, the stronghold of Poles and other Slavonic peoples. Hamtramck, named for the army officer of Polish birth who commanded the garrison at Detroit in 1803, is an independent entity and, though located practically in the heart of Detroit's industrial district, remains a city within a city. For, as the automobile industry pushed Detroit's limits out farther and farther to absorb small towns on the perimeter, Hamtramck refused to be absorbed. The Poles of Hamtramck were eager to become Americanized, but, as they learned English and the 'American way of life', they preferred to govern their own municipality. An excellent local school system, adapted to the temper and background of these new Americans, helped preserve Hamtramck's determination to keep her independence of the larger city that today completely surrounds her. Polish customs and Polish societies thus survive to give Hamtramck on church feast days or other special occasions a colorful and engaging Old World atmosphere lacking in Detroit. Another village to reject incorporation in Detroit was Highland Park, where Henry Ford had built his factory in 1908, and from which in 1920 he moved all operations when he built a huge plant further west in the village of Dearborn. Thereafter Ford's influence on Detroit's development was indirect, albeit still powerful. His assembly-lines had given new form to industry, built up a great city and remade America. Now Detroit was not wholly loath to lose him. Highland Park, though crippled for a time by the loss of the Ford factory, preferred to manage her own affairs apart from Detroit.

Detroit of the post-war era, nevertheless, was a distinguished municipality. After Mayor Pingree's death in 1901, the city administration had reverted to the practices that Lord Bryce had described in the late 1880's as the chief threat to all American democracy. In the first years of the twentieth century, while the city was growing at a totally unpredictable rate, citizens preoccupied with personal affairs had permitted the old forces of political corruption to return to power. The liquor interests, entrenched in the corner saloon, had a stranglehold on the city government which made the police their subservient tool and enabled them to use appointments to posts in the public schools and awards of city contracts as weapons with which to browbeat. It was a regime known as the 'Swap Voters' League'. It seemed impossible to break. But Henry Leland, always a devout Presbyterian and now an official of General Motors and a person of great influence in Detroit's business world, was determined to smash it. Pingree, Mayor of Detroit for four terms and Governor of the state for two, had laid the groundwork upon which reformers succeeded in building a new state constitution in 1907. Thereafter no city in Michigan need observe national or state party affiliations in municipal primaries or elections. Non-partisanship in municipal government, in the phrasing of the day, was now permissible. In sponsoring an organization to fight Detroit's political machine Leland made initial errors by taking a sectarian approach and by giving the association the unfortunate name of the Detroit Civil Uplift League. Experience, however, soon taught him and his associates. They renamed their organization the Citizens' Association and, instead of restricting membership to 'Evangelical Christians', opened it to all people anxious to have decent government in Detroit. Experience also taught them that the way to develop honest administration was to align good votes to oppose 'bad' at the polls. The Citizens' Association's publication, the *Civic Searchlight*, repeatedly broadcast its precept 'Vote as you please, but VOTE.' The paper pushed its program of citizen education by articles analysing the costs to every resident of municipal maladministration and then appended a careful factual statement about the record of every candidate for office.

The campaign took time. But in 1916, when, in spite of personal tastes, citizens voted to bar liquor sales in Detroit, they destroyed the saloon men's power. The

Mayor hastily forced the resignation of the Commissioner of Police and appointed James Couzens, one-time director of the Ford Motor Company and a lawyer of ability and conscience. Two years of enforcing the law as Police Commissioner then placed Couzens in the City Hall as Mayor. A new city charter dispensed with the 'Gray Wolves', the forty-four ward aldermen, and centralized authority and responsibility in the hands of the Mayor and a nine-man Council elected by the city at large. The principle, the Citizens' Association declared, was 'Put all your eggs in one basket and then watch the basket.' Results were astonishing. Corruption all but disappeared, the schools ceased to be a political football, streets were kept clean, public health supervision became a reality, and city officials, obliged to submit itemized budgets, found public expenditures for many services shrinking. Observers from other American cities came to speak of Detroit as the incredible municipality that had no political machine.

Some of these benefits were attributable to the Detroit Bureau of Governmental Research, a fact-finding body established in 1916 and initially financed by individual public-spirited citizens who had noted the performance of a similar bureau established in New York. Good will, its sponsors averred, was insufficient for a well-run city without factual knowledge to guide policy. From the Bureau's first reports came the reorganization of the city's accounting procedures. A series of studies of local conditions, of the effects of experimental measures, and of probable wise moves for the future made the Detroit Bureau a valuable instrument of good government. When Wayne University emerged from the Detroit Teachers' College into the status of a municipal university, additional useful studies of civic problems and wider understanding of city needs followed. The Prohibition era, when bootleggers made the most of Detroit's proximity to Canada, brought new troubles, the depression another variety, and the tremendous expansion of the city during the second World War still other difficulties. But in spite of occasional lapses from the high standards the city had set for herself in 1916, municipal government operated generally with efficiency and honesty. Over the years Detroit on the whole has earned the honor implied in one student's comment: 'Detroit rules itself'.

Detroit's growth to a city of a million and a half people by 1930 was the direct result of the expansion of the automobile industry. Nearby cities shared in Michigan's monopoly of car manufacture, but plants in Flint and Pontiac were offshoots of Detroit companies and were controlled in Detroit. Early in the 1920's the industry had assumed the shape it bears today. Walter Chrysler, engineer and former executive in the General Motors Corporation, had branched out to form his own company, whose well-designed, well-built cars grew rapidly in popularity. Though lesser companies survived, Ford, General Motors, and Chrysler became the 'big three' who ruled the industry. Because competition between the 'big three' was vigorous, the public escaped the worst ills of monopoly.

Not only had Ford, now located just outside Detroit, made and sold over 13,000,000 Model T's before 1927, but inexpensive cars by the million had rolled out of factories within the city. By 1929 most householders in the United States regarded as a necessity a car of some sort, new or second-hand, equipped with a variety of gadgets or starkly utilitarian. Americans marked as an eccentric the man who chose to go without an automobile. If you could not buy outright, you bought on the instalment plan. If you had to skimp on food and wear the shabbiest of clothes, a car was still an essential. Tractors were replacing the horse-drawn seeder, the cultivator, and the reaper on America's farms. Where individual farmers could not manage purchase alone, three or four, or whole communities, pooled their funds and shared the mechanized equipment. Acres of parking lots for workmen's cars surrounded every factory in Detroit. With distances between home and job lengthening as city housing neared exhaustion, with buses and street railways unable to transport more than part of the city's working people, and with numbers of workmen to produce motor vehicles perpetually mounting, cars for driving to and from work were indeed nearly a necessity.

The depression of the 1930's revised Americans' concepts of necessity. Purchasers of new cars grew fewer and fewer as 1930 turned into 1931 and 1931 into 1932. Automobile companies reduced payrolls; men left on the job wondered when they would follow their fellows already laid off. It was no moment to press demands upon employers, even had collective bargaining been a recognized procedure in Detroit. An AF of L union, the United Automobile, Aircraft, and Vehicle Workers' union, had enlisted a large membership in Detroit during World War I, but, in attempting to hold war-time wages and new privileges after the war, the organization had been nearly annihilated. Throughout the twenties mechanization of production had steadily replaced skilled men with semi-skilled or unskilled in the automobile plants, with the result that industry-wide organization of labor, including the 41 per cent unskilled and the 58 per cent semi-skilled, was essential to success in negotiating with employers. Detroit companies had resolutely clung to the open shop, a position strengthened in 1927 by a shutdown at the Ford Motor Company while engineers retooled its River Rouge plants to make the new Ford Model A. The 100,000 jobless men from Dearborn so glutted Detroit's labor market that employers could dictate terms.

Nevertheless, by 1933 the American Federation of Labor again dared attempt organization. Unhappily, the Central Committee of the AF of L forbade the new Automobile Workers of America to enroll members over whom existing craft unions claimed jurisdiction, and not until 1936, when the CIO broke with the AF of L and the UAW threw in its lot with the CIO, did matters progress.

The critical year was 1937. The new strike device of sitting down within a plant and refusing to admit strike-breakers did not originate in Detroit. In Michigan the United Automobile Workers first used the scheme in Flint where in February 1937 the union won a collective bargaining agreement from the General Motors Corporation. That victory inspired a series of similar strikes in Detroit. At that moment Detroit's working people focused the attention of the entire country upon the city. When the first sit-down strike began at the Chrysler plants, Americans hitherto indifferent to local 'labor squabbles' became alarmed. The air was brittle with explosiveness that spring. Newspaper men called the city the 'Powder Box of America'. The least imaginative person could believe that social revolution might break out any day. And then the Governor of Michigan, Frank Murphy, formerly Mayor of Detroit and later an Associate Justice of the United States Supreme Court, stepped in, arranged a meeting between John L. Lewis, president of the CIO, and Walter Chrysler, and the upshot was contracts with the United Automobile Workers signed by all the major motor companies in Detroit. In Dearborn, violence and Ford Company defiance of the National Labor Relations Board continued for another four years. Subservient company unions staved off legal action. Most newspapers preferred to ignore the methods used by the Ford Company against union organizers or suspected 'trouble-makers'. Workmen naturally preferred employment with any other automobile company despite the good wages the Ford Company paid. Within Detroit the open shop was gone, and eventually the federal government forced Henry Ford to comply. After the second World War, strikes for a workers' pension plan and for wage increases adjusted to the cost of living took place at both the General Motors and the Chrysler plants; the union won most of its demands. In Detroit today labor holds a recognized, honorable place.

By 1940 labor conflicts in Detroit had subsided. The air had cleared for production on a scale never before dreamed of when orders for army trucks and tanks began to multiply, coming first from British and French purchasing missions, then from the United States government. American industrialists elsewhere watched with attention to see how the mighty automobile industry would respond. Were the 'big three' to resist pressure to abandon manufacture of passenger cars and commercial trucks and to protest the immediate expense and

A Detroit Factory, 1931

probable ultimate high cost of conversion of tools and assembly lines, that refusal might set an example which other industries would follow. It was Walter Reuther of the United Automobile Workers who published the famous Reuther Plan showing how the automobile companies could effect conversion to war production rapidly and economically. Though business men have frequently denied that the Reuther plan carried great weight, many informed people believed that the union leader's widely publicized proposal forced the hand of the automobile companies. With some astonishment, the American public saw Detroit's automobile executives accept the challenge, cancel their lucrative peace-time programs, in a matter of months turn their plants to military production, and admit uniformed officers to management counsels. What the automotive industry was willing to do others would undertake as best they could. The efficiency of Detroit's factories during World War II became an eighth wonder of the industrial world. The numbers of airplane engines, trucks, armored cars, half-tracks, tanks, and spare parts turned out before mid-summer 1945 ran into millions. As Detroit had been the key to big industry's attitudes in 1941, so her magnificent production record thereafter made her a symbol in men's mind of what effective organization, coupled with determination, could accomplish in a democracy.

Wherein American democracy has failed most completely was also brought home by events in Detroit. The CIO unions' full recognition of all workers, irrespective of race, had settled the question of Negro employees in Detroit's industries. In factories white and black worked side by side harmoniously. But union rulings could not guarantee full acceptance of the black man throughout the city, and some Negroes displayed at times an uncomfortable aggressiveness. The war had brought a fresh wave of Negroes from the deep South, where colored people were not permitted such freedoms and economic opportunities as they had here. At the same time a large number of southern whites came, so-called 'red necks' from Georgia, Mississippi, and Alabama, 'hillbillies' from Kentucky and Tennessee. Whites of this breed, ill-educated when not wholly illiterate, and long inured to a lowly social status in their native states, for generations had nursed their self-esteem by despising the Negro, the one element of society to which they felt surely superior. This combination of newcomers—and there were thousands of each kind—heightened immeasurably already existing racial antagonisms. Emotional and physical weariness born of personal anxieties and long hours of work built up in many better-established citizens an irritability conducive to hysteria. By 1943 the stage was set for trouble.

The Detroit race riot of the summer of 1943 makes a shameful and deeply

Detroit and Windsor, Ontario, 1932

depressing story. Later investigation proved that native fascist agitators of the worst species provoked the incidents that touched off the battle on the Belle Isle bridge that hot Sunday evening in July. Youngsters of high school age were leaders in the fighting and looting that spread through the city and lasted for nearly two days. The roots of the conflict, thoughtful men knew, went far into the past. The guilt lay upon all America, not Detroit alone. Northerners, having abolished slavery and enfranchised the Negro, for the next seventy-five years had washed their hands of him. Failure to educate the white majority in racial tolerance and respect for minority rights left a void where solid foundations were essential if the nation were to build a peaceful bi-racial civilization. The more immediate causes of Detroit's 'Bloody Week', men later concluded, lay in the shocking living conditions in the city's Negro slums and the want of decent recreational facilities in those neighborhoods. The first results of the riot were an increase in mutual distrust and a sharpening of race hatreds. Detroiters found no comfort in the knowledge that theirs was not the only American city in the 1940's to have an open and bloody clash between whites and blacks. Out of the bloodshed and violence came one good: formerly oblivious citizens were obliged to consider the meaning and consequences of racial hostilities. Careful study of how to check them and earnest endeavors to teach men how to live peacefully in a bi-racial community held out some hope for the future. *Promising Practices in Intergroup Education*, a report issued in 1946 by the Board of Education, discussed the methods tried and the progress achieved in 152 public schools in the city. Parents and teachers, as well as school children, were beginning to learn.

As the racial conflict presents Detroit's most sombre side, so the Detroit Tigers represent her most light-hearted. The Tigers are the city's big league baseball team. For the last sixty years the Tigers' victories and defeats have been of vital importance to the true Detroiter. In other American cities baseball fans follow their teams' careers with attention, but the Detroit Tigers command a city-wide devotion equalled only by that of Brooklyn, New York, to the Dodgers, and in 1953 exceeded by Milwaukee's fanatic pride in her new team. Any temptation to ascribe Detroit's passionate enthusiasm and loyalty to the youthfulness of her population is destroyed by discovery that octogenarians share the excitement of ten-year-olds when the Tigers win a game. Gloom settles over the city when the team loses. If the Tigers stand near the top place in the league, as the World Series draws near in the autumn, street corners and buses, bar-rooms, offices, and kitchens buzz with discussion of the Tigers' chances of winning the pennant. Detroit newspapers carry front page streamers when a star pitcher sprains his wrist. Batting averages are as ready on the tongue of the big business executive as on his office-boy's. When the team is playing in Detroit, it is Detroit tradition that the number of grandmothers' funerals which employees request leave to attend will mount rapidly. If the 'boss' then encounters the bereaved at the ball-park, neither feels embarrassment. For weeks of the year pride in the Tigers makes all Detroiters kin.

Apart from loyalty to the Tigers, social bonds between Detroiters are frail. The industrially powerful no longer live in the city; they have built large houses along the river to the east at Grosse Pointe, in country places to the west and north, or in Ann Arbor, seat of the University of Michigan forty miles southwest. Their business interests tie them to Detroit, and, as patrons of the arts, they contribute to her cultural opportunities. The Detroit Museum of Art today possesses a priceless collection; thousands of people yearly throng to see it and the special collections on loan. People of taste and wealth support the Detroit Symphony Orchestra. Wayne University is earning increasing recognition as an institution of national importance. Yet the nearly two million residents of Detroit lack a sense of civic cohesion. Men endeavor to elect honest city officials, because experience has proved the costs of corruption. But no one brags proudly of being a Detroiter. Impersonality enshrouds the community. The city constitutes a geographical expanse within which, for a price, householders receive city water, gas, electricity, and transportation. Growth has been too recent to give permanence to any neighborhood, and apartment houses lining miles of streets shelter a perpetually shifting succession of families who move as their economic status improves or as the breadwinners change jobs. Most big American cities of mid-century see a somewhat similar shifting of population, but in New York, Philadelphia, Boston, and even Chicago, the flux appears to leave some sections stable by comparison. While Hamtramck preserves its independence and some of its Polish flavor, in Detroit the distinctive national colonies of the first World War era and earlier are disappearing; restricted immigration for the past thirty years has prevented the arrival of new foreign-born and hastened the process of wiping out cultural differences deriving from differences in national origin. Because of the extensive exodus of the well-to-do to outlying residential towns, citizens of Detroit proper are primarily working men and their families, minor executives of the city's commercial houses and industries, and the army of clerks. The taxes levied upon business property supply most of the funds for city administration. Detroit has thus become a city inhabited by people of limited means, many of them possessing meagre cultural backgrounds.

Outwardly, much of Detroit is drab. The visitor may at first sight be incredulous that for twenty years this can have been the fourth city of the United States, or, now that Los Angeles has pushed into fourth place, that Detroit still ranks fifth. Though automobiles jam wide streets and miles of two- and three-story buildings house shops, warehouse goods, or people, signs of a great metropolis are few. Near the river an area of skyscrapers, huge hotels, and department stores is impressive; a similar business center at the city's edge where the offices of the General Motors Corporation have arisen is dignified, but haphazard expansion has left Detroit with half a dozen business sections, instead of a lower Manhattan Wall Street or a Chicago Loop. The nearest semblance of a subway consists of the tunnels under the Detroit river, one for automobiles, the other for railroad trains running into Canada. Architecture, generally a mélange of everything, attains its chief distinction in the one-story, scientifically planned automobile factories located in various parts of the city. Here at night ghostly blue lights cast eery shadows into the streets, whence the onlooker can watch mammoth machines feeding conveyor belts and phantom men assembling parts. Otherwise, little picturesque remains. The smoke of modern industry grays all outer things into monotone.

Yet however commonplace the city may look, Detroit's vitality is unmistakable. The stranger can best sense it by observing what happens near an automobile factory at the end of a workshift. A prosaic, empty-looking neighborhood suddenly comes alive. At the shriek of factory sirens, a flood of men spill into the streets, filling them in a few seconds from curb to curb. Out of the factory yards and parking lots stream hundreds and hundreds of cars, 'on the steering wheel of each the calloused hands of a working man'. Writers have truthfully described this as 'the most exciting spectacle in all Detroit'.

Henry Ford died in 1947, leaving his grandson Henry II, still a very young man, to succeed him as president of the Ford Motor Company. The older man, chief exponent of extreme individualism, for forty years had stood in the way of every move toward collective bargaining; he had exercised a feudal despotism. Only at the very end of his life had national laws forced him to yield somewhat. Of his grandson men have had hopes for a more enlightened view. But in spite of the might of Ford, Detroit in the last fifteen years has effected a social revolution, virtually bloodless and the more solid for that reason. For a century a center of conservatism, the city has accepted a totally new order. Although citizens' feeling for Detroit as a community runs low, she embodies much of what is vigorous in modern America. If Reuther of the United Automobile Workers and now President of the CIO appears to have become more big business man than representative of the little fellow of his union, Detroit in the 1950's, unlike Seattle, shows few signs of succumbing to a dictatorship. Recognizing the vulnerability of her position on the 'great circle' route from northern Siberia, Detroiters are less isolationist in sentiment than once they were. On domestic issues facing the country, Detroit may well shape the liberalism of the United States of tomorrow.

# IX

# Washington, the Federal City

LIKE men the world over, Americans built their towns and cities where geographic conditions promised the first settlers and later promoters a profitable future. The single notable exception in American history is the capital of the United States, Washington in the District of Columbia, founded for the sole purpose of serving as the national capital. For a European it may be hard to comprehend that the seat of government of a world power is not also inescapably the vital center of the country. The Briton looks upon London, the Frenchman upon Paris, as the embodiment of national feeling, but Washington in American eyes epitomizes only one phase of American life, national politics. Today when men on Capital Hill, the President of the United States from the White House, and the Secretary of State from his office in Foggy Bottom appear to Americans to exercise greater influence on world affairs than people in any other one city on earth, Washington still represents neither the heart nor the brain of America. Men of intelligence and genuine humanity are gathered here, but citizens of the District of Columbia have had no vote in national elections since 1800, have had no local self-government since 1878 and have acquired political experience only by observation. The perceptive American in Washington knows that Washington residents, permanent or temporary, by no means determine or even greatly affect national sentiment. So widely do Americans share this view that even in mid-twentieth century proposals occasionally recur to move the capital to the Midwest where, men contend, the federal administration could better feel the pulse of the American people.

In the 1780's when plans to found a national capital took shape, leaders of the new Confederation believed that the Congress could maintain freedom of action only by establishing a seat of government where no local pressures could obtain, in short, in a locality exclusively under the control of Congress. In drafting the federal Constitution in 1787, the founding fathers, in fact, incorporated a provision for a federal city outside the jurisdiction of any one state. Citizens of a federal district, though citizens of the United States, would not be citizens of a state; therefore, in keeping with a basic principle of federalism, whereby votes in national affairs were restricted to enfranchised residents of the states, citizens of a federal area claiming no state citizenship could not upset the delicate balance of

216

the new union. An occasional contemporary statement revealed awareness of the consequences for residents of the district to be formed, but in 1788 and 1789 statesmen of the new federal Union were too concerned with evolving a sound method of putting the hard-won Constitution into effect to borrow trouble about the political rights of a still unborn federal city. The question was rather where to locate it. Congress empowered the President, George Washington, the one man universally trusted in the United States, to select the site.

Washington had been a surveyor in his earlier years and thus combined some technical knowledge of ground suitable for a city with understanding of political considerations. To keep as close touch as possible between the states at either extremity of the two-thousand-mile stretch along the Atlantic seaboard, the capital must be located mid-way. Washington's choice fell upon a site on the Potomac river about a hundred miles from its mouth, part of the land in Virginia, part in Maryland. Some of the area was swampland and most of it was low-lying. But the river, though impeded by falls just above tide-water, offered a link through Cumberland Gap to the trans-Alleghany country, and that fact loomed large in Washington's mind. Moreover, location near the sea where coast-wise ships could provide easy access was a virtual necessity in days when roads were non-existent or nearly impassable for months of the year. And, finally, anyone with a smattering of geography could see that this location on the Potomac was more nearly central for the nation of 1790 than any northern site.

Nevertheless, although conflict between slave states and free had not then assumed the proportions it would attain thirty years later, men of the North were apprehensive at having the capital placed in slave-holding territory. Furthermore, Philadelphia and New York, the first capitals and cities of great importance in the nation, were reluctant to be passed over. Perhaps Philadelphians and New Yorkers would have contended less eagerly for the honor had they believed Congress would dare, the constitutional provision notwithstanding, to strip them of their state citizenship. Certainly belief was general that wherever the capital city arose, there a powerful commercial and financial center would also develop. Jefferson's papers describe the compromise that induced Congress to accept President Washington's choice. Jefferson, Virginia-born and Secretary of State in Washington's first cabinet, believed strongly in the desirability of a southern site, just as he opposed the proposal of the Secretary of the Treasury, Alexander Hamilton, to have the new federal government take over the debts incurred by the individual states during the Revolution. A small dinner party in New York arranged between the two cabinet members resolved the problem: Jefferson's friends promised to persuade Virginia representatives to support assumption of state debts, and influential proponents of Hamilton's plan under-took to align Northern votes for a southern capital. So the votes passed, with the provision that for a ten-year period Philadelphia should be the seat of the government. Virginia and Maryland then ceded to the United States all claim to land included in a ten-mile square, Congress voted to name this square the District of Columbia, and the President agreed to undertake arrangements for building the federal city there. Until Congress decreed otherwise, the laws of Virginia and Maryland were to continue to run in the District.

Washington, as the agent of Congress, chose Pierre L'Enfant, a gifted French engineer, to plan the projected city, and appointed three Commissioners to supervise construction of public buildings and to stake out lots for sale. Benjamin Banneker, a Negro engineer and mathematician, served on L'Enfant's staff. Washington himself negotiated the purchases of property for federal purposes from individual owners. The price was £25 an acre. Two incorporated communities already existed within the limits of the District, Alexandria at its southern tip, and Georgetown lying north of the Potomac between the river and Rock creek, a small tributary. Fortunately L'Enfant had no wish to place the government city at either location. He selected the highest spot north of the Potomac between the Anacostia river and Rock creek as the focal point where the Capitol building should stand and from which broad avenues should radiate. The President's house was to be built a mile to the west near the shores of the Potomac. In 1790, if a painting made fifty years later were not wholly romanticized, wooded knolls and open fields covered most of the area of L'Enfant's choice; the grounds selected for the President's house lay near the tidal estuary formed by Tiber creek where it emptied into the Potomac below Georgetown. Since small plantations, previously within Maryland, occupied most of the site of Washington City, no problem arose over clearing the land of buildings. Nevertheless, the inevitable soon occurred. L'Enfant and the Commissioners quarrelled, and the Frenchman retired in indignation at changes in his layout. Years afterward, officials revived the partially executed plan, and the Washington of today follows in general the original pattern L'Enfant had conceived.

Meanwhile the Commissioners proceeded with their business. In September 1791 they named the federal city Washington. One feature of the transactions which was to prove of utmost importance to residents of Washington City was the extent of the land set aside for streets and federal buildings; the President had reserved over half the total acreage within the city limits for streets and 541 acres for public buildings. As national property all that was tax-free. The remaining 1,964 acres, when sold to private individuals, would have to carry the whole tax burden of running the city, except in so far as Congress might vote money to the municipality. Though no one foresaw that difficulty in the 1790's, to the ruination of speculators lots in Washington sold slowly. By 1800, however, inhabitants numbered over 3,000 souls, 623 of them slaves. By summer the Commissioners had the Capitol near enough completion to warrant moving the government from Philadelphia. A few sloops sufficed to transport all official documents and the household effects of government employees to the new capital. Despite the Commissioners' efforts to have everything in readiness, federal functionaries, arriving fresh from the elegance of Philadelphia, beheld a discouraging sight. Pennsylvania Avenue, intended to be the great thoroughfare from the Capitol to the Executive Mansion, was a broad swathe cleared of trees but still overgrown with swamp alder; lumber and debris cluttered the innumerable vacant lots; a few shops had opened on the Hill, and scattered dwellings stood ready to turn into boarding houses. It was scant consolation that the Capitol and the President's house, not yet finished, looked solid and dignified. Disorder was everywhere. But the federal city, however depressing, was now a reality.

When Congress convened in November, the problem postponed during the preceding decade became pressing. What form was the government of Washington City and of the District to take? Congress could presumably delegate power to a municipality of its own creation, but, men asked, might it not also leave matters as they were, keeping Maryland laws in force in the District north of the Potomac and Virginia's in the part south of the river? Citizens of Alexandria, a busy commercial port, were particularly vigorous in opposing any plan that would disenfranchise them. Congressmen countered: 'It was undoubtedly the intention of the framers of the Constitution that after this territory became the seat of government no authority but that of Congress should be in force.' In a series of able articles in the *National Intelligencer*, Augustus Woodward, later a territorial judge in Michigan but in 1800 a resident of Washington, argued that if the Constitution needed amendment to permit District citizens to vote, then an amendment must be enacted at once, for otherwise Congress would be denying 'natural law' and flouting the very principle for which Americans had fought the Revolution—no taxation without representation. Congress hesitated. Temporarily it vested executive power over the District in the President and judicial authority in courts modelled on Maryland's. While the scramble for appointments to federal office went forward as Thomas Jefferson took over the Presidency from the defeated John Adams, the question of a permanent system of local government hung in the balance. At length, in May 1802, Congress granted the federal city a charter of incorporation giving local white property-owners and

'Georgetown and Federal City, or City of Washington', 1801

The three-arched bridge on the left spanned Rock creek. The artist has heightened the hills and romanticized the scene

householders with a $100 estate the right to elect a city Council, but denying them a vote for the President and Vice-President or for a District representative in Congress. The property qualifications corresponded to those in effect in most of the states; the extraordinary fact is that a proposal for universal manhood suffrage in the city failed of passing the House of Representatives by only two votes. The President appointed the Mayor. Mayor and Council levied local taxes. In 1804 Congress empowered the city to establish schools, while new charters for Alexandria and Georgetown confirmed most of their former political rights, except participation in national elections. Over the next sixty years Washington City won a few added privileges—in 1820 an elective mayoralty and in 1848 white manhood suffrage in local elections, but Congressional authority still loomed in the background, and citizens felt their political status a matter of Congressional favor, not assured right.

While the blurring of federal and city responsibilities created confusions, these held less significance for the community than other features of life in Washington. Five factors more immediately affected the character of the antebellum city: the climate, the poverty of the municipality, the meagreness of industrial and commercial growth in the District, the large proportion of transients, and the existence of slavery.

Americans who are obliged to spend June, July, or August in the District of Columbia frequently wonder at the insensibility of so sensible man as George Washington in deliberately choosing this spot for the site of a city. Some evidence suggests that the climate has worsened since the eighteenth century, for Jefferson wrote of sharp winters in the 1780's when the ice lay thick over Chesapeake Bay, and no letters of that era mention the oppressive heat of summer in the region. Yet drainage was poor at best, and the swampy land near the Potomac bred mosquitoes and disease. The White House, standing near the tidal marshes at the mouth of Tiber creek, was less comfortably located than were the government buildings to the east on Capitol Hill. As the Tiber was an open sewer until 1871, the occupants of the White House and of all the buildings nearby were exposed in warm weather to nauseous odors. Engineering, in time, could alter the sewerage system; it could not improve the climate itself. Modern Washington is healthful, but perspiring government employees today curse her summer climate, as their predecessors have done for five generations. In the antebellum period, offices closed at three in the afternoon, and long after the turn of the century the tempo of the city slowed every summer to the langorous pace suited to the semi-tropics. Before 1933 no one expected anyone to do anything in Washington between late May and October.

The second problem, the impoverishment of the municipality, was the result of having few tax-payers to provide for a tremendous layout. True, the city before 1860 covered only a small segment of her present-day area, but Congress appropriated nothing at all for maintenance of streets during her first twenty years and niggardly sums thereafter. While Congressmen complained about the mud of winter and the dust of summer, they left to private property-holders the obligation of supplying money through taxes to improve conditions. City health supervision was in similar case. Up to 1856, volunteers manned the Board of Health. Until Congress belatedly agreed to finance an aquaduct, completed in 1863, residents had to rely upon cisterns and wells; Philadelphia's water works went into operation in 1801, New York's in 1842, Boston's in 1848. Again, anxiety about city finances interfered with development of public schools in Washington. Indeed, in view of the demands upon the city budget and in view of the Southern tradition of private schools, supplemented in some communities by 'poor schools' maintained by charity, the action of the city Council in 1805 must rank as highly liberal: the Council imposed a luxury tax on wines and spirits, slaves, carriages, and the like and assigned the proceeds to the support of two schools; poor white children might attend without any fee, well-to-do must pay tuition, but the trustees and the principals were pledged to strict secrecy about who were charity pupils, who paying. Opposition nullified the scheme before it was well started. Taxpayers objected to its extravagance, the Council halved funds, and citizens, humble and wealthy alike, soon refused to send their children to 'the pauper schools'. Thirty years later a survey revealed that 75 per cent of the city's children were receiving no education whatsoever. Free Negroes meanwhile established their own schools and, in the face of some white hostility, maintained them. Public schools free for all white children first appeared in the 1840's. Thereafter a senator who brought his family to Washington might enter his children in a public school, but he still was not ready to fight for Congressional appropriations to support an adequate local school system, although federal land grants to the territories for that purpose were customary.

The third feature that marked nineteenth-century Washington was her restricted economic development. The hopes of permanent residents of building an economy independent of federal government activities were repeatedly dashed. George Washington had selected the site on the Potomac partly because it promised to permit commercial ties with the new West. In response to his urgings, as early as 1785 Virginia and Maryland had chartered the Potomac Company to improve navigation from the river's headwaters, more than 220 miles inland, to tidewater, and by 1802 engineers had completed canals and locks around the series of falls above Georgetown. Unfortunately the alternate turbulence and shallowness of the river made it unsafe for boats laden with fifty barrels of flour, the load the charter required the Company to provide for. Unable to raise the funds needed to enlarge its work, the Potomac Company expired in 1825. But the dream of making the capital a great commercial center did not die. In that year a new company obtained a charter calling for the construction of a canal along the river to the mountains and thence over the 1,900 foot elevation to the Ohio. Despite the scruples of 'strict constructionists' in Congress who questioned the constitutional powers of the federal government to undertake 'internal improvements', Congress invested $1,000,000 of federal money in the Chesapeake and Ohio Canal Company, Maryland $500,000, the three cities of the District $1,500,000, and private individuals another few thousands. On 4 July 1828, the very day on which Baltimore began construction of the Baltimore and Ohio railroad, President John Quincy Adams turned the first spade of earth to inaugurate the start of the waterway designed to connect the Potomac with the Ohio. But an over-elaboration of the original plan brought the city close to bankruptcy and slowed the work. In the 1840's, as the canal neared Cumberland at the base of the mountains, canal boats brought down increasing quantities of up-country farm produce into Georgetown or on to markets in Alexandria. Nevertheless by 1846 Alexandria felt her commerce so hampered by District rule that she persuaded Congress to re-cede her to Virginia. At the same time all the section of the District south of the Potomac reverted to Virginia. Georgetown similarly sought reincorporation into Maryland, but Congress rejected that plea. Although the canal reached Cumberland in 1850, the Company, faced with the competition of the Baltimore and Ohio railroad, abandoned the project of carrying the waterway over the mountains to the Ohio. Thus, while the canal helped the up-country farmers, it failed to become the commercial artery hoped for.

Meanwhile, residents of Washington and Georgetown planned to channel water from the canal through water wheels to build industrial enterprise in the District of Columbia. After 1837, when Congress granted the Company the right to sell surplus water, the Company, eager to raise capital, sold water to several Georgetown flour mills and a foundry, but in Washington no significant industry developed. Even in Georgetown, though the power available exceeded that used by most mills in New England, industrial growth was slight. If men occasionally grumbled that Congress, preferring to conduct its business in a non-industrial city, was to blame, the accusation was patently unjust. Why, if District citizens were anxious to promote industrialization, they so neglected opportunity remains to this day a puzzle. Perhaps the answer lies in their background:

**VIEW OF WASHINGTON.**

*Published and sold by E. Sachse & Co., Baltimore, Md.*

View of Washington, 1851

The portrayal of the proposed new wings of the Capitol and the still unfinished Washington Monument is imaginative, and the Tiber canal is idealized. The towered building on the Mall in front of the Monument is the Smithsonian museum. Pennsylvania Avenue stretches from the Capitol to the White House

permanent residents were chiefly Southerners whose training ill-equipped them for organizing large industrial ventures and whose direct contacts with sources of credit were few.

For all their local influence, Congressmen were not permanent residents of Washington. Though sometimes a representative, re-elected again and again, would spend a number of winters in the city, his home remained elsewhere. His political career required him to keep close touch with his constituency and to view Washington as a temporary abode. Before 1860 it was the exception rather than the rule even for senators, with six-year terms of office, to rent or buy houses here. Instead, most government officials lived in boarding houses or hotels and felt neither responsibility for nor keen interest in the city as such. Official life, on the other hand, for many years was both agreeable and dignified. Under the Virginia dynasty from Thomas Jefferson's Presidency up to and including James Monroe's, men of distinction and cultivation held government posts in the new capital, and John Quincy Adams, President from 1825 to 1829, also appointed men of cosmopolitan tastes.

Hence when the election of Andrew Jackson brought to the federal city his vociferous supporters from the backwoods and raw settlements of the West, the shock to Washington society was overwhelming. Receptions at the White House, once conducted with due formality, turned into truly public affairs attended by all and sundry who had helped put 'Old Hickory' into office and who regarded their President's house as partly their own. A story, doubtless apocryphal, tells of a small child lost during one of the White House receptions, whose parents at length found her jumping upon a handsome old sofa; in response to her mother's anxious cries, the little girl exclaimed: 'Just think, Mamma! this sofa is a millionth part mine.' All Washington stirred to satisfaction or indignation, depending upon the political sympathies of each group in turn, when the President chivalrously determined to protect the fair name of the wife of one of his cabinet members and insisted that she be received by Washington hostesses who knew all too well Peggy Eaton's reputation when she had still been a gay widow about her father's tavern and hotel. Thereafter, social affairs in the capital lost in grace, while they gained in 'democracy'. Conservative households, now cut off from official functions, found themselves, like 'Cross-patch, draw the latch', doomed to drink their tea alone and even then refuse to call the neighbors in. After 1830, moreover, to a greater degree than formerly, permanent residents of the capital saw about them a perpetual shifting, a succession of new faces, other minds. The continuity felt under earlier administrations disappeared. This change emphasized the seasonal character of the city's life, where the difference in tempo, winter and summer, was as pronounced as at a seaside hotel of the seventies. Washington was a winter resort when Congress was in session, a slow-moving southern village in summer.

The fifth circumstance to form community patterns was the existence of slavery. To New Englanders, the sight of coffles of slaves moving along Penn sylvania Avenue, the rattle of their chains sometimes penetrating into the chambers where Congressmen sat on the Hill, never ceased to be intensely repellent. Before mid-century Washington was a slave market of some importance. The city permitted traders to house slaves in the public jail before shipping them south by coastal vessels, and the District was easily accessible to the Maryland and northern Virginia plantations whose soil, exhausted by years of tobacco-growing, was no longer productive and whose owners had for some decades raised slaves as their principal saleable commodity. The Compromise of 1850, whereby Congress sought to check the growing disunity of North and South, included an act abolishing the slave trade in the District of Columbia, but slave-owning Congressmen were still allowed to bring their servants with them, and many well-to-do Washingtonians kept two or three slaves. Even an order of Catholic Sisters owned a few. It was anxiety lest educated Negroes stir up trouble among slaves that fostered local opposition to Negro schools. Shocked and disapproving Northerners and slightly defiant Southerners, obliged to mingle somewhat in ordinary course, together created an air of uneasiness in the city years before the outbreak of war between the states.

The Civil War changed many things in Washington. In the spring of 1861 the city became, and for the duration of the war remained, not so much an armed camp as the gathering place of camp followers, furloughed or hospitalized soldiers, and swarms of Northern business men and place-seekers. Boarding-house rooms were at a premium. The few hotels and the bar-rooms were filled with vulgar people, newly rich from profits on army contracts, with anxious parents come to inquire for their sons, with harried-looking, tired officers and unseasoned swaggering new recruits. Anyone with anything to sell could command a price for it. A hectic gaiety pervaded public places, until, as occurred several times, the Confederate army in Virginia threatened the capital; then gaiety gave way to alarm bordering on panic. In 1862 Congress decreed the emancipation of all slaves in the District. The next year, President Lincoln's Emancipation Proclamation announced the freedom of all Negroes held in servitude in states in rebellion. Thereupon, an endless stream of black people, whose owners could no longer feed them or who escaped from the South, poured into the city. There had long been a number of free Negroes in the District—some

3,000 as early as 1820, over 11,000 in 1860—self-respecting householders, small business men, barbers, draymen, cooks, and the like. But the newly freed slaves were in a different position; few of them knew how to fend for themselves. Some found menial jobs in the army, a few enlisted as soldiers, and some simply waited for 'de white folks' to take care of them. The burden of giving some form of assistance to thousands of helpless Negroes added to the difficulties of the municipal administration, already taxed by problems of policing and running the suddenly expanded city.

Then came Appomatox, brief wild celebration, the assassination of President Lincoln, grief and vindictive anger. Vice-President Johnson, sworn in as President, and members of the Cabinet joined efforts that spring of 1865 to keep the city calm. Company after company of disbanding army units marched through the streets toward the railroad station and home. Badly wounded men still filled the hospitals, and jobless Negroes thronged the streets, while the newly established Freedmen's Bureau endeavored to help colored people to help themselves. Army contractors and office seekers no longer crowded the bar-rooms and city streets, but the anticipated general exodus of newcomers failed to occur. On the contrary, according to one estimate, by 1866 the white population of the city was 40 per cent larger than in 1860 when Washington had had 50,000 white residents. Perhaps the excitements of the war-time capital persuaded some that the city would offer new peace-time opportunities. Colored people and Northern philanthropists eager to promote the well-being of the Negro continued to flood into the city. In December 1866, Congress thrust upon the District a measure that local voters had overwhelmingly rejected in 1865, namely enfranchisement of Negroes. Here was a bitter blow to a community still Southern in feeling that the Negro was an inferior race. But within the District, Congress held the power elsewhere exercised by state governments, and white men in Washington had no recourse but acquiescence. A group of radical Republicans in Congress was clearly intent upon trying out locally legislation later to be applied to the whole country.

White residents in Washington, anticipating an immediate new influx of colored people, envisaged a Negro-controlled city, and, in light of conditions developing in a state like South Carolina, where Northern 'carpet-baggers' were encouraging irresponsible Negro rule, the prospect was disquieting. Between 1866 and 1867 Washington's Negro population had increased 12 per cent. One estimate figured that Negroes owned a fifth of all privately held real estate in the city, obviously a reference to ownership of Negro-occupied property, or possibly to area, certainly not to value. Educated Negroes themselves were uneasy about the new order; law notwithstanding, local white hostility could affect them adversely in a dozen ways, most particularly in provisions for schools for Negro children. Hence Negro leaders were at pains to see that their people behaved with circumspection. Though for the first election in which both races participated Negro registration was 70 per cent of white, the colored people did not immediately put a Negro into office. In the next three years, they elected first one, then seven, and then six Negro Councilmen out of twenty-one, only one Negro Alderman. The white Mayor, elected in 1868 and 1869, was put in office by the Negro vote, and, his enemies charged, delayed needed work on city streets because of his attempt to give black men the jobs. The city debt increased by a million dollars and there was little to show for it. When Congress repealed the property qualifications for holding municipal office the wrath of white property-owners reached new heights, but proposals on the floor of the House of Representatives to move the seat of government altogether out of stiff-necked Washington frightened local business men into silence. Some way out of the morass of conflicting opinions and wants had to be found.

As in earlier years, the municipality lacked the money to provide adequate services. Only Pennsylvania Avenue and parts of other main thoroughfares had street lights; cobblestones paved only a few blocks here and there. Most sections of the city had no sewerage system whatsoever. Tiber creek, ostensibly a canal for moving freight barges between the Potomac and Anacostia rivers, served as a sewer for the area adjoining Capitol Hill; elsewhere householders still had to depend upon public scavengers to collect offal. The understaffed Board of Health and the police could not enforce the sanitary regulations. Householders dumped their garbage into the streets. Truancy left schools ill-attended, though the principal of a school in Georgetown had devised his own solution of that problem in 1853. Boys, so the story runs, had been 'playing hooky' by offering the excuse of having toothaches. The principal bought a pair of dental pincers, extracted a tooth from each complainant, and school attendance improved. As early as 1860 nearly 1,200 Negro children were enrolled in private schools, and although men now admitted the public obligation to provide for Negro education, officials were tardy or remiss in paying out public money for colored schools. The threat of higher taxes in order to open new colored schools was unwelcome to every resident.

In fact, for the capital of a vigorous and wealthy nation, the Washington of 1870 was a disgrace. She had potentialities, to be sure. Public buildings had multiplied in the seventy years since the government's move to the Potomac. Most of them were well-proportioned, solid structures built in the classical style.

Poised on the new Capitol dome, a bronze Freedom now looked eastward. South of the White House rose the 150-foot marble stub of the Washington Monument and still farther south the enchantingly ugly red-brick crenellations of the Smithsonian museum. At an angle of Pennsylvania Avenue stood Andrew Jackson's Treasury, placed, according to persistent popular legend, at the President's insistence where it would block off from the White House the sight of the Capitol. Grass now covered most of the public squares and the Capitol grounds on which soldiers had bivouacked during the war. Charming private gardens, usually walled off from the street, occasionally permitted a glimpse of roses and crepe myrtle. Still the city as a whole was too unconnected and too unfinished to have dignity. Foreign diplomats poked fun at the pretentious sweeps of the avenues, alternately thick with dust and deep in mud, and at the very emptiness of the broad vistas that one day would delight the visitor in Washington.

Although all Americans were sensitive to European ridicule, disappointment over foreigners' lack of appreciation of the city was not responsible for the campaign of the seventies to improve conditions. The sheer physical discomforts of life in Washington impelled Congress to act, and the despair of local citizens at their inability to carry through unaided any major program led them to propose drastic changes. Residents reasoned that if the federal government was determined to interfere with local wishes on important local issues, then let the federal government take some responsibility for the federal city. The Board of Trade, a group of businessmen formed in 1865 to struggle with the city's post-war unemployment problems, sponsored the plan that went into effect in 1871. Congress abrogated the city charter and made the District a federal territory with a government like that established for all national territories before admission to statehood. The President appointed a governor and members of an upper house; District voters elected a lower house and a delegate to Congress. Unfortunately, Congress made no specific appropriation of money, so that uncertainty endured about who would foot the bills for modernizing the city.

Nevertheless, under the driving force of Alexander Shepherd, the head of the new Board of Public Works, the face of Washington changed extraordinarily in the next three years. Sewers, street paving and lighting, trees planted along the avenues, the removal of unsightly nuisances, and the rerouting of the railroads that had run their tracks across the Mall at the foot of Capitol Hill had transformed the most noticeable aspects of the city before the end of 1873. The Board of Public Works, however, left the alleys untouched. L'Enfant had planned a city of large blocks, the deep lots of which presumably would allow for spacious gardens, but to simplify and conceal from daily view the unpleasant work of public scavengers, the city had split the blocks with alley-ways. Along these, shanties had sprung up where thousands of Negroes lived in utmost squalor. Shepherd and his associates, like Baron Haussmann in Paris, were less concerned with behind-the-scene improvements than with over-all effect. The effect was pleasing. The hitch was the cost. By 1874 Shepherd had run the city's indebtedness up to $19,000,000, although Congress had imposed a $10,000,000 limit. The panic of 1873 added to people's alarm at this lavish spending. Congress thereupon called a halt, substituted a temporary commission form of government, and subjected Shepherd to prolonged investigation. Washington residents were bitter. Return of a city charter with the Negro voting was distasteful to men who, one newspaper charged, were 'willing to surrender their own rights rather than respect the rights of others'. The upshot was the passage in 1878 of the so-called 'Organic Act'.

By the terms of the Organic Act, Washingtonians lost all self-government. Congress placed administration of the District in the hands of three Commissioners appointed by the President of the United States. This revolutionary change brought order out of chaos and eliminated any opportunity for graft in letting city contracts. With the advice of a Congressional committee and supported by annual Congressional appropriations or other special legislation, the Commissioners rule the District of Columbia today as they have for the last seventy-five years. In many ways they administer it well. The city streets are clean, the parks well-tended, taxes reasonable. But the District of Columbia is the only place in the United States where responsible adults have no voice in their government. The Secretary of State himself has no vote, if he be a citizen of the District. The Board of Trade, dominated by powerful real estate interests, has consistently opposed return of a city charter because of fear of the Negro vote. That fear has repeatedly helped to defeat Home Rule bills before Congress. Voters in the rest of the country fail to realize that Congressional supervision of District affairs is costly to themselves since representatives and senators elected to legislate for the nation are obliged to devote long hours to purely local problems.

Meanwhile, long before the conflicts of the seventies over Home Rule had subsided, another significant change was slowly taking shape. Little by little, Washington was beginning to lose the character of a federal city and becoming the seat of a more nearly centralized government. Adroit political manipulation during the Reconstruction period after the Civil War had initiated this change by securing the ratification of two amendments to the federal Constitution. The Radical Republicans in the saddle in Congress had determined to force the

Southern states to admit Negroes to full citizenship. Negro voters in the South would keep in power the party that had brought them freedom. The Radicals, therefore, had hurried through Congress the amendments that denied to any state the right to limit its citizenship on the basis of race, color, or former condition of servitude, or to restrict the privileges of any citizen without due process of law. By refusing to seat in Congress representatives of any state recently in rebellion until it had ratified the fourteenth amendment, the Republican extremists had assured ratification by the number of states required to make the amendment law. Confronted with these 'steamroller' tactics, supporters of 'states' rights' were helpless. The fifteenth amendment aimed at forcing Negro suffrage upon all the states. The 'due process' clause of the fourteenth amendment, ostensibly designed to protect helpless new citizens, in the 1880's and 1890's turned into a powerful weapon in the hands of corporations seeking to protect their monopolies and battling labor organizations. But the immediate effects of the new constitutional provisions were to weaken the control of the states over their citizens and to vest much of it in the federal government. For Washington, the heightening of the power of Congress and the President at the expense of the states at first made little difference, but gradually, as the prestige of the federal government increased, residents of the city began as never before to bask in reflected glory. Residence in the capital came to seem desirable to people of means even if they had no official function here.

Thus as Washington ceased to be an independent municipality, she found new compensations in serving as the national capital. Growing wealth in the nation brought an ever mounting number of affluent senators who, like 'Haw' Tabor of Colorado, found the glitter of official society a prize worth angling for. Diamonds and elegant gowns adorned their wives and daughters on state occasions, and private parties again became as correct and formal as in the first years of the nineteenth century. If the day book of the wife of a government clerk be any clue, minor officials also led a pleasant life. Menus for the dinner parties given by relatively insignificant underlings in the early 1880's list at least six courses, beginning, perhaps, with Chesapeake Bay oysters and moving on *via* woodcock or quail to a savory, each course accompanied by a suitable French wine. Nor was life in Washington devoted exclusively to government business and frivolity. Men of letters gathered here, sometimes to observe and report upon the political scene, sometimes to participate in the brilliance of a society in which great international figures appeared at intervals, and perhaps always in order to enjoy the serenity that Americans in the United States of the Gilded Age could find only in a non-commercial, non-industrial community. Henry Adams, the most distinguished of this literary group, later explained that he came to live in Washington 'partly to write history, but chiefly because his seven years of laborious banishment in Boston convinced him that, as far as he had a function in life, it was as stable-companion to statesmen'.

Other scholars, moreover, were beginning to discover in the Library of Congress resources for the study of American history hitherto little tapped. Thomas Jefferson's books formed the original backbone of the Congressional Library, though a fire in mid-century destroyed two-thirds of that priceless collection as well as many volumes acquired later. But after the Civil War acquisitions by gift and purchase made the Library the repository of both valuable Americana and important government publications. The Peter Force collection alone, books and papers which Force, one-time Mayor of Washington, editor, antiquary, book-lover, and magpie, had accumulated over a life-time, contributed to turning the Library into the American equivalent of the British Museum library. Upon the completion in 1897 of a large, new, ornate Italian Renaissance building to house the collections, the Congressional Library offered facilities for historical research such as were available nowhere else in the United States. Under the direction of an eminent Librarian appointed by the President the importance of the Library to scholars increased with every year.

Five universities within the District of Columbia added to the city's stature. George Washington had hoped to see the federal government sponsor a national university in the capital and had requested that his shares in the canal company be used to help found such an institution. It never materialized, partly because the shares became worthless a few years after Washington's death in 1799, but chiefly because later Presidents and Congresses lost interest in the plan. Georgetown University, however, emerged from a Catholic seminary founded before the District of Columbia came into existence, and in 1821 Baptists opened the Columbian College which became a university in 1873 and later took the name George Washington University. The Catholic University of America was incorporated in 1887, and Methodists organized American University in 1893. More notable still in many respects was Howard University, established in 1866 by Northern humanitarians to enable Negroes to obtain professional training. Its founders, eager to prove the feasibility of a bi-racial institution, entered their own sons in the first class. In time, Howard became more largely a Negro than a mixed university, but some white students enrolled yearly.

Yet these new interests and broader culture changed Washington only superficially. The influences that had shaped her before the Civil War still operated, although in somewhat different form. By 1880, citizens of the District of Columbia had resigned themselves to having no industry and only such other business as would cater for the comfort of government officials. The narrowness of other economic opportunity now became an accepted fact. On the other hand, while Congress after 1878 voted more generous funds than formerly for public services in the District, many civic needs remained unfilled, because of too little money from either federal appropriations or local taxes. The summer heat, heavy with moisture, was still unrelieved, and not until the government in the late 1930's began to install air-conditioning units in new federal buildings could government employees work in some comfort between May and late September. Changes in administrations and the limited numbers of federal jobs covered by the provisions of the Civil Service Act of 1884 kept the turnover of householders in Washington high and perpetuated the sense of impermanence among most residents of the capital. And finally, though slavery was no longer a question, the problem of the Negro in the city took its place as a recurrently troublesome issue.

After the mid-seventies, Congress, despite its one-time ardor for Negro rights, successfully shut its eyes to the plight of Washington's growing colored population; a small annual appropriation to Howard University apparently soothed Congressmen's conscience. Southern sentiment among white citizens of this abidingly Southern community decreed that Negroes must be 'kept in their place'. Consequently, where no specific law forbade, segregation continued. 'Jim Crow' cars no longer ran upon the city's trolley tracks, but white restaurants refused to serve Negro customers, a form of discrimination which continued until prohibited in 1953 by a Supreme Court ruling. Colored schools were few, ill-equipped, and staffed with an inadequate force of Negro teachers. Occupations open to colored people multiplied discouragingly slowly; illiteracy or meagre schooling barred many of them from well-paid jobs. Nevertheless, in the face of these handicaps, the Negro community came to include a growing number of relatively well-to-do families who developed a gentle culture of which white people knew little or nothing. Graduates of Howard University entered the professions and served their people well. Whatever the restrictions on their freedoms, colored people in Washington probably fared better than in other urban centers where any considerable number of black people had congregated. Here they constituted 33 per cent of the population in 1890, a larger proportion than in any other big city in the country. Nation-wide concern over the status of Negro citizens of the United States would not appear until the 1930's.

At the turn of the century, Washington, for all her new air of cosmopolitan sophistication, remained curiously provincial. Learned societies made the capital their headquarters without deeply affecting the life of the city. The dynamic

The Arlington Memorial Bridge, Lincoln Memorial, and
Washington Monument, 1931
The round open plot at right is the site of the Jefferson Memorial completed in 1939

Theodore Roosevelt entered and departed from the White House, leaving behind
him a more vigorous government and a new conception of public responsibilities;
but Washingtonians had seen a long succession of Presidents come and go and
were less stirred with excitement than men elsewhere in the country. More
absorbing to Washington than 'trust-busting' programs and national conservation legislation was the outcome of a conference of American architects held in
the city in 1900, on the occasion of her first centennial. A commission appointed
to prepare recommendations for an improved park system submitted a report in
1902 which called for sweeping changes in the layout of the whole city. Three
members of the special commission had shared in planning the grounds and
buildings for Chicago's Columbian Exposition. Daniel Burnham, its director,
Frederick Olmstead, the noted landscape architect, and Augustus St Gaudens, the

most widely recognized of American sculptors, had learned from experience what enthusiasm and concerted effort could accomplish. If determination and skill could convert the dreary swamps of South Chicago in two years into a 'White City', well directed effort could effect permanent improvements in Washington which would transform her into the stately capital L'Enfant had dreamed of more than a century before. Political embroilments prevented prompt action upon some features of this new plan, but over the years the National Capital Planning Commission and allied bodies have carried out its essentials.

A new Union Railroad Station was a first utilitarian step. After 1907, the new-comer arriving in the city by train emerged into the street not from any one of a series of train sheds but from an imposing spacious hall on to a porticoed plat-form from which his view of the Capitol on the Hill was interrupted only by great fountains. At the western end of the Mall beyond the Washington Monu-ment, a memorial to Abraham Lincoln was to be erected, but engineers had to fill the swampy tidal land along the Potomac at that point, before the Greek temple to house the marble statue of the 'Great Emancipator' could arise. When finished in 1922, the Lincoln Memorial became at once the spot which every American tourist visited while in Washington. Even Southerners, with memories of the Civil War still strong within them, came to look at Daniel French's portrayal of the man who had preserved the federal union. Beyond the Lincoln Memorial stretches the Arlington Memorial bridge across the Potomac to the national cemetery and Robert E. Lee's mansion. Projected in the 1840's, included in the architects' plan in 1902, the bridge was built and opened in 1932. Linking, as it does, the memorial to the hero of the North with the home of the great Virginian, Robert E. Lee, General of the Confederate armies and the idol of the South, the bridge for the historically minded American today symbolizes the healing of once bitter cleavages. In 1942, the federal government completed the Jefferson Memorial, built on tidal fill downstream from the Arlington bridge. On the inner walls of the slightly modified reproduction of the Rotunda of the University of Virginia, which Jefferson himself designed, bronze letters spell out passages from the most noble and moving of Jefferson's writings. Set among the Japanese cherry trees lining the 'Tidal Basin', the Jefferson Memorial constitutes a fitting and beautiful shrine to the first great American democrat.

Well before the completion of this extensive architectural and landscaping program, Americans from every nook and cranny of the United States had begun to regard a visit to Washington as a goal to achieve at some time in their lives. Perhaps not quite a case of 'See Rome and then die', Americans still felt that a trip to the capital was a privilege of which every citizen should avail himself. Schools

'At the Neptune Fountain', about 1899

organized spring holiday tours for students and teachers who came by train or chartered bus every year. As automobiles made family expeditions easy, the procession of tourists' cars grew in length, at first rolling in when the cherry trees were in bloom or during the summer months, more recently at all seasons. Second only to government itself, the main business of Washington has become the tourist trade. Specially trained guides, thoroughly instructed in the history of the institution to which they are attached, explain to eager tourists the origins of the paintings and sculpture in the Capitol on the Hill, the growth and tasks of the Bureau of Engraving and the Mint, the functioning and procedures of the United States Supreme Court sitting in its marble halls. Every Saturday morning, rain or shine, a queue of men, women, and children string out along Pennsylvania Avenue waiting their turn to walk through the public rooms of their White House. While the observer will see incongruously posed groups being photographed at the threshold of one national shrine or another and will overhear from the crowds absurd comments on American history, he can hardly fail to be moved by the passion of pride and interest in their national capital which these hordes of tourists display.

However admirable this national enthusiasm for the sights of Washington, it raised in the minds of sober citizens of the District questions of whether the resulting stress upon the outer and visible in the city did not hamper the growth of an inner and spiritual grace. Save during war time, when their motto became 'Beauty Can Wait', the Commissioners and the District Committee of Congress never considered sharp curtailment of expenditures for the maintenance of the parks, for keeping fountains playing, or for floodlighting the Capitol dome, the Washington Monument, or the statue of Lincoln. But public schools, particularly colored schools, were overcrowded, playgrounds in the most densely populated sections of the city were wanting, and welfare services were of a meagreness that Cincinnati or Denver, Seattle or even Holyoke would not have tolerated. Visitors, charmed by flower beds, trees, and gleaming white marble buildings, were not likely to see the primitive, insanitary slums stretching out southeast of the Capitol or in scattered areas northeast. In the 1920's government funds redeemed Foggy Bottom, near the Potomac below Georgetown, to serve as a site for new State Department buildings, and cleared Swampoodle, one of the Negro quarters of the late nineteenth century, in order to make place for more rentable houses. But innumerable spots remained in the District, where poverty-stricken Negro families dwelt in misery. In the Smithsonian Institution a pen sketch recently hung, dated 1934 and entitled 'Five Blocks from the White House'. It showed a Negro wash-woman standing over a tub in the yard, a dilapidated, sagging-roofed outhouse at her back. Similar sights are still visible in the capital of the nation known the world over for its dedication to plumbing. An Alley Dwelling Authority established in 1934 undertook the razing of the worst of these breeding places of disease and crime, but the second World War stopped the program before it was more than well started. While Citizens' Associations, made up of white residents, and parallel separate Civic Associations of Negroes grew up in many neighborhoods endeavoring to better conditions, complaints or petitions to the District Commissioners often fell on deaf ears. As always, the Negroes suffered most from this neglect, and Washington's 'big business', the real estate companies, employed every subtle device conceivable to keep Negroes' living quarters confined to the least desirable sections of the city. Hundreds of discouraged Washingtonians concluded that until Home Rule returned control to local residents, the less patently visible needs of the District would go unheeded. Federal administration of the federal city cloaked local governmental anachronisms.

As the political center of national affairs, on the other hand, Washington in the twentieth century swiftly grew in importance. The process begun with the ratification of the fourteenth and fifteenth constitutional amendments now gained momentum rapidly. Within fifty years of Appomatox *federal government* had come to be rather a phrase accepted by custom than a term valid in fact. Yet national legislation was strengthening the hold of the central government at the expense of the states' when World War I broke out. The mobilization of national resources to meet that emergency then widened the area of national power as over against state until, when America looked about at the end of the war to find herself a world power, state authority, if not *de jure*, nevertheless *de facto* had dwindled to a shadow of its former importance. Boston's and Albany's, Denver's and Sacramento's loss was Washington's gain. Industrialists and bankers, groups of educators, and labor unions seeking favors or special legislation now looked to Capitol Hill instead of nearer home. In the black year 1932 'armies of the unemployed' marched toward the White House as the one source whence help could come.

Into this situation in 1933 moved Franklin D. Roosevelt and his supporters. With vigorous hand and sure political insight the President began a revitalizing of the national government, fallen into a slough of despond and impotence by the overwhelming disasters of the depression. Money poured out upon hundreds of federal projects directed by tens of new government agencies, each with headquarters in Washington. 'Braintrusters' from the country's leading universities appeared to take charge of a vast spending program and to map out new undertakings. Hope, welling up in the hearts of men who had despaired of the future of this materialistic, seemingly foundering nation, brought to government service in Washington a host of able, idealistic, professionally trained men and women eager to share in the rebuilding the New Deal promised. Federal employment assumed now dignity in America's eyes. In time, disillusionment with what they felt to be the ineptitudes of a growing bureaucracy took many of the first comers away but the imprint of the New Deal remained. Washington after 1933 never resumed her earlier placid imperturbability. As growing numbers of Negroes, encouraged by official policies of non-discrimination, passed Civil Service examinations and found government jobs in the city, white people who worked with them side by side began to see that color was no bar to competence. While white prejudice still kept Negroes out of the better paid jobs, and occasional anger flared out at 'Nigger lovers', many citizens of the District learned to shed some of their racial antagonisms.

Washington during World War II, in the American language, was a 'mad house'. To Army, Navy, and Air Force, War Production and Price Control Boards, the War Manpower Commission and innumerable other American agencies, every allied government added special missions, all centering their activities in the District of Columbia. An acid jest described murders committed to dispose of occupants of apartments or rooms into which the triumphant murderer would promptly move. Government employees jammed streetcars and buses morning and evening, as petrol- and tire-rationing made use of private cars an unthinkable luxury. On the main avenues where nothing less decorous than horse-drawn carriages and automobiles had been seen since 1900, bicyclers appeared in swarms, pedalling to and from offices within the city or out across the bridge to the mighty Pentagon, the new home of the War Department in Arlington. Typists and stenographers, recruited fresh out of high school, came from every small town in the country. Hotel lobbies, the rendezvous of all sorts and kinds of people, important and insignificant alike, revealed the kaleidoscopic quality of Washington's war-time busyness. Of the older hotels where similar crowds had milled about in Civil War days and after, only the Willard still commanded prestige, while huge new palatial structures far uptown vied with each other to boast of the most distinguished patrons. In these hotel lobbies the accelerated pace of life was more perceptible than anywhere else in Washington. Though Americans called the city the greatest 'rumor factory' in the world, people worked hard at their jobs. Even the 'cliff-dwellers', the self-adopted name of well-to-do, long-established Washington families unconnected with government posts, were obliged to see themselves in these years as only a small segment of an international community bending every effort to win the war.

Post-war adjustments were slower to take effect than in 1919. The dominant position of the United States in world affairs justified continuation of some erst-while war agencies, and while many Americans thankfully hastened home to resume their former occupations, others were reluctant to leave the capital. Apart from the sections of Virginia and Maryland which compose Greater Washington, the city in the decade of the 1940's added nearly 150,000 inhabitants to the 663,000 at the end of the 1930's. Official society resumed its round of cocktail and dinner parties where men arranged many of the preliminaries of plans that later became officially endorsed measures. Men came and went. In the next seven years the capital under two administrations faced a succession of grave national problems. Anxieties followed one after the other, forgotten briefly amid local amusement over the unexpected outcome of the Presidential election of 1948. Washington newspaper men who had predicted Harry Truman's overwhelming defeat gave a dinner for the President where the guest of honor enjoyed turkey while his hosts 'ate crow'. But shortly thereafter, the conviction of the former State Department official, Alger Hiss, for perjury raised doubts in the minds of many Americans in the District and out who only two years before had ridiculed the notion of Communist infiltration into government posts. The trial and its outcome shook the capital to its core and gave force to Senator McCarthy's in-quisitions. With the outbreak of war in Korea, official life in Washington became increasingly uneasy; the truce three years later lightened the atmosphere very little. And throughout, citizens of the District remained bystanders, knowing they could not influence policies in the making for either nation or city. Until the federal government saw fit to return Home Rule, citizens of Washington would continue to regard the future like the past, with fortitude qualified by indiffer-ence.

Life in modern Washington in many particulars is little different from life in the capital of the eighties. The city is bigger and contains more varied elements. The cliff-dwellers, too self-contained a group to be known to most of Washing-ton, lead their own social life, as do the university faculties. Otherwise, social affairs are semi-official. Wives, regardless of their individual gifts and interests, make a business of forwarding their husbands' careers or missions, and a party given or attended for sheer pleasure is an utmost rarity. In most other great capitals of the world a stimulating society exists independent of government circles. Not so in Washington. For officialdom, participation in the perpetual round may be exciting in its endless jockeying for position. To an astonishing extent, among federal employees a social compartmentalizing has grown up based less upon rank than upon agency. Thus people with posts in the State

Department tend to associate primarily with other State Department employees, lawyers of the Justice Department with other lawyers, and officers and civilians of the Department of Defense largely with their Pentagon neighbors. For humble people social life may be leaner and less satisfying than in any small town in the country, but many of them appear to find vicarious pleasure in the rumored doings of the great. Minor government employees sometimes contrive a pseudo-Bohemian give-and-take reminiscent of America in the 1920's, but, like the family gatherings of self-sufficient householders, these are forms of social life outside the main current. While colored people enjoy opportunities for employment here, many of them resent white condescension. Negroes and whites rarely exchange hospitalities, and few Negroes, however distinguished or cultivated, mingle freely with any group not of their own race.

Europeans in some numbers live in the city. Embassies of every important nation on earth might be expected to add a foreign flavor. But in spite of the diversity of background thus offered by residents born and bred abroad, the startling truth is that Washington preserves a singularly American and peculiarly Southern flavor. The capital is far less cosmopolitan in feeling than New York or San Francisco or New Orleans. The theatre is makeshift, the local symphony orchestra struggles to survive, and patronage of painters and sculptors is largely limited to an occasional glance at gallery exhibits. Night clubs are an innovation. People entertain at home. Today, as in the past, Washington is rooted in a provincialism as surprising as it is alternately annoying and refreshing.

In spite of these singularities, and indeed partly because of them, Americans regard the capital as a monument to national enterprise. Out of the tidal marshes and open fields has come an architecturally beautiful city containing, it is true, few evidences of artistic originality, yet presenting a planned harmony rarely found elsewhere in the country. And just as every state in the Union contributed stones to complete the obelisk of the Washington Monument to its full 555-foot height, so Americans feel they individually have built the city. Even while they object to the detachment of Washington from the rest of the United States, they take pride in having created this splendid isolation. Depressions, cushioned by government activities, never strike here with the severity other big cities experience. Political crises are so frequent they become everyday fare. Utterly a-typical of American cities, unrepresentative of American customs and thought, Washington still embodies the essence of the nation.

# X

# Epilogue

THE United States first emerged as a nation preponderantly urban in the early years of the twentieth century, but the influence of cities upon American life had been mounting steadily throughout the century preceding. As immigration from the Old World and natural increase of native population swelled the numbers of the American people, older cities grew in power, while migrations westward brought new cities into being as rapidly as farmers brought virgin land under cultivation or as miners, ranchers, and lumbermen developed new sources of wealth. Indeed, frequently it was the rise of new cities and their promoters' efforts to make them grow greater that hastened the peopling of the country roundabout. The ideas and aspirations that created an urban America originated not on the farms and in the forests of the backcountry but in the cities themselves.

American urban civilization had begun to take form in the seventeenth century. With land everywhere available and transport the chief problem to consider, commercial centers had arisen where good harbors provided safe anchorage for ocean-going ships. Local custom early gave these communities the name of *city*, although they were neither bishops' seats nor in all cases governed as corporations. Modelled at first upon European communities, by 1800 the cities of the United States had achieved a distinctively American quality. They were less crowded than English seaports, and trees lined many of their streets, but their most American feature lay not so much in appearance as in the spirit that animated their citizens. Boundless confidence in their future and in the destiny of the United States lent an excitement and a certain dignity of purpose to the activities of men who beheld a vision of a noble new nation.

At the opening of the nineteenth century, the cities scattered along the coast were necessarily the focus of national economic life. Householders still depended upon Europe for many essentials, as well as for luxuries, and imports naturally came through the Atlantic ports. Wealth, accumulating from this commerce, and the intellectual stimulus that derived from the exchange of ideas among men of varied interests and experience early created in these seaboard communities a culture rarely equalled in richness elsewhere in America. Here appeared the first journals, the first literary groups, the earliest schools of painters, and here architects found their principal patrons. While the new lands in the West beckoned to men of one turn of mind, the seaboard cities irresistibly drew others, those as eager for fame as much as for money, and people attracted by the diversity of city life. Agrarians like Jefferson feared the consequences of swift urbanization, disciples of the Enlightenment with faith in the perfectibility of man, they saw in the crowding and the competitive spirit of the city a threat to the growth of the free institutions that alone would make progress possible. But with the passing of the generation schooled in that eighteenth-century creed, this philosophy gave way to that of men who believed with Alexander Hamilton in quickly peopling the country, enlarging its commerce, developing manufactures, and completing its independence of Europe. Before 1816 the Atlantic seaports were encouraging the spread of population inland; merchants anxious to balance imports with exports were sponsoring improvements in transportation to bring to their wharves the produce of new lands in the interior.

The rise of the river cities marks the next stage in this reaching for greater national stature. Although most men were concerned less with the advance of the nation than with the bettering of their own fortunes, the self-seekers, perhaps unwittingly, served both ends simultaneously. Since farmers in remote places of the West could not market direct, new cities grew up quickly to forward to eastern distributing points the products of the hinterland and to supply to homesteaders and local city-dwellers articles unobtainable at home. The westward flow of capital from the metropolitan centers on the seaboard abetted, when it did not actually initiate, new enterprises in the West, and before mid-century local capital also had accumulated, serving to develop both commerce and industry in the vicinity and in the country beyond. Again in cultural realms, the pattern of urban influence here repeated that of the seaboard, and the cities of the New West became magnets attracting the ambitious and gifted who felt stifled on the farms.

While the force of the westward movement was carrying men into the trans-Appalachian country and creating new cities on the inland waterways, Bostonians were taking steps to ensure a future for infertile New England and, in the process, to enhance their own prospects. Manufacturing, already well-established in and about Philadelphia, promised Massachusetts a prosperity she could not otherwise maintain. Hence New England mercantile capital built factory towns inland wherever streams offered power. Because labor was as scarce as land was abundant, the new industrialists imported mill hands from Europe, skilled operatives and unskilled alike bound by contract to work off their passage money in company factories. Agents similarly combed Quebec Province to find French

Canadian peasants willing to man New England mills. Bostonians connected the development of manufactures with the extension of railroads into the interior and, successfully ignoring the blights industrialism brought in its wake, persuaded themselves that they were diffusing the blessings of their culture in the rest of the country. In the course of stressing the value of domestic manufactures to the entire United States, New Englanders popularized among Northerners the concept of an industrialized nation. Protective tariffs, improved steam engines, and abundant supplies of coal in Pennsylvania and Ohio soon enabled communities without water power to undertake manufacturing.

The coming of the railroads opened another era. In the early fifties the spreading network of rails inaugurated a period of national growth unparalleled by any former expansion. No community in America illustrates the effects of this new form of transport so well as Chicago. Using the railroads as means of tying a vast hinterland securely to her own interests, she showed other cities how an urban empire could develop. Her newspapers, her innovating methods of marketing, and her infectious belief in her own significance in national affairs long gave her a unique position in the United States. She came to symbolize the vitality, the vulgarity, and the violence of urban America. But her strength was impressive. Few Americans needed further proof of the benefits railroads would bring. Mining towns in the mountains, agricultural villages in the plains, and settlements in the forests of the far Northwest all saw in railroads their hope for the future.

The railroads, the industrialists, the land speculators everywhere dedicated their energies to populating the country: more people meant more traffic, larger markets, and greater profits for investors. In response to the alluring words of special recruiting agents, and stirred also by inner compulsions to start life anew, people from every nation of Europe poured into this 'land of opportunity', the 'cradle of liberty' and the 'home of the free' where law promised the protection of life, liberty, and property, and guarantees of free speech, religious toleration, and, after 1865, full racial equality. Partial disillusionment of early comers to the United States failed to stop others from immigrating. Some found place for themselves on the land; more lingered in the eastern cities or gravitated toward the large inland cities. In the seventy-five years between the great migration of the 1840's and the imposition of restrictions in the 1920's, incoming Irish, Germans, Scandinavians, French Canadians, Bohemians, Poles, Russians, Italians, Greeks, Armenians, and a lesser host of other nationalities changed the make-up of the American people. Americans, it is true, speak a form of English, and in the 1950's foreign language colonies in American cities are rare. But the original English and Scottish stock underwent modification. Americans, in absorbing, or at least partly assimilating, a variety of cultures, ceased to be an extension of the British people and became a wholly new amalgam. Negroes, transplanted early and in spite of themselves, added still another element. It was largely the cities that had to cope with this infinite diversity. Bewildered newcomers readily succumbed to the blandishments of scalawag politicians in every big city, and the immigrant vote helped keep them in office even while they exploited the foreign-born. Small wonder that injustice and corruption darkened the record of many municipalities. Amid the confusions of perpetual change, Americans of good will lost their way.

Moreover, from the mid-1830's onward, voices arose in protest over hurrying the growth of national power by encouraging immigration. Working men denounced the system of protecting manufacturers while permitting free importation of labor. Samuel Finley Breeze Morse, portrait painter and later inventor of the telegraph and originator of the Morse code, published his criticisms under the title *Imminent Dangers to the Free Institutions of America*, a plea to forbid naturalization of foreigners. By the 1850's the Know Nothing Party was resorting to violence and intimidation in its campaigns to keep America for Americans. A later generation added arguments. Henry Cabot Lodge of Massachusetts, in 1896 on the floor of the Senate, after extolling the virtues of Anglo-Saxon civilization, pleaded for legislation to halt the 'new barbarian invasion'; Henry Fairchild's volume *The Melting Pot Mistake* and Lothrop Stoddard's *Re-forging America* repeated the theme. The dissidents, however, could not turn the tide. Only fears of over-population in the years after the first World War closed the doors at Ellis Island to all foreign comers save a select few. Whatever the drawbacks of this limitation for the country and for the world, within the United States thereafter a new homogeneity developed.

Meanwhile, in the first decades of the twentieth century, the automobile was revolutionizing life in the United States. The growth of the industry produced not only the giant Detroit but new concentrations of wealth as well. More important, throughout the country automobiles forged stronger links between rural areas and urban than the railroads had ever created. Extending telephone lines also aided in breaking down rural isolation and contributed to the result completed by the cinema, the radio, and eventually television. City ideas of culture have today permeated every section of the United States from the southern tip of California to the forests and remote farms of Maine. Yet the new forms of communication and transport are also weakening the position of cities as the dominant force in American life. The family automobile, country 'stores' supplied by lorry and van, telephone communication with doctors, hospitals, repairmen, or friends, and the rural electrification service that permits use of labor-saving devices are combining to give life outside the great urban centers an ease and charm that is yearly inducing city-dwellers to be city-dwellers no more. While small industrial plants, fed power from electric power transmission lines, are appearing in villages inaccessible even a generation ago, people are spreading out into the country nearby. Large cities are doubtless destined to remain, but a less purely urban culture is also taking form, one distinguished by awareness of the rest of the world but lacking the tensions and anxieties that mar city life in the United States. The middle years of the twentieth century thus may constitute the last period of American history in which city influence will overshadow every other in the nation.

# Bibliographical Note

Published material on American cities, while abundant, is frequently difficult of access even in the United States. Local newspaper files, census reports, municipal records, and contemporary studies prepared by civic organizations or students concerned with some special phase of the city are the most obvious sources. Yet when available, these, too, often leave disconcerting gaps that only diligent search among unpublished papers can fill. Consequently the volumes named below constitute not so much a bibliography as a list of books from which a foreign reader may obtain additional factual information and, occasionally, sound interpretive data as well.

## ATLANTIC SEAPORTS, 1800–1930

John Krout and Dixon Ryan Fox, *The Completion of Independence*, vol. v, *A History of American Life*. New York, The Macmillan Co., and London, Macmillan & Co. Ltd, 1944.

Clement Eaton, *A History of the Old South*. New York, The Macmillan Co., 1949.

John H. Franklin, *From Slavery to Freedom*. New York, Alfred A. Knopf, 1947.

Ulrich Phillips, *Life and Labor in the Old South*. Boston, Little, Brown and Co., 1929.

Sidney I. Pomerantz, *New York, An American City 1783–1803*. New York, Columbia University Press, 1938.

Robert G. Albion, *The Rise of New York Port, 1815–1860*. New York and London, Charles Scribner's Sons, 1939.

Van Wyck Brooks, *The World of Washington Irving*. Philadelphia, The Blakiston Co., 1944.

John A. Kouwenhoven, *The Columbia Historical Portrait of New York: An Essay in Graphic History in Honor of the Tercentennial of New York City and the Bicentennial of Columbia University*. New York, Doubleday & Co., 1953.

American Philosophical Society, *Transactions*, vol. 43, part 1, 'Historic Philadelphia'. Philadelphia, 1953.

Ellis P. Oberholtzer, *The Literary History of Philadelphia*. Philadelphia, G. W. Jacobs and Co., 1906.

Hamilton Owens, *Baltimore on the Chesapeake*. Garden City, N.Y., Doubleday, Doran and Co., 1941.

Dieter Cunz, *The Maryland Germans, A History*. Princeton, N.J., Princeton University Press, 1948.

Mrs St Julien Ravenel, *Charleston, The Place and the People*. New York, The Macmillan Co., 1906.

Samuel G. Stoney and Bayard Wootten, *Charleston, Azaleas and Old Brick*. Boston, Houghton Mifflin Co., 1937.

Josiah Quincy, *A Municipal History of the Town and City of Boston during Two Centuries*. Boston, C. C. Little and J. Brown, 1852.

*The Memorial History of Boston*, ed. Justin Winsor, 4 vols. Boston, J. R. Osgood and Co., 1880–1.

Samuel E. Morison, *The Maritime History of Massachusetts, 1763–1860*. Boston, Houghton Mifflin Co., 1941.

# BIBLIOGRAPHICAL NOTE

Oscar Handlin, *Boston's Immigrants, 1790–1865*. Cambridge, Harvard University Press, 1941.

Van Wyck Brooks, *The Flowering of New England*. New York, Random House, The Modern Library, 1941.

Dirk J. Struik, *Yankee Science in the Making*. Boston, Little, Brown and Co., 1948.

Cleveland Amory, *The Proper Bostonians*. New York, E. P. Dutton, 1947.

## THE RIVER CITIES, 1800–1860

Carl Fish, *The Rise of the Common Man, 1830–1850*, vol. vi, *A History of American Life*. New York, The Macmillan Co., 1927.

Edgar Martin, *The Standard of Living in the United States in 1860*. Chicago, University of Chicago Press, 1943.

Leland D. Baldwin, *The Keelboat Age on Western Waters*. Pittsburgh, University of Pittsburgh Press, 1941.

Louis C. Hunter, *Steamboats on the Western Rivers*. Cambridge, Mass., Harvard University Press, 1949.

George W. Pierson, *Tocqueville and Beaumont in America*. New York, Oxford University Press, 1938.

Isaac Lippincott, *A History of Manufactures in the Ohio Valley to the Year 1860*. New York, the Knickerbocker Press, 1914.

James T. Flexner, *Doctors on Horseback: Pioneers of American Medicine*. New York, Garden City Publishing Co., 1939.

Frances Trollope, *Domestic Manners of the Americans*, ed. Donald Smalley. New York, Alfred A. Knopf, 1949.

Alexander Mackay, *The Western World, or, Travels in the United States in 1846–1847*, 3 vols., especially vol. iii. London, 1849.

Charles Lyell, *A Second Visit to the United States of North America*, vol. ii. New York, Harper and Brothers, London, J. Murray, 1849.

Clara Longworth de Chambrun, *Cincinnati: Story of the Queen City*. New York and London, Charles Scribner's Sons, 1939.

*Cincinnati, A Guide to the Queen City and Its Neighbors*, compiled by the Workers of the Writers' Program of the Work Projects Administration in the State of Ohio. Cincinnati, Ohio, Wiesen-Hart Press, 1943.

Isaac H. Lionberger, *The Annals of St Louis and a Brief Account of its Foundation and Progress, 1764–1928*. St Louis, 1930.

John Hogan, *Thoughts about the City of St Louis*. St Louis, 1854.

Logan U. Reavis, *St Louis: The Future Great City of the World*. St Louis, 1870.

Thomas E. Spencer, *The Story of Old St Louis*. St Louis, 1914.

John S. Kendall, *History of New Orleans*. Chicago and New York, The Lewis Publishing Co., 1922.

Harold Sinclair, *The Port of New Orleans*. Garden City, N.Y., Doubleday, Doran and Co., 1942.

Eliza Ripley, *Social Life in Old New Orleans*. New York and London, D. Appleton and Co., 1912.

Lyle Saxon, *Fabulous New Orleans*. New Orleans, R. L. Crager, 1950.

248

## BIBLIOGRAPHICAL NOTE

*New Orleans City Guide*, written and compiled by the Federal Writers' Project of the Works Progress Administration. Boston, Houghton Mifflin Co., 1938.

### NEW ENGLAND MANUFACTURING CITIES

Grace P. Fuller, *An Introduction to the History of Connecticut as a Manufacturing State*. Smith College Studies in History, No. 1, Northampton, Mass., 1916.

Caroline F. Ware, *The Early New England Cotton Manufacture*. Boston, Houghton Mifflin Co., 1931.

William G. Lathrop, *The Brass Industry in Connecticut*. Shelton, Conn., W. G. Lathrop, 1909.

Dirk J. Struik, *Yankee Science in the Making*. Boston, Little, Brown and Co., 1948.

Vera Shlakman, *Economic History of a Factory Town*. Smith College Studies in History, vol. xx, Northampton, Mass., 1936.

Constance McL. Green, *Holyoke, Massachusetts, A Case History of the Industrial Revolution in America*. New Haven, Conn., Yale University Press, and London, Oxford University Press, 1939.

Mary D. Curran, *The Parish and the Hill*. Boston, Houghton Mifflin Co., 1948.

Constance McL. Green, *History of Naugatuck*. New Haven, Conn., Yale University Press, 1949.

### CHICAGO

Bessie L. Pierce, *A History of Chicago*, 2 vols. New York and London, Alfred A. Knopf, 1937 and 1940.

Bessie L. Pierce, *As Others See Chicago, Impressions of Visitors, 1673–1933*. Chicago, University of Chicago Press, 1933.

Lloyd Lewis and Henry Justin Smith, *Chicago, The History of its Reputation*. New York, Harcourt, Brace and Co., 1929.

Homer Hoyt, *One Hundred Years of Land Values in Chicago*. Chicago, University of Chicago Press, 1933.

Elmer A. Riley, *The Development of Chicago and Vicinity as a Manufacturing Center Prior to 1880*. Chicago, 1913.

Edgar Lee Masters, *The Tale of Chicago*. New York, G. P. Putnam's Sons, 1933.

Jane Addams, *Forty Years at Hull House*. New York, The Macmillan Co., 1935.

Edith Abbott, *The Tenements of Chicago, 1908–1935*. Chicago, University of Chicago Press, 1936.

Paul W. Gates, *The Illinois Central Railroad and its Colonization Work*. Cambridge, Harvard University Press, 1934.

Henry David, *The History of the Haymarket Affair, A Study in the American Social-Revolutionary and Labor Movements*. New York, Farrar and Rinehart, 1936.

Almont Lindsey, *The Pullman Strike, The Story of a Unique Experiment and of a Great Labor Movement*. Chicago, University of Chicago Press, 1942.

Peter Finley Dunne, *Mr Dooley in Peace and in War*. Boston, Small, Maynard and Co., 1898.

St Clair Drake and Horace Cayton, *Black Metropolis*. New York, Harcourt Brace and Co., 1945.

Theodore Dreiser, *Sister Carrie*. New York and London, Harper and Brothers, 1912.

Theodore Dreiser, *The Financier*. New York and London, Harper and Brothers, 1912.

# BIBLIOGRAPHICAL NOTE

Upton Sinclair, *The Jungle*. New York, Harper and Brothers, 1951.

Frank Norris, *The Pit. A Story of Chicago*. Garden City, N.Y., Doubleday, Doran and Co., 1930.

Richard Wright, *Native Son*. New York and London, Harper and Brothers, 1940.

## CITIES OF THE GREAT PLAINS

Walter Webb, *The Great Plains*. Boston, Ginn and Co., 1931.

Everett Dick, *The Sod-House Frontier, 1851–1890, A Social History of the Northern Plains from the Creation of Kansas and Nebraska to the Admission of the Dakotas*. New York and London, D. Appleton-Century Co., 1937.

George F. Willison, *Here They Dug the Gold*. New York, Brentano's, 1931.

Glenn Chesney Quiett, *They Built the West, An Epic of Rails and Cities*. New York and London, D. Appleton-Century Co., 1934.

Stuart Henry, *Conquering Our Great American Plains*. New York, E. P. Dutton and Co., 1930.

Joseph G. McCoy, *Historic Sketches of the Cattle Trade of the West and Southwest*. Glendale, Calif., The Arthur H. Clark Co., 1940.

Ora B. Peake, *The Colorado Range Cattle Industry*. Glendale, Calif., The Arthur H. Clark Co., 1937.

*Cowboy Songs and Other Frontier Ballads*, collected by John A. and Alan Lomax. New York, The Macmillan Co., 1938.

Clyde L. King, *The History of the Government of Denver, with special reference to its relations with Public Service Corporations*. Denver, Col., The Fisher Book Company, 1911.

Nolie Mumey, *History of the Early Settlements of Denver*. Denver, Col., The Range Press, 1942.

Orsemus H. Bentley, *History of Wichita and Sedgwick County, Kansas*, 2 vols. Chicago, C. F. Cooper and Co., 1910.

Arnold Lau, *Community Life and Development*. Wichita, Kans., The Wichita Eagle Press, 1920.

Juliet Reeve, *Friends University, The Growth of an Idea*. Wichita, Kans., 1948.

## SEATTLE

Oscar O. Winther, *The Great Northwest*. New York, Alfred A. Knopf, 1947.

James B. Hedges, *Henry Villard and the Railways of the Northwest*. New Haven, Conn., Yale University Press, and London, Oxford University Press, 1930.

Glenn C. Quiett, *They Built the West, An Epic of Rails and Cities*. New York and London, D. Appleton-Century Co., 1934.

Victor L. O. Chittick, ed., *Northwest Harvest. A Regional Stock-Taking*. New York, The Macmillan Co., 1948.

Archie Binns, *Northwest Gateway, The Story of the Port of Seattle*. Garden City, N.Y., Doubleday, Doran and Co., 1941.

George Leighton, *Five Cities, The Story of their Youth and Old Age*. New York and London, Harper and Brothers, 1939.

Curtis C. Aller, *An Industrial Survey of Seattle*. University of Washington Bureau of Industrial Research, Bulletin No. 3, Seattle, 1918.

Calvin F. Schmid, *Social Trends in Seattle*. University of Washington Publications in the Social Sciences, vol. 13, Seattle, 1944.

R. H. Thomson, *That Man Thomson*, ed. by Grant H. Redford. Seattle, University of Washington Press, 1950.

## DETROIT

George B. Catlin, *The Story of Detroit*. Detroit, News, 1926.

Arthur Pound, *Detroit, Dynamic City*. New York and London, D. Appleton-Century Co., 1940.

Silas Farmer, *History of Detroit and Wayne County and Early Michigan*, 2 vols. Detroit, Mich., S. Farmer and Co., 1890.

Arthur Pound, *The Turning Wheel; The Story of General Motors through Twenty-five Years, 1908–1933*. Garden City, N.Y., Doubleday, Doran and Co., 1934.

Henry Ford, *My Life and Work*. Garden City, N.Y., Doubleday Page and Co., 1922.

Keith T. Sward, *The Legend of Henry Ford*. New York, Rinehart, 1948.

Ulysses W. Boykin, *A Handbook on the Detroit Negro*. Detroit, The Minority Study Associates, 1943.

Walter White and Thurgood Marshall, *What Caused the Detroit Riot?* New York, The National Association for the Advancement of Colored People, 1943.

## WASHINGTON, D.C.

Wilhelmus B. Bryan, *A History of the National Capital*, 2 vols. New York, The Macmillan Co., London, Macmillan & Co. Ltd., and Toronto, The Macmillan Co. of Canada, Ltd., 1914 and 1916.

*Washington, City and Capital*, compiled by the Federal Writers' Project of the Works Progress Administration. Washington, D.C., the Government Printing Office, 1937.

George A. Townsend, *Washington, Outside and Inside*. Hartford, Conn., and Chicago, J. Betts and Co., 1873.

Charles Moore, *Washington Past and Present*. New York and London, The Century Co., 1929.

Margaret (Bayard) Smith, *The First Forty Years of Washington Society, portrayed by the Family Letters of Mrs Samuel Harrison Smith*, ed. Gaillard Hunt. New York, Charles Scribner's Sons, 1906.

Charles Hurd, *Washington Cavalcade*. New York, E. P. Dutton, 1948.

Katharine E. Crane, *Blair House, Past and Present*. Washington, D.C., Department of State, 1945.

Walter S. Sanderlin, *The Great National Project: A History of the Chesapeake and Ohio Canal*. Baltimore, Johns Hopkins Press, 1946.

# Index

# INDEX

New England, industrialism in 37–8, 79–99, 243

New Orleans, La., 2, 36, 45, 56, 57, 58, 61, 65, 110; location and origins, 66–7; Creole society of, 67–8; and Louisiana Purchase, 68–9; slave trade, 69, 71; sugar planting, 71–2; trade, 69, 72, 73; development of banking and railroads, 75; climate, 74–5; city government and social characteristics, 74, 77–8

New York, N.Y., 2, 6, 10, 36; Dutch influence, 7; early commercial preeminence, 8–9; captures cotton trade, 22, 73

Noble, John, 165

Non-Intercourse Act, 21, 28

Norris, Frank, 125

Northern Pacific Railroad, 174, 175–6

Northwest Land Ordinance (1785), 39

Northwest Ordinance (1787), 195

Nullification Ordinance, South Carolina, 25

Ogden, Utah, 141

Ogden, William B., 103, 104, 105, 107

Ohio, state of, 39, 42, 53

Ohio Associates, 40

Ohio river, 17, 36, 39, 40–1, 101, 114

Oil industry, at Wichita, 161, 162

Olds, Ransom, 201

Olympia, Wash., 168, 172, 185

Olympic mountains, 167

Oregon, state of, 61, 168, 170

Orient, trade of, with Seattle, 177, 179, 181

Panama Canal, and Northwest, 181

Paper industry, in Holyoke, 83, 85, 89–90

Paulding, James Kirke, 8

Peale, Charles and Rembrandt, 12, 17

Penn, William, 11

Pennsylvania, state of, 10; University of, 12

Pennsylvania, Academy of Fine Arts, 12

Philadelphia, Pa., 2, 6, 7, 9; early commercial importance, 10–11; architecture and social characteristics, 10, 12

Pike's Peak, 133

Pinckney, Charles and Charles Cotesworthy, 24

Pingree, Hazen, 200, 206

Pittsburgh, Pa., 40, 114

Poles, in Detroit, 205

Pony express, 139

Pork packing industry, in Cincinnati, 48–9, 55; Chicago, 110, 114

Portland, Oreg., 168, 169

Potomac river, 217, 222–3

Powers, Hiram, 51

Public Works Administration, 163

Pueblo, Col., 134, 139

Puget Sound, 167, 168, 169

Pullman, George M., 108–9, 122; Palace Car Company, 122–4

Puritan influence in Kansas, 156

Quakers, in Philadelphia, 10, 12; Kansas, 157, 158

Railroads, development of; Baltimore and Ohio R., 17–18; Charleston to Savannah river, 22; in New England, 38, 80; from the river cities, 49, 62, 75, 78; in Illinois, 104–7, 113–14; in Colorado, 139–41; in Kansas, 149, 151, 152; in Northwest, 174–6; in Michigan, 198

Rainier, Mt, 167

Retail trading methods, development of in Midwest, 109–10

Reuther, Walter, 211, 215

Rice planting, in South Carolina, 20–1, 24

Richard, Father Gabriel, 196

Rittenhouse, David, 12

River traffic, on Mississippi and Ohio, 41, 43, 44–5, 57–8, 61, 65, 72, 78

Robb, James, 75

Rockefeller, John D., 118

Rocky Mountains, 129

*Rocky Mountain News*, 137, 138

Roman Catholicism, 56, 58, 67, 88–9, 196–7

Roosevelt, Franklin D., 238

Roosevelt, Theodore, 50, 234

Rubber industry, in Naugatuck, 92–8

Rush, Benjamin, 12

Russell, Green, 133

St Louis, Mo., 2, 55, 78, 104, 113, 114–15, 116; origins, 56–7; city government, 58, 62–3; growth as river port, 58, 59, 61, 62; 'Gateway to the West', 56, 61–2; the Dred Scott case, 63; social and cultural characteristics, 63, 65, 66; architecture, 59, 65

St Clair, General Arthur, 41

# INDEX

70 71 72 73   12 11 10 9 8 7 6 5 4

# About the Author

Constance McLaughlin Green was awarded the Pulitzer Prize for History in 1963 for her book *Washington, Village and Capital, 1800–1878.* Her father, Andrew Cunningham, received the same prize in 1936.

Born in Ann Arbor, Michigan, Mrs. Green spent her childhood years in Chicago, was graduated from Smith College, and taught at the University of Chicago and Mount Holyoke. During World War II, she was director of the Smith College Council of Industrial Studies and a historian for the Ordnance Department, U.S. Army, at the Springfield Armory, Massachusetts.

Following her husband's death, in 1946, she moved to Washington to help prepare a history of the American Red Cross and soon after became chief historian of the Ordnance Corps, writing a volume in the series, *U.S. Army in World War II.*

*American Cities in the Growth of the Nation* developed from Mrs. Green's Commonwealth Fund lectures in history at University College, London, in 1951. Later she was appointed historian for the Department of Defense Research and Development Board in Washington. A Rockefeller Foundation Grant for her history of Washington, D.C., led to the Pulitzer Prize, given for the second of two volumes.

At present Constance Green lives in Washington, D.C., and is working on a book on the Negro in Washington.

# COLOPHON BOOKS ON AMERICAN HISTORY

\*In Preparation

25-401